FRIENDS *of the*
Livingston Public Library
Gratefully Acknowledges
the Contribution of

Sandy & Len Goodman

For the 2018-2019 Membership Year

GODLESS CITIZENS
IN A
GODLY REPUBLIC

GODLESS CITIZENS IN A GODLY REPUBLIC

★

Atheists in American Public Life

R. LAURENCE MOORE
AND
ISAAC KRAMNICK

W. W. NORTON & COMPANY
Independent Publishers Since 1923
NEW YORK   LONDON

For information about permission to reproduce selections from
this book, write to Permissions, W. W. Norton & Company, Inc.,
500 Fifth Avenue, New York, NY 10110

For information about special discounts for bulk purchases,
please contact W. W. Norton Special Sales at
specialsales@wwnorton.com or 800-233-4830

Manufacturing by Quad Graphics Fairfield
Book design by Helene Berinsky
Production manager: Anna Oler

ISBN 978-0-393-25496-9

W. W. Norton & Company, Inc., 500 Fifth Avenue, New York, N.Y. 10110
www.wwnorton.com

W. W. Norton & Company Ltd., 15 Carlisle Street, London W1D 3BS

1 2 3 4 5 6 7 8 9 0

*To our grandchildren, who,
we hope, may freely choose to believe in
one God, twenty Gods, or no God.*

The matter of "faith" has been in the papers again lately. President Eisenhower . . . has come out for prayer and has emphasized that more Americans are motivated (as they surely are) by religious faith. The *Herald Tribune* headed the story "President says prayer is part of democracy." The implication in such a pronouncement, emanating from the seat of government, is that religious faith is a condition, or even a precondition of democratic life. This is just wrong. A President should pray whenever and wherever he feels like it . . . but I don't think a President should advertise prayer. That is a different thing. Democracy, if I understand it at all, is a society in which the unbeliever feels undisturbed and at home. If there were only a half a dozen unbelievers in America, their well-being would be a test of our democracy, the tranquility would be its proof. . . . I hope that Belief never is made to appear mandatory. . . . I hope my country will never become an uncomfortable place for the unbeliever, as it could easily become if prayer was made one of the requirements of the accredited citizen.

—E. B. White, 1956, author of *Charlotte's Web* and
Stuart Little, Cornell University, class of 1921

CONTENTS

ABOUT CITATIONS AND SOURCES

To keep our book as accessible as possible, we have dispensed with footnotes. Many of the primary sources we have used have been published in multiple editions and can easily be accessed online. To cite a page number in a specific edition of Jefferson's *Notes on the States of Virginia* is superfluous and in fact not very helpful. It's far simpler for our readers to "Google" important quotations. Dates and page numbers from secondary sources and from some primary material, including newspaper articles, are contained in chapter notes at the end of the book. Also in those chapter notes are short lists of books we have not cited that may interest readers.

PROLOGUE

To the ears of many Americans, the word "atheist" has a hard, unpleasant ring to it. Describing oneself with that label has never been a recommended way to court popularity. For that reason, many non-theists prefer to describe their beliefs with a different term. They call themselves agnostics, or freethinkers, or humanists, or secularists, or simply nonbelievers. Statisticians have invented the term "nones," referring to the answer given by many people when asked for a religious preference.

These less confrontational-sounding words connote a variety of meanings, but people who embrace them share a deep skepticism toward the doctrines of Christianity, which has been the religious persuasion of most Americans over the course of the nation's history, despite the fact that at the beginning of our national experiment most of the ex-British colonials who had just forged a union didn't regularly attend church. Many of the prominent white men who wrote the nation's fundamental documents called themselves deists. They believed in a designer Creator, but in none of the core beliefs of Christianity. The virgin birth, the miracles attributed to Jesus, his resurrection and saving grace, heaven and hell—all of these ideas, they thought, flew in the face of reason. So did the belief that the Bible was the revealed word of God. For deists, reason always trumped faith. Deists saw their belief system as irenic. It eschewed the theological squabbles that had caused too many bloody wars in Europe.

Thomas Jefferson believed in progress. For him the peaceful intention of deism marked an important human advance in his revolutionary generation. He saw it, or perhaps Unitarianism, becoming the settled religious view of the American nation. Unitarians remained committed to Christianity even though they professed a skeptical attitude toward many of its central doctrines, including the divinity of Christ and the reality of biblically recorded miracles. Thomas Jefferson's view on this point proved to be as mistaken as his notion that American slavery would die a natural death. Deism faded away. Americans turned their energies to building and populating churches. In the early nineteenth century, a new generation of American leaders branded nonbelief in a God who intervened in human affairs and who judged humans as fit or unfit for heaven as a scandalous position bordering on moral turpitude. However illogically, they equated deism with atheism. Atheism became a pejorative, a blanket term that covered all forms of religious skepticism. Ministers and politicians used it to attack threats, often more imagined than real, on social order and the rule of law. Individual states had laws that placed a premium on traditional theistic beliefs.

Those laws in part reflected the nervousness attendant to our democratic experiment. We easily forget that our early history was not a period marked by strong national self-confidence or greatness. If it seemed plausible that atheism undermined social stability, that fact justified laws that discriminated against nonbelievers. It didn't strike most early Americans as controversial that people who denied the existence of a divine creator could not hold public office. In many states they could not testify in court, even in their own defense. If they published treatises proclaiming their nonbelief or spoke about it publicly, they could face criminal charges that subjected them to heavy fines or jail terms.

A different point of view remained embedded in the United States Constitution. Its First Amendment, along with a provision in Article

6 banning religious tests for federal offices, suggested that Americans shouldn't face discrimination because of what they believed or didn't believe about God and religion. But until 1940, when the Supreme Court in *Cantwell v. Connecticut* held that the concept of "due process of law" embodied in the Fourteenth Amendment made the religious clauses of the First Amendment applicable to the states, states could follow their own notions of what constituted religious liberty. They were free to write laws based on the assumption that atheism, deism, or religious skepticism posed a danger to the safety and morals of the community. Denied basic civil rights available to most Christians, and usually to Jews, nonbelievers were relegated to second-class citizenship.

American state laws have changed over the years, and nonbelievers have more legal security in the twenty-first century than they had one hundred years ago. Even so, a belief based on theistic religious teachings may still carry more legal weight than a belief based on a secular philosophy. Moreover, on the playing field of public opinion, the rules for believers and nonbelievers are not equal. Whatever the law says, an avowal of atheism effectively disqualifies a person from the nation's highest public offices and many local offices in much of the country. More than half of polled Americans state without equivocation that they would never vote for anyone who doubts the existence of God, whatever his or her qualifications. People who have no use for religion may run for public office, but no political adviser would tell them to declare openly their nonbelief in God.

The view that godless people are dangerous troublemakers received solid reinforcement from America's long engagement in the Cold War. We advertised ourselves as a godly nation locked in doctrinal combat with the atheistic Soviet Union, casting the terms of the engagement in amazingly apocalyptic terms. If evil disbelief triumphed over godly pietism, the free world would end. In this era Congress, with bipartisan enthusiasm, inserted the phrase "under God" into the Pledge of Allegiance and in 1956 adopted "In God We Trust" as the national motto (replacing "E pluribus unum"—"Out of many one") and for the first time placed it on all American currency. But as we shall see, the fierce popular identification of godliness as the basis of American citizenship predated the Cold War. It has lasted well beyond the Cold War's end.

In the second half of our book, we will discuss how jurists have used the phrases "ceremonial deism" or "American civil religion" to condone government-sponsored God references that both formally and informally define a concept of American citizenship. In some important court rulings government-sponsored references to God become not affirmations of a truth espoused by churchgoing citizens but simple affirmations of a common patriotism. That usage flies in the face of plain language and ignores the offense that references to God carry to nontheists on public occasions. It excludes them from full participation in ceremonies that are supposed to join Americans together.

The time has come for a serious reassessment of what it means to continue practices that ground citizenship in theistic belief. Whatever memories of a religious America we have carried from our past, the religious nature of the population is changing. It's true enough that for most of the nation's history the United States was a Christian country. No law declared that in explicit terms, but the general body of laws as well as cultural practices took it for granted. The great majority of Americans, whether or not they attended church, identified themselves as Christian. In the newspapers and books they read, in the lectures they attended, in their public encounters with fellow citizens, they rarely heard or saw anything that challenged the basic tenets of Christianity. Village atheists existed. Sometimes they drew crowds to their lectures. But numerically they were an oddity. In contrast to many nations of Europe, where religious faith seemed to be waning by the end of the nineteenth century, Americans appeared to be capable of combining their country's strong economic growth and startling technological advances with an unwavering commitment to a belief in God, in the resurrection of the dead, and in an eternal life won by the sacrifice of "Jesus Christ our Lord."

That world no longer exists. The percentage of Americans who describe themselves as atheist remains small—perhaps 4 percent of the population—while the percentage of Americans who profess belief in some kind of God is still large. But that god is not necessarily the sort of personal god worshipped in most of the world's religious traditions. According to the Pew Research Center, 23 percent of adult Americans describe themselves as atheists, agnostics, or belonging to no religion. The number of those militantly indifferent to the teachings of any of America's organized religions swells to eight in ten among millennials. To put these figures in perspective, the number of Americans who are nonbelievers approaches the percentage of Americans who call themselves Christian evangelicals and exceeds the combined total of Methodists, Lutherans, Presbyterians, Episcopalians, Jews, and Muslims. We are witnessing the rapid rise of a "New Atheism," a social movement that made best sellers out of Sam Harris's *The End of Faith*, Christopher Hitchens's *god is not Great: How Religion Poisons Everything*, and Richard Dawkins's *The God Delusion*. These uncompromisingly strident treatises unfortunately point to yet another cultural division that plagues this country's democratic system. But not all American nonbelievers are especially militant, if militancy is defined by open hostility to organized religion. In fact, atheist Jews often celebrate Jewish high holidays. Atheists who were once Presbyterian may put a star atop their Christmas tree.

Yet militant or not, nonbelievers are building a movement. They are rude enough to say something else that has never before been so manifestly true. Our nation's religious leaders no longer constitute a moral elite. The American experience began with an assumption shared even by deists that religion fueled the country's moral supremacy. Even in recent times many nonbelievers sent their children to church to learn moral standards. That has become less and less a reliable strategy. Religious leaders who once were the presidents and trustees of colleges founded by their denomination no longer are academic leaders. Theology that once was the Western world's dominant subject of philosophy and was the subject of best-selling literature into the twentieth century excites little public interest. Many of the most popular religious leaders in America use the pulpit to fight equality for women, demonize women who often face an agonizing choice about ending a pregnancy, or cast as sinners people of the same sex who fall in love. The clientele for such moral instructions is diminishing, especially, as all polling data show, among young Americans.

In our present climate, religious Americans and nonreligious Americans square off against one another and complain about their threatened status. The former see the court-mandated elimination of school prayer and Bible reading as constituting a government glorification of "secular humanism." The latter regard any government-sponsored prayer or references to God on public occasions as an unconstitutional establishment of religion. Our government is supposed to be secular. Hearing a president end a speech with the phrase "God bless the United States of America" may seem small potatoes compared to what religious dissenters once faced when forced to pay taxes to support an established church. Nonetheless, it violates the idea of a secular state and contributes to the notion that nonbelievers are outsiders and don't quite belong in the American family. Male atheists may learn that lesson early in life. They can't join the Boy Scouts.

When George H. W. Bush served as vice president under Ronald Reagan, he supposedly brushed aside a reporter's question about whether atheists were good citizens with the remark: "I don't know that atheists should be regarded as citizens, nor should they be regarded as patriotic." Bush later denied using those words. He needn't have. The opinion would not have shocked most Americans, both the educated and the uneducated. Bush, a Yale graduate with a Phi Beta Kappa key, was the epitome of the American establishment, and atheists didn't belong in his world.

We cannot write off Bush's comment as an offhand remark made carelessly by a politician seeing an easy way to gratify one set of supporters. In 1984 Richard John Neuhaus, a respected Lutheran pastor who founded the journal *First Things*, published *The Naked Public Square: Religion and Democracy in America*. The title of the book became a popular term that summarized the book's thesis: courts had banned religion from American public life and as a result had put American democracy in peril. Neuhaus compared the American situation to what happened in Nazi Germany. Writing in his journal seven years later, when Neuhaus had become a Roman Catholic priest, he addressed the same question put to George Bush: could an atheist be a good citizen. His answer was "No." "A good citizen," according to Neuhaus, "is able to give an account, a morally compelling account, of the regime of which he is part." In Neuhaus's intellectual universe only a theist could do that.

Neuhaus was wrong, and in several inexcusable ways. For one thing religion has hardly been driven from the public square. Public ceremonies are riddled with references to God. But more important, there is nothing about the philosophy of atheism that would prevent its adherents in contemporary America from presenting secular reasons to justify the importance of democracy and from positing a secular moral framework necessary to sustain it. Neuhaus's contrary assertion borders on dishonesty. Atheism is not typically a philosophy of nihilism stripping all meaning from human existence but a position of principled conscience grounded on commitments to reason and science and open debate. Hypocrisy is what empties the public square of moral purpose, and nothing encourages hypocrisy more than a god of convenience who finds sin not in what we do but in what our political opponents do.

All of the above points, spelled out in more detail, are the subjects of our book. The main arguments rest on a principle we share with people who may disagree with us on other issues. Religious liberty, which includes the liberty not to believe in God, is a precious right that must be defended along with a more general commitment to equality and equal protection under the law. Where we begin to part company with many religious Americans is over our belief that "E pluribus unum" is a much better national motto than the more recently substituted "In God We Trust." The former promotes the hopeful expectation that every generation of Americans will find common ties that can bind together a singularly diverse population. The words of the latter strike at the idea of unity. In our present age dividing Americans into theists and atheists, or churchgoers and religious skeptics, creates a serious gulf that our democracy can ill afford. To understand fully what is at stake, we need to look at our history, since past attitudes toward nonbelief have persisted into our own day. They won't disappear by magic. We need to understand why atheism was demonized. That story is complicated, but the premise of our book is easily summarized: the reasons used to denounce atheism in America at the beginning of the republic just don't make sense anymore.

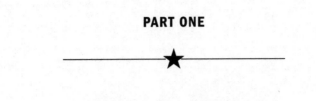

PART ONE

ATHEISTS IN AMERICA:
THEIR PAST

1

The Invention of Religious Liberty

BY THE END of the seventeenth century, Europe had had its fill of the religious wars that began in 1517 with Martin Luther's protest against what he viewed as corruption within the Catholic Church. While Christendom had long before that date engaged in holy crusades against Muslims and heretics in its own ranks, the spread of Luther's doctrines opened a new era. Ending Rome's position as Europe's undisputed center of religious authority, the Reformation provoked political schisms that during the sixteenth century redrew the political map of Europe in blood. States and principalities engaged in constant battles over the true form of Christianity. Doubtlessly, Europe's leaders would have found reasons other than religion to rouse their subjects to internecine slaughter, but religion served as the most useful way to give a noble purpose to otherwise base motives of financial greed, the desire for power, and, in the case of the English monarch Henry VIII, divorce.

Henry VIII's decision to break with Rome and place his realm in the Protestant camp carried beyond his desire to end his marriage with Catherine of Aragon, the Spanish daughter of Ferdinand and Isabella. His wooing of Anne Boleyn was only part of his game. In 1535 he required all public officials to take an Oath of Supremacy that proclaimed him to be England's only supreme governor in matters both ecclesiastical and temporal. The Catholic prelates who refused to take the oath saw their wealth confiscated and their monasteries burned. They fled England or lost their heads on the executioner's block.

Henry's actions to put his island nation beyond the reach of papal authority hardly settled matters. Over the next 150 years, England's domestic religious disputes carried momentous political consequences. In her brief reign, Mary, the daughter of Henry and Catherine of Aragon, attempted to turn England back to her mother's Catholic faith. She won the epithet "Bloody Mary" because of her enthusiasm for executing Protestant "heretics." Many of them fled England to seek a safe haven in the Netherlands or in John Calvin's Geneva. Queen Mary's replacement, the long-reigning Elizabeth I, put England back on its Protestant course, but she was less interested in the content of religion than in using religion to consolidate opposition to the Catholic monarchies in France and Spain. Many church reformers who were dubbed "Puritans" remained unhappy with the form of the English Church and the ecclesiastical leaders who managed it. The vestiges of Roman practice in church rituals and government remained far too pronounced for their taste. In the early seventeenth century, under the reign of James I, the Calvinist-informed party of Puritans gained the upper hand in Parliament and began what became under Charles I a crisis in English governance. The Puritans propelled England into its civil war that led to the beheading of Charles and the interregnum rule of the Lord Protector Oliver Cromwell that lasted from 1653 until 1659.

The Restoration in England of the Stuart monarch Charles II in 1660 raised again the threat of a Catholic conspiracy. Charles II and especially his brother and successor James II were judged to be soft on Catholicism and likely to form an alliance with France. James II in fact converted to Roman Catholicism and produced a Catholic heir with his second wife, an Italian princess. In the ensuing turmoil, many English Catholics and English Protestants died, as James II vied with the Protestant Parliament for supremacy. The trouble ended with the flight of James from England to escape an invading force led by William of Orange and his wife Mary, James's Protestant daughter.

In 1688 Parliament declared that James had abdicated and gave the throne to William and Mary in a peaceful transition of power. This was England's so-called Glorious Revolution and the setting for legislating new, and for the time revolutionary, rules for the practice of religion.

The reign of William and Mary instituted a number of important changes, but none had more lasting consequences than the Act of Toleration. It took effect in England and its American colonies in 1689. Under its provisions, Protestants who separated from the Church of England but who were prepared to swear that they believed in the Trinity and the divine inspiration of Christian scripture gained important rights and were freed from formerly enacted fines and penalties. These "Dissenters" would henceforth be able to worship peacefully in their own churches so long as they didn't lock the doors during services in order to prevent surveillance. Catholics were accorded no protections under the act, nor were non-Trinitarians, non-Christians, and nonbelievers.

In the same year John Locke published "A Letter Concerning Toleration," a document he had written four years earlier in Holland. Louis XIV of France had just revoked the Edict of Nantes, which for almost one hundred years had granted substantial rights to France's Protestants, or as they were better known, Huguenots. This bloody reassertion of Catholic supremacy, which led to a mass exodus of Huguenots, who were among France's best-educated citizens, helped to define Locke's views on toleration. Locke argued that no church had the authority to interfere with the religious beliefs of any person who was not within its own congregation. To Locke Unitarian Christians and "pagan" non-Christians should enjoy the same status as Trinitarian Christians. All people should be allowed to worship freely so long as their religious practices and beliefs posed no threat to public peace and violated no laws that applied to all citizens.

Although Locke's provisions for tolerance were more generous than the ones enacted by England's Parliament, he retained two of the exceptions written into the Act of Toleration. Catholics, unless they found a way to take the Oath of Supremacy and sever any bonds of allegiance to the Pope, a foreign power, did not qualify for rights as Dissenters. Although Locke viewed Catholicism as a threat to England's sovereignty, he at least gave Catholics a way back into the fold. It wasn't their religion that made their churches illegal, but their politics. He offered no such hope to nonbelievers. He singled them out and was more specific than the Act of Toleration in saying why the idea of religious toleration could never apply to "those . . . who deny the being of a God." They were a threat to public order because "promises, covenants, and oaths which are the bonds of human society can have no hold upon an atheist." Thus, "those that by their atheism undermine and destroy all religion, can have no pretense of religion whereupon to challenge the privilege of toleration." To the English philosopher who is often named as the founder of the "modern" idea of religious toleration, persons who didn't believe in God didn't belong in the discussion.

Locke's reasoning would not be forgotten even after England and its colonies had moved toward his view that people should not be molested because of the way they chose to worship God. But that would take another century or more. We can make better sense of what England's Act of Toleration did and did not do in 1689 if we bear in mind that the concept of religious toleration did not grow out of an eagerness to embrace different points of view. To our own ears the word "tolerant" often connotes a generosity of spirit that was mostly absent from the men who wrote England's law. They weren't driven by curiosity or an interest in novel ideas that might open new vistas of the mind. Their "toleration" resulted instead from the exasperated conclusion that putting up with someone or something distasteful causes less trouble than engaging in perpetual, expensive, and finally unsuccessful efforts to eradicate the source of their distaste. Two hundred years of warfare provided that much of a lesson, but the idea of toleration was hedged with limits and qualifications.

England's Act of Toleration did not eliminate a state church or the belief that an "established" religion was an essential component of social peace. It did not eliminate the obligation of everyone, whatever church they attended, to pay tithes to support the official church. It did not extend full civil liberties to "tolerated" Dissenters. Nonconformists, as they were labeled, could not sit in Parliament or attend Oxford and Cambridge. Nor did the Act end all punishments, fines, and imprisonment for certain religious beliefs. Blasphemy remained a part of English law until the twentieth century and formed the basis of prosecutions of persons charged with denying the being of God, "contumelious reproaches" of Jesus Christ, or profane scoffing at Holy Scriptures. Although England abolished the death penalty for blasphemy in 1676, Unitarians and Methodists ran afoul of the law even after they achieved legal status as Dissenters and faced fines and imprisonment if they spoke publicly against the Church of England. As late as 1921, an English court sentenced John Gott to nine months of hard labor for comparing Jesus Christ to a circus clown.

Even so, England's Act of Toleration made a big difference. It effectively eliminated the idea of "heresy" as a punishable offense and provided free worship for most of England's population. Although it didn't confer dissenting status on Catholics, Unitarians, and non-Christians, the Act much reduced the state's interest in people who kept their religious opinions and practices to themselves. English officials did not hunt down Catholics and Unitarians to throw in prison unless something they said or did was viewed as a threat to public order. In effect the Act of Toleration created a distinction between people's private religious views, which were left alone, and people's public practice of religion, which was regulated and subject to punishment.

Moreover, this first important implementation of the principle of religious toleration forced unwanted changes in the practices of some of England's North American colonies. The Puritan founders of Massachusetts Bay Colony and Connecticut may have sailed to New England in search of religious freedom for themselves, but they never intended to found a haven for people whose religious practices differed from their own prescribed and rigid ways. To them freedom of worship meant that anyone who didn't like their rules of orthodoxy was free to leave the colony. Those who persisted in their errors faced forced exile or, in the case of repeated acts of recalcitrance, the gallows. Three members of the Society of Friends, remembered as the "Boston martyrs" in Quaker tradition, were executed by public hangings in Boston, in 1659, 1660, and 1661. Other Quakers had their death sentences commuted but were severely whipped. For the leaders of Massachusetts Bay and Connecticut, religious differences were not welcomed. England's Act of Toleration was the first in a line of unpopular measures shoved down the throats of Puritans whose descendants would one day throw tea into the Boston harbor and push for a war of independence.

The forced acceptance of Dissenters as a protected category did not mean that Baptists and Quakers were exempt from social prejudice. They were a minority and suffered the verbal taunts of people who charged them in colorful language with hypocrisy and mean-spiritedness. They were "enemies of god," "fanatical crackpots," and troublemakers. The verbal scorn often turned into physical assaults, and colonial records contain numerous accounts of the beatings of men and women who wanted to separate their religious practices from those of the established church.

It is somewhat remarkable then, especially given Locke's placement of atheists outside the social contract, that not a single nonbeliever was executed or imprisoned in colonial America. They had no rights under the Act of Toleration as Dissenters, but the quarrels in the colonies about the limits of toleration were quarrels among believers in Christianity. The absence of attention to nonbelief shouldn't surprise us if we consider the following. Western history is filled with executions of religious heretics, but heresy almost never involved anyone who actually denied a belief in God. The targets of persecution were not atheists but people who posited the wrong sort of God and deviated from the teachings of church orthodoxy. Heretics might say that God was a woman, or that he was fallible, or that he had made the world out of blue cheese, but only rarely did they claim that there was no God at all. In simple fact, an actual atheist was hard to find in seventeenth-century Europe and its colonies. John Locke stigmatized nonbelievers, but the practical consequences of his excluding them from toleration were minimal. In the late seventeenth century and early eighteenth century the orthodox clergy in North America used atheism as a straw man to keep in line not the rare godless colonist but men and women whose zeal for the Holy Trinity or the authority of Scriptures was at best tepid.

Just about the only colonial leader who discussed nonbelief as a position deserving toleration was Roger Williams. Williams, a prominent minister in Massachusetts Bay who was cast out of the colony for his refusal to countenance infant baptism, received authorization to found his own colony next door. He practiced in Rhode Island what he construed to be the true pattern of life that God had ordained for his sinful creatures. He held very strict views about what constituted the correct form of church government, even if he changed his mind over time. For that reason he insisted on a "wall of Separation between the Garden of the Church and the Wilderness of the World." Unlike Massachusetts Bay, Rhode Island gave magistrates no power to interfere in or to enforce the practices of individual churches. Williams endorsed the Baptist form of church organization that did away completely with hierarchies and held that no church council or synod could dictate policy to an individual congregation of God's saints.

His strict separation of church and civil matters put Williams in a class by himself. The godly had authority only over religious opinion and only in their own churches. Secular leaders had a colony to govern, and in doing that they played by rules that had nothing to do with religious doctrine. Their personal religious beliefs had absolutely no bearing on their talents as civil magistrates. In his book *The Bloody Tenet of Persecution*, Williams was way ahead of his time. He upheld a position that even today has not been accepted by a majority of Americans: "A pagan or anti-Christian pilot may be as skillful to carry the ship to its desired port as any Christian mariner or pilot in the world, and may perform that work with as much safety and speed." To profess the "right" religion did not make one an expert in the arts of governing. The purpose of government was not to create a Christian nation. That was a sinful illusion. Government existed to maintain peaceful arrangements among God's fallen creatures. Civic duties were the same in Asia and Africa as in London and Boston. The main danger to public peace was not so-called "false and idolatrous practices" but people who claimed to represent true religion and tried to convert the heretic "by weapons of wrath and blood."

Roger Williams died in 1683, six years before England's Act of Toleration, and what that act prescribed ignored his views. By eliminating the category "dissenter," Williams, prematurely, tried to transform the idea of toleration into a modern idea of religious liberty where people don't suffer a civic disability because of what they believe or don't believe concerning God. To be sure, Williams's view that atheists and theists had equivalent status in the civic sphere was never really put to the test since no pagan or nonbeliever presented himself for public office in the colony. But even if one had, Williams's singular belief would not have taken hold beyond the boundaries of Rhode Island. Until the end of the colonial era, most of the other colonies maintained an established church and collected tax money to support it.

Pennsylvania was the most important of the colonies to resist that general pattern of state-supported churches, although even there only Christians could participate in its government. Maryland, which was founded by the Catholic Calvert family, passed an Act of Toleration in 1649 that, by extending free religious practice to all Trinitarian Christians, was meant to provide a haven for English Catholics. Though it predated England's Act of Toleration and is often celebrated in textbooks of American history as a milestone in the advancement of religious liberty, it hardly exemplified a remarkable generosity of spirit, even by seventeenth-century standards. Modern readers will have to look closely at the text before they find anything that is actually tolerated. Its first provision decreed that persons who "blaspheme God, . . . or deny our Saviour Jesus Christ to be the sonne of God, or shall deny the holy Trinity . . . shall be punished with death, and confiscation or forfeiture of all his or her lands and goods." Its second provision prescribed whippings, imprisonment, and heavy fines for people who "utter any reproachful words concerning the blessed Virgin Mary." Only toward the end of the document does language guarantee the "free exercise of religion for all who believe in Jesus Christ." Catholics were the principal beneficiaries of the Act, although the protection accorded them didn't last. In 1654, just five years after its passage, a new governor, who was a staunch supporter of the Church of England, oversaw the repeal of the law.

Until the American Revolution, the Church of England was the established church in most of the colonies except for New England, which maintained a different religious order. Dissenters failed in almost all of the colonies to end the collection of ecclesiastical taxes that supported a religious establishment. But in the eighteenth century some of them were able to have the religious taxes they paid directed toward the support of their own churches. Baptists and Quakers were not content with this half measure, and in some places succeeded in winning exemption from religious taxes altogether if they were able to demonstrate that they supported their places of worship with voluntary contributions. However, colonial laws remained complicated and provided no reliable continuity in the way they treated the members of dissenting churches. In no colony was it easy or automatic to qualify for a tax exemption, and Dissenters didn't enjoy a status under the law equal to the people who belonged to the majority churches. Often, in fact, the successful petition for tax exemption carried with it the cost of social stigmatization.

Nonbelievers, it goes without saying, had no standing to claim a tax exemption. If there were any in colonial towns and cities, they apparently kept their mouths shut. Historical records don't record their complaints. That did not stop leaders of the established churches from using atheism as an abstract noun to exemplify a myriad of social horrors. The Reverend Samuel West argued that for the people to "enjoy full liberty of conscience does not imply that men shall have liberty to have no conscience at all." Any measure that might accord respectability to atheists would amount not to religious liberty but to "irreligious liberty."

Attitudes changed slowly, if at all. In 1780, after the colonies had won their independence from England, Massachusetts, which many regarded as the seedbed of the Revolution, wrote a state constitution.

What rights were granted were permanent and not subject to the whims of future legislative assemblies. The document begins with an expansive Bill of Rights that aimed to be generous in the way it protected religious conscience. The second article mandates that "it is the right as well as the duty of all men in society, publicly and at stated seasons, to worship the Supreme Being, the great Creator and Preserver of the universe. And no subject shall be hurt, molested or restrained, in his person, liberty, or estate, for worshipping God in the manner and season most agreeable to the dictates of his own conscience, or for his religious profession or sentiments, provided he doth not disturb the public peace or obstruct others in their religious worship." Another article added this language: "Every denomination of Christians demeaning themselves peacefully, and as good subjects of the Commonwealth, shall be equally under the protection of the law: And no subordination of any one sect or denomination to another shall ever be established by law."

It sounded good, and the establishment of constitutional guarantees was in fact an important step forward in creating nonrevocable principles of religious liberty. But from our contemporary perspective, the Massachusetts Constitution in limiting religious protection to Christians did not go nearly far enough. Its strong language granting equality among Christian denominations did not seem inconsistent to the magistrates of Massachusetts with collecting tax money to support an established church. Nor did the magistrates see anything in their ideas about toleration that was incompatible with requiring all office holders to swear: "I do declare that I believe the Christian religion, and have a firm persuasion of its truth." Jews, other non-Christians, and nonbelievers simply fell outside the boundaries of Massachusetts's constitutional provisions. In the years just after the American Revolution ended, Massachusetts was as progressive in its practices of "toleration" as most of the other colonies.

However, a few years later, a sea change in opinion affected the men who gathered in Philadelphia to draft a document to replace the Articles of Confederation. Largely because of the efforts of Thomas Jefferson and James Madison, who successfully fought for the end of church tax support in their home state of Virginia, the Massachusetts Constitution did not become the model for the American Constitution. Madison was the principal architect of America's "Godless Constitution," a framework of government unlike any other comparable document because it made no reference to a divinity of any kind. Ten years before, in 1777, Jefferson had drafted Virginia's Statute for Religious Freedom and after a difficult fight finally managed in 1786 to get it enacted by Virginia's lawmakers. The Statute for Religious Freedom remains the most impressive set of principles on any subject passed by an American state government from the end of the Revolution to the present. It has no close competitor. Therefore it's worth paying attention to how Jefferson pushed the idea of religious toleration to a new level, one very close to what prevails now. At the same time, it's important to note how the religious climate of his generation was reflected in his principles.

In strong language Jefferson's Statute for Religious Freedom proclaims that "no man shall be compelled to frequent or support any religious worship, place, or ministry whatsoever, nor shall be enforced, restrained, molested or burthened in his body or goods, nor shall otherwise suffer on account of his religious opinions or belief, but that all men shall be free to profess, and by argument to maintain, their opinions in matters of Religion, and that the same shall in no wise diminish, enlarge or affect their civil capacities." It rejected Patrick Henry's proposal for a "general establishment," permitting Virginia to collect taxes that people could direct to the church of their choice. Jefferson's language put a stop to government's role in funding churches, allowed the expression of all religious opinions, and stipulated that the state could not take any action to reward or punish people because of their religious opinions.

But did the Virginians who supported the Statute regard nonbelief or atheism as a religious opinion? Definitely not, though in one sense it didn't matter because the Statute prohibited the state from forcing anyone to attend church or to pay for the construction of church buildings or the salaries of ministers. What about Jefferson? He seemingly endorsed the freedom "not to worship God" when he wrote in his *Notes on the State of Virginia* that it was a matter of indifference whether his neighbor believed in twenty gods or no god ("It neither picks my pocket nor breaks my leg.") He didn't mention atheism in his statute, but he didn't mention Islamic or Hindu beliefs either. Still, the omission of non-Christian opinions and nonbelief signified that for most of the time they weren't at the forefront of his thinking. Although he was later to endure many personal attacks upon his character as an "infidel" and atheist, he usually equated religious liberty with the manner of "worshipping God." When he talked about religion, he addressed himself to a population of believers in which he included himself. Already in his Declaration of Independence he had tied the "unalienable rights" of human beings to a Creator's endowment. That was not an offhand remark. The brief phrase encapsulated his philosophy. Likewise, in the Statute for Religious Freedom he connected the particular right of free religious worship to the design of a Creator. His famous document begins with the statement, "Whereas, Almighty God hath created the mind free: that all attempts to influence it by temporal punishments or burdens, or by civil incapacitations, tend only to beget habits of hypocrisy and meanness, and therefore are a departure from the plan of the holy author of our religion. . . ."

James Madison, Jefferson's good friend who was equally liberal in his views about religious toleration, expressed a similar philosophy in penning his "Memorial and Remonstrance against Religious Assessments," a justly famous argument for church and state separation. Addressed to Virginia's General Assembly in 1785, Madison's tract defended the unalienable right of people to follow their own religious conscience. But because the religious world in which he lived affected his views, as it had those of Jefferson, he grounded that "unalienable" right in divine authority, writing: "It is a duty of every man to render to the Creator such homage and such only as he believes to be acceptable to him. . . . Before any man can be considered as a member of Civil Society, he must be considered as a subject of the Governour of the Universe." Public support for churches interfered with the plan of the "Universal

Sovereign." Madison wrote the same idea into the First Amendment of the American Constitution. It forbade the federal government from enacting laws respecting an "establishment of religion."

Madison's endeavor was in no way meant to discourage religion. Rather, he turned the notion that ending tax support for churches would weaken them on its head. All efforts to legally establish Christianity had been counterproductive and bred "more or less in all places, pride and indolence in the Clergy, ignorance and servility in the laity, in both, superstition, bigotry and persecution." Later, Madison persuaded the men who gathered in Philadelphia to draft a new framework of national government that the Constitution they wrote, which made no reference to God, wasn't unfriendly to religion or likely to encourage the spread of atheism in the young republic. The ban on religious tests in Article 6 of the federal Constitution along with the ban on religious establishments in the First Amendment was meant to accomplish what Virginia's Statute for Religious Freedom was meant to accomplish, the "leveling, as far as possible, of every obstacle to the victorious progress of Truth."

The religious language that Jefferson and Madison used was not the language of conventional Christians, but it was rooted in theism. It expressed their view that all people owed duties "to our Creator" and that if government tried to dictate those duties "it was an offence against God, not against man." Old habits died hard. Madison and Jefferson more than any other two men wrote the principle of government religious neutrality into the American Constitution, a concept that ended the need to define anyone as a religious "dissenter." Nonetheless these two deists used language that kept them part of a population that was overwhelmingly Christian. In 1802, when Jefferson wrote his often-cited letter that enunciated the idea of a "wall of separation" between church and state, he wrote not to an assembly of "howling atheists" or to a group of fellow deists, but to Baptist ministers in Danbury, Connecticut. They were his allies in his effort to convince Americans in states that continued to collect ecclesiastical taxes after the adoption of the Constitution that ending such taxes based on a more generous concept of religious liberty would not "destroy religion, introduce immorality, and loosen all bonds of society."

In another important particular, Madison and Jefferson were very much part of their times. They believed that a proper understanding of divine plans built into nature formed the basis of human morality. Whatever different ideas the founders had about the wisdom of ending government religious establishments, or exactly what that requirement meant, they agreed that religion was the essential component of moral behavior. Democracy could not survive without it. The late eighteenth century remained a world where nonbelievers were in short supply. Enlightened ideas had prompted a revolution in the political order in England's North American colonies and in France. Yet English deists and most of the French *philosophes* judged many existing religions as superstitions not because they posited a Creator but because they relied on Scripture to prove his existence rather than on human reason. Deism, as it circulated among thinkers in the American colonies, had a God, and a remarkable one at that. Ordinary Americans saw a clear difference between their new republic of religious citizens and the one established by atheistic Frenchmen who spoke about a "religion of humanity" while keeping the guillotine in operation night and day.

Madison's and Jefferson's notion that churches would prosper despite ending tax support for them proved to be correct. True, Massachusetts and Connecticut continued to use public funds to support religion into the nineteenth century. And many of the other states adopted constitutions that in the first fifty years of the republic explicitly favored Christianity or more narrowly Protestantism over other religions and required officeholders to profess belief in God. However, even though the federal Constitution's First Amendment didn't apply to state action, religious competition turned churches into engines of free enterprise. They didn't need state money. True, the membership rolls of the largest church denominations protected by the old orders in colonial America declined. But those numbers were more than made up for by the churches that embraced the enthusiastic revivals in antebellum America that collectively have been labeled America's Second

Great Awakening. (The first had happened in the eighteenth century.) Baptists, Methodists, and even Catholics proved to be expert in adapting to a changed landscape where churches looked beyond the government for funds to stay in business. Their efforts "churched" in an unprecedented way the American population.

This religious energy in the early nineteenth century, however, was accompanied by a new phenomenon—the appearance of nonbelievers. They were not numerous but they were often vocal and unafraid to assert their rights as American citizens. As we shall see in the next chapter, they complained not because they faced legal troubles for refusing to attend church but rather for expressing their religious opinions publicly. John Locke had placed atheists outside the protection of religious freedom, and most Americans continued to agree with his reasoning. Atheists faced a hard task as they struggled to make themselves part of the debate about religious liberty. In doing that, at least in the nineteenth century, they turned not to Jefferson and Madison but to another voice of the American Revolutionary era, that of Thomas Paine. Paine believed in a deity, but his fervent commitment to "Reason," and the persecution he suffered as a result, made him a champion of human rights to many of America's first generation of nonbelievers.

2

Atheism Becomes Un-American

ANYONE WHO BELIEVES that ideas act as powerful motivating forces in history can cite as an example Thomas Paine's pamphlet *Common Sense*, published in January 1776. Selling over 100,000 copies in three months, with sales rising to half a million in its first year, it gave a decisive spark to the American Revolution. Men and women discussed Paine's explosive polemic in scattered forums across the thirteen colonies. Paine had absolute faith in human reason. He used it to question the supposed benefits of colonial ties to England and to unmask the pretenses of the English monarch. He succeeded in convincing many of his fellow colonials that George III and royal sovereigns everywhere usurped power rightly belonging to the people. "Of more worth is one honest man to society, and in the sight of God, than all the crowned ruffians that ever lived." That inspired sentence perhaps captured better the American spirit of rebellion than Jefferson's famous line about unalienable rights in the Declaration of Independence. To the citizens who took up arms and fought with Washington to achieve independence from the Mother Country, Paine was a well-known name and a hero.

The passage of time is an act of forgetting salient facts and is often cruel to the reputations of men and women once revered. When Paine died in 1809, not more than a dozen people showed up for his funeral. His deeds after the American Revolution ended by erasing the esteem he had once enjoyed. His big mistake was going to France, where his confidence in human reason failed him badly. Caught in the cross-currents of the French Revolution, he was arrested in Paris during the period of the Terror and went to prison with other opponents of Robes-pierre. Surviving his internment with his head still on his shoulders, he continued to live in Paris and to champion the Revolution. But in the newly launched United States, French radicalism had fallen out of favor. Paine's admirers who applauded the use he made of "common sense" in mocking the British monarch took a much dimmer view of how that principle informed a book that Paine wrote in prison and published its first part in 1794. Dedicated to "My Fellow Citizens of the United States," it raised a firestorm of criticism.

The Age of Reason was about religion. Paine was a deist, the same religious position espoused by Jefferson, Madison, and a host of other Founding Fathers. But most other deists professed their views dis-creetly and did not write sarcastic treatises renouncing the authority of Scripture and the creeds of all existing Christian faiths. Paine's boldness and his outspokenness in deploying common sense to reveal not this time the foolishness of monarchy but the inconsisten-cies contained in the Bible, the flimsy historical basis of the stories it recorded, and the absurdities of laws credited to divine inspiration, obliterated the popularity he had once enjoyed. Jefferson, who knew what it felt like to be excoriated by clergymen, warned Paine not to publish the book. Despite its initial brisk sales, the detractors of *The Age of Reason* quickly outnumbered its partisans, and they were sav-age in their attacks on Paine. Called a "loathsome reptile," he was branded an atheist. He wasn't one, but to his critics Paine's mockery of Christianity was equivalent to atheism. The label stuck. Over one hundred years after the publication of *The Age of Reason*, President Theodore Roosevelt dismissed Paine as a "filthy little atheist." The man whose words inspired colonials to defy the fiction of the divine right of the British monarch to rule became a villain when he suggested that the God who informed the religious beliefs of most of his countrymen was also a fiction.

Paine published his book in England, a country where the crime of blasphemy was regularly and severely punished from the sixteenth century until the middle of the nineteenth century. Under English law, blasphemy encompassed statements that denied the being or the providence of God, "contumelious" (insolently abusive) reproaches of Jesus Christ, and profane scoffing at Holy Scriptures. It wasn't blasphemous to speak contemptuously of non-Christian religions, or of atheism, or, at least in seventeenth- and eighteenth-century England, of dissenting Christian sects cut off from the Church of England. Blasphemy laws existed to protect the official Christianity of England's established church. The law left room for interpretation, but by almost any reading of it, Paine and anyone who sold his book was guilty of a crime. Paine wisely steered clear of England once his book was published.

When Paine returned to the United States from France, he didn't face charges of blasphemy, just reproach and ostracism. Compared to Great Britain, with its established church and no Bill of Rights, the crime of blasphemy in North America had a much sketchier legal foundation. However, it was far from an irrelevant concept. While only some states enacted laws against blasphemy, in all of them it was a term of opprobrium used by ministers, politicians, and newspapermen to destroy reputations. Events in the United States in the nineteenth and early twentieth century worked to forge a strong link between the concepts of blasphemy, atheism, and social radicalism. Thomas Paine's fall from grace formed the beginning of that story. To his many detractors Paine's attack on Christianity made him not only a contemptible nonbeliever but also a champion of a dangerous sort of radicalism unleashed by the French Revolution. Questioning the authority of God's revealed word quickly became in the first decades of American democracy the same as a destabilizing challenge to social order and the rights of property.

Massachusetts was the site of an early episode that elected officials used to illustrate the harmful fallout from Paine's attack on biblical religion. It was one of the states that had a law of blasphemy on its books. The statute, a holdover from the state's colonial past, was enacted in 1697 in the aftermath of the Salem witch trials; but its sordid lineage was not a sufficient embarrassment to force a repeal of the law. It remains unrepealed in the Bay State to this day, as is the case with similar laws in Michigan, Oklahoma, South Carolina, Wyoming, and Pennsylvania. The Massachusetts law prescribes fines and/or jail time for "whoever willfully blasphemes the holy name of God by denying, cursing or contumeliously reproaching God, His creation, government or final judging of the world, or by cursing or contumeliously reproaching Jesus Christ or the Holy Ghost, or . . . the holy word of God contained in the holy scriptures."

Abner Kneeland was the most famous, or infamous, person convicted in the nineteenth century for violating the Massachusetts law. Born in 1774, Kneeland dropped his first career as a Baptist minister to become a Universalist minister. That move represented a step away from orthodoxy because Universalists were widely maligned in the early decades of the nineteenth century as un-Christian. They were anathema, especially to Calvinists, because they rejected the idea of predestination and preached the universal redemption of all humankind. Hell didn't exist. On further reflection, especially after reading Paine, Kneeland decided that Universalism didn't go far enough in discarding what was unreasonable in Christianity. Everything about Christianity, he came to believe, rested on a fable. In Boston, in 1831, he founded *The Investigator*, a journal devoted to free thought and social reform, and he contributed to Fanny Wright's journal the *Free Enquirer*. Wright, the outspoken, Scottish-born proponent of abolition and women's rights, had in 1825 founded the Nashoba Commune near Memphis, where she hoped to educate slaves and prepare them for freedom.

Wright's doomed commune was inspired by her admiration for the Welsh-born social activist Robert Dale Owen. In 1825, his father Robert Owen had founded the socialist utopian community at New Harmony, Indiana. New Harmony was a continuation of the senior

Owen's work in Scotland to create a model factory at New Lanark, a mill operation based not on profit but on the well-being of workers. The enterprise eventually failed, as did the cooperative enterprise at New Harmony on the banks of Indiana's Wabash River. But Owen passed to his son a dislike of the profit motive on which capitalism depended. It was a dislike shared by Wright and Kneeland.

Kneeland, like Owen and Wright, became a visionary utopian. Like them he was a religious freethinker who questioned the truth of all existing creeds. Freethinkers gathered in several American cities every January to celebrate Paine's birthday. These "Paine Days" were not a community event akin to a celebration of Washington's birthday but a move by outsiders to declare their proud distance from the Christian religion professed by most other Americans. In January 1833, admirers of America's still-reviled patriot toasted the trio of Kneeland, Owen, and Wright as "champions of the cause of human emancipation." Kneeland welcomed his association with Paine and boasted that *The Age of Reason* had inspired an article he published in *The Investigator* in December of that year. The article, which spelled out the reasons why he rejected his former faith in Universalism, was the one that got him into trouble:

> Universalists believe in a God, which I do not; but believe that their God, with all his moral attributes ... is nothing more than a chimera of their own imagination.
>
> Universalists believe in Christ, which I do not, but believe that the whole story concerning him is as much a fable and fiction as that of the God Prometheus.

He added in similarly dismissive language that he didn't believe in miracles or in a life after death.

These words, despite their provenance in the eighteenth-century Enlightenment, propelled Boston's authorities into action. They arrested Kneeland, charged him with blasphemy, and rushed him to trial in January 1834. Legal complications resulted in a new trial that delayed his prison sentence. In fact, Kneeland's fate wasn't finally resolved until a guilty verdict in a trial four years later resulted in Kneeland's imprisonment for sixty days.

A number of prominent Bostonians came to Kneeland's defense, including William Ellery Channing, one of New England's most respected clergy, and Ralph Waldo Emerson, America's famous transcendentalist philosopher and poet. Emerson especially had reason to speak up in Kneeland's behalf because Kneeland greeted Emerson's "scandalous" Divinity School Address at Harvard in 1838, a talk to a small group of divinity students but immediately published, as a pronouncement that helped clarify his thoughts. In the year he went to jail, Kneeland claimed inspiration from Emerson equivalent to what he had taken from Paine. He declared at his trial that he was not an atheist, but a pantheist—"God and nature are synonymous terms." According to Theodore Parker, himself an unorthodox religious thinker, Kneeland read Emerson's lecture to his followers and said it was "better infidelity" than his own words.

Kneeland's prosecutors didn't cite the defendant's intellectual closeness to Emerson, which had come late in the game, but they made a great deal out of his association with Robert Dale Owen and Fanny Wright, and his adoption of "their pernicious doctrines." The prosecuting attorney was not embarrassed by zealous exaggeration. He urged the jury not to let anything prevent them from "abhorring Abner Kneeland and his detestable dissemination of obscenity and impiety and blasphemy—this defendant who may be considered from his acts and doctrines to be the common enemy of the human race." The language was strong but no worse than the obloquy once aimed at Thomas Paine.

It's easy to see in retrospect that the prosecutor overstated his case, and some contemporaries recognized that fact. Owen and Wright were socialist reformers who supported communitarian enterprises, better wages for workers, birth control, greater freedom for women, including their right to own and manage their property, liberalized divorce laws, and the gradual emancipation of slaves. They were not, however,

any more radical in their views and actions than many other antebellum utopians who wrote treatises, held meetings, and founded socialist communities in the years preceding America's Civil War. These
included George Ripley, who masterminded the transcendental commune of Brook Farm; Bronson Alcott, the father of Louisa May and
the founder of the agrarian commune he called Fruitlands; John Hum-
phrey Noyes, who practiced the very unorthodox system of "complex
marriage" at his society at Oneida but who succeeded by manufacturing animal traps and then silverware; and the several hundred German Pietists who built the Amana Community, a place now famous
for making washing machines and refrigerators. Claims that Kneeland
and his friends favored "unlimited lasciviousness," adultery, the elimination of marriage, and an "invasion" of property rights that would
result in "universal misery" went well beyond any reasonable interpretation of their social radicalism. Owen twice served in the Indiana House of Representatives, and voters in Indiana elected him to
the United States House of Representatives in 1842. There he drafted
the bill for the creation of the Smithsonian Institution and served on
its first board of regents. Kneeland was a social radical who admired
Paine, but hardly a wild-eyed one.

Ridiculous or not, the association of Kneeland's nonbelief with
social chaos worked to convince the jury. Moreover, without engaging in the hyperbole used by Boston's prosecuting attorney, Lemuel
Shaw, chief justice of the Massachusetts high court, upheld Kneeland's
conviction, rejecting the argument of Kneeland's attorney that his cli-
ent's right to free speech and free religious practice, guaranteed by the
Constitution of Massachusetts, had been violated. Shaw disagreed. By
his reasoning, the Massachusetts law against blasphemy, although it
was not intended to make criminal the "simple and sincere approval
of the disbelief . . . of a supreme intelligent being . . . nor to prevent
or restrain the formation of any religious opinion," justified Kneeland's prosecution. He had gone beyond the proper rules of dissent.
His conviction rested on his "denial of God made with bad intent."
Kneeland, that is, could believe anything he wanted, but he could not

express his belief with a malice directed at his fellow citizens. Read in its entirety, the provision of Massachusetts's Bill of Rights regarding religious liberty held that no subject "shall be hurt, molested, or restrained for his religious professions . . . provided he does not disturb the peace or obstruct others in their religious worship." Kneeland, according to Shaw, had disturbed the peace of God-fearing citizens. In Shaw's judgment, Kneeland intended his article to give offense and stir social unrest.

Thus it was that Kneeland's blasphemy helped forge in the minds of many Americans a strong connection between social disruption and radicalism. It's a connection that remained strong for the following 150 years. Even if blasphemy trials in the United States, compared to England, were rare, public attacks on religion were presumed to lead to the advocacy of other dangerous ideas. In 1810 the appeal of a case involving John Ruggles came before James Kent, a respected American jurist who was the chief justice of the New York Supreme Court. Ruggles had been convicted of shouting in public that "Jesus Christ was a bastard, and his mother must be a whore." Even Paine would have balked at that pronouncement. New York had no specific statute outlawing blasphemy, but for Kent that didn't matter. Christianity, he asserted, was part of the common law and provided the "moral discipline" that held society together. The case assumes "we are a Christian people." Citing the English jurist William Blackstone, Kent ruled that the right of people to a "free, equal, and undisturbed enjoyment of religious opinion . . . and the free and decent discussions on any religious subject" ended when the expression "reviled with malicious and blasphemous contempt the religion professed by almost the whole community." Then it constituted a "gross violation of decency and good order," in a way that "attacks upon the religion of Mahomet or of the Grand Lama" were not.

The same logic underlay nineteenth-century Sabbatarian laws that required businesses and places of entertainment to close their operations on Sundays. Being Jewish didn't provide a merchant with an exception. In 1817, the Pennsylvania high court upheld the conviction of a Jewish shopkeeper who tried to keep his business going on Sunday, writing that the right of religious conscience "was never intended to shelter those persons, who, out of mere caprice, would directly oppose those laws for the pleasure of showing their contempt and abhorrence of the religious opinions of the great mass of the citizens. . . . Whatever strikes at the root of Christianity tends manifestly to the dissolution of civil government." We can be certain that the last thing on the mind of that Jewish merchant was "the dissolution of civil government," but Pennsylvania's officials were operating on the principle that the insult to Christianity didn't have to be intentional to wreak social havoc.

By the end of the nineteenth century, laws were changing to accommodate the practices of non-Christians, and scoffing nonbelievers only now and then faced legal charges. Not everything changed, however, and the social stigma attached to nonbelief if anything increased. The reason was a wave of new immigration in the late nineteenth century. It filled the ranks of American labor with men and women who came from non-English-speaking countries. Most of them obeyed the law, strove to be good Americans, and were deeply religious. Nonetheless, labor unrest grew and often turned violent. A series of turbulent events gave a new face to social radicalism. Exploding bombs and talk of overthrowing the capitalist system through "direct action" rather than the ballot gave reality to fears about social chaos caused by the joining of nonbelief in God to dangerous social radicalism. Blame for the trouble fell on the ideas of atheism and anarchism, two foreign imports, invariably paired in the minds of nativist alarmists, that struck at the heart of middle-class America.

Chicago's Haymarket Affair or, as it was often misnamed, the Haymarket Riot, more than any other event set off the new wave of warnings about the threat of "radical anarchism" and its ideological twin "atheism." It shook the city of Chicago and the nation on May Day, 1886. Arguably, it was the first act of domestic terrorism in the history of the United States. While Kneeland, Wright, and Owen were social radicals who championed the anti-Christian ideas of Thomas Paine, the working-class anarchists who were charged with setting off

a dynamite bomb that killed eleven people, most of whom were police-
men, and injured seventy others at a crowded labor rally in Haymarket Square were something else altogether. Four of them were born in
Germany. There was never convincing proof that any of the anarchists
had set off or built the bomb. They had called a labor rally in behalf of
an eight-hour day, and it remained peaceful until police tried to break
it up. Then the bomb exploded. In the trial that followed, seven anarchists were condemned to hang and an eighth, who was not at the rally,
was sentenced to fifteen years in prison. Although the Illinois governor
commuted the sentence of two of the condemned and one committed
suicide in prison, four anarchists went to the gallows.

American newspapers and bipartisan political commentary
quickly reached a panicked consensus linking Haymarket to what had
happened in France in 1871. In that year following France's humili-
ating defeat in the Franco-Prussian War, the Paris Communards
threw down barricades in the nation's capital and with the support of
radicalized workers established a government in Paris that to many
recalled the "horrors" and "crimes" of the Reign of Terror during the
French Revolution. An editorial in the *New York Times* on May 31,
1871, described the "spectacle of a city governed by its *classes dangere-
uses,*" who declared property "a robbery" and religion "a superstition."
The Communards, according to the editorial, sacked and desecrated
churches, broke business and marriage contracts, and banished or
murdered ministers of religion. They exemplified what happened when
anarchism and atheism operated in coordinated action. The Commune
and then Haymarket were the delayed poisoned-fruit consequences of
Thomas Paine's effort to replace Christianity with something called a
"religion of humanity."

American editorial writers sensationalized the excesses of the Commune and much else besides, but they did not invent the way its leader,
Louis Blanqui, attacked private property and religion together. Nor did
American politicians and clergymen engage in simple lies when they
drew a connection between anarchism and atheism. Mikhail Bakunin
and Peter Kropotkin, two of the best-known European theorists of

anarchism, were hostile to religion. Johann Most, a self-declared anarchist who immigrated to the United States in 1872, befriended August
Spies, another German-born immigrant, who was one of the Chicago
anarchists hanged on charges of conspiracy. Most was not among the
Haymarket defendants, but he made popular the anarchist concept of
direct action that he called "propaganda of the deed." He justified violence as a means of bringing down the capitalist system.

Most remained a firebrand, and his speeches and writings kept
alive the fears associated with Haymarket. On several occasions he
went to prison, but after every jail term he resumed his calls for revolution. On April 21, 1892, the *New York Times* reported on a speech
he made at a mass meeting of German-speaking workers at Cooper
Union in New York. He declared: "I am an atheist. I believe in no God.
But I am not satisfied to deny God alone. I deny the right of any man
to govern me. I am a Communist and deny the right of private property. I am an anarchist." He was in trouble again in 1901 for printing
an inflammatory article in his journal *Freiheit* justifying the murder
of despots. The article was badly timed because it appeared on the day
an anarchist shot President William McKinley at an exposition in Buffalo, New York. Most was arrested but managed to get his bail reduced
when he proved that he wrote the article well before McKinley's assas-
sination and that it could not have served as provocation for the attack.
To most Americans it didn't matter. Most's words were incendiary—
the equivalent of crying fire, falsely, in a crowded theater.

The association of nonbelief with radical political activity made life
difficult for freethinkers who played no part in the labor movement
and who were not socialists. One of them was Robert Ingersoll. We
shall hear much more about Ingersoll in the next chapter, but he played
a small role in the Haymarket Affair when the defense lawyer asked for
his help. Known as the "great agnostic" and for a time a leading Republican politician, Ingersoll combined his very successful legal practice
with tours of America delivering powerful "blasphemous" speeches.
These popular performances were never prosecuted, although an editorial in the *Chicago Tribune* on September 16, 1879, derided a "so-

called liberal convention" that Ingersoll organized, as a collection of "atheists, spiritualists, free-lovers, communists, misogynists, demagogues, and monomaniacs," whose aim was to establish "Atheism as a state religion." The article continued: "Socialism knows no religion, no Bible, no God, and no sentiment of any kind but the wildest license which is the very essence of Atheism."

In the same year as the Haymarket episode, Ingersoll defended Charles B. Reynolds, who resigned his position as a Seventh-day Adventist minister to become a "free thought" lecturer. He toured the country and spoke to audiences under a huge tent he carted from place to place. The state of New Jersey indicted him on two counts of blasphemy after one of his appearances. Ingersoll's summation to the jury drew a packed courtroom who listened with apparent approval to his defense of free speech: "It was holier than any book . . . more sacred than any creed man has made." Reynolds, according to Ingersoll, was the victim of religious persecution that was "monstrous, fiendish, savage, and devilish." The judge instructed the jury that the law was the law, and it found Reynolds guilty of treating the Christian religion in a "scoffing and railing manner . . . calculated to wound the feelings of the Christian community." For that, he was fined $25.

Ingersoll concluded that if he was powerless to get Reynolds off the hook, Reynolds being a man with many allies and not tied to any radical movement other than free thought, he could do absolutely nothing for the Haymarket defendants. Thus, when William Black, the chief attorney of the defendants, asked him to serve as a co-counsel, he refused. He told Black that "the tocsin has already been sounded by the press and the pulpit that Anarchism is the logical fruit of Ingersollism, and that the doctrine of no God, no accountability to a Supreme Being, must inevitably lead to no government, no authority on earth." He might have quoted the speech on August 24, 1886, by Reverend Calvin T. Blackwell, an altogether typical voice among Chicago's Protestant ministers, that teachers of atheism were more deeply "dyed in guilt" than the seven "assassins" now under sentence in Chicago "because by their assaults on God and sacred institutions they made it possible for the Anarchist followers to gain a hearing for bloodthirsty assaults on secular institutions." Ingersoll advised Black "to get a lawyer of national reputation who is a pillar of the church."

Still another incident in 1886 is relevant. Just after the bomb exploded in Haymarket Square, the Massachusetts legislature debated a measure, not for the first time, to repeal a statute stating that disbelief in the existence of God could be used to impugn the credibility of witnesses who testified at trials. Opponents of the measure called it the "Atheists' Bill." The law that made atheism a relevant factor in weighing the truthfulness of testimony was admittedly an advance over earlier laws that in almost all states totally excluded the testimony of witnesses who did not believe in God, or in his divine judgment, or in the life to come, when liars could expect to spend eternity in hell. In most states by the end of the nineteenth century, nonbelievers along with Quakers and other religious objectors to oath taking didn't have to swear to God to tell the truth in order to take the witness stand. But Massachusetts law still placed the testimony of atheists, and only that of atheists, in a special category. Their nonbelief in God was a relevant consideration in evaluating the truthfulness of their testimony.

The debate was heated. In opposing the repeal that would have erased the distinction drawn between the testimony of believers and that of nonbelievers, Clement Fay, a representative from Brockton, found a lesson in the Haymarket Affair. He conceded that not all atheists were anarchists. Even so, he was certain, without bothering to cite any proof, that "all the Chicago anarchists, as well as their brethren in Europe, and men generally who seek to upheave society and who promote revolutionary methods are disbelievers, every one of them." The corollary flowing from his statement was that atheists were social revolutionaries who could not be trusted to give truthful testimony. Fay didn't call upon the authority of John Locke to uphold his point of view. He didn't need to. The motion to repeal the law failed.

After Haymarket and for the rest of the nineteenth century and into the twentieth century popular rhetoric connecting the "un-American" and foreign concepts of anarchism and atheism continue to spread.

Leon Czolgosz, McKinley's assassin, was in fact born in Detroit, but his parents were Polish and his name sounded foreign and seemed unpronounceable to those of western European background. Senator John Dolliver of Iowa, speaking at a memorial service for McKinley in Chicago, drew the lesson (quoted by the *New York Times*, September 23, 1901) that "the fatal word in the creed of anarchy is atheism." Almost as if following Dolliver's script, Czolgosz refused spiritual counsel on the eve of his execution.

It's true that an impressive list of men and women associated with radical trade unionism in the United States were outspoken critics of religion. What follows are only the highlights. The Russian-born anarchist Alexander Berkman tried to assassinate Henry Frick six years after the Haymarket Affair. Berkman chose Frick as his target after the industrialist directed a police assault on striking workers at the Homestead plant of Carnegie Steel. Berkman was also the companion of Emma Goldman, a woman whose radical activities stopped short of violence but who nonetheless defended the actions of Czolgosz. Even Berkman urged her not to do so. Goldman, while Jewish by birth, rejected all forms of religion. In addition to her essay "The Philosophy of Atheism," she published "The Failure of Christianity" in her journal *Mother Earth*. In it she wrote, "Never can Christianity . . . bring us relief from . . . the weight of poverty, the horrors of our iniquitous system. Christianity is the conspiracy of ignorance against reason, of darkness against light, of submission and slavery against independence and freedom, of the denial of strength and beauty, against the affirmation of the joy and glory of life."

In addition to her advocacy of labor militancy, Goldman crusaded for equality for women and for birth control. Finally, during World War I, her antiwar activities gave the United States government a reason to deport her. In 1918, she, Berkman, having served his jail term, and two hundred others were put on a boat to Russia. Neither she nor Berkman ever returned to the United States.

Not all atheist radicals were immigrants. The most militant labor leader in the United States in the early years of the twentieth century was William Haywood. Born in Salt Lake City, he became radicalized while working in the western mining industry, both in Idaho and Colorado. The latter state was the scene of a series of violent confrontations between the Western Federation of Miners and mine owners. The violence was centered in the Cripple Creek area. In 1905, Haywood formed the Industrial Workers of the World, a union opposed to trade unionism and committed to one large labor organization representing all workers, skilled and unskilled. He also served on the executive committee of the American Socialist Party, led by Eugene Debs, until a dispute over his espousal of "direct action" led to his ouster. To other American socialists, direct action meant violence, which the Socialist Party condemned, and Haywood was in fact often implicated in labor violence. He also opposed organized religion and wrote in his autobiography: "To me Christianity was all nonsense, based on the profane compilation of fables called the Bible." That statement helped the prosecution when during the Red Scare that followed World War I, it rounded Haywood up with one hundred other members of the I.W.W, and charged him with hindering the draft and sponsoring union activity detrimental to the American war effort. Facing twenty years in prison, he fled the United States for Russia, where he lived until his death in 1928.

In 1926, two years before Haywood died and nine decades after Kneeland served his time in jail, Massachusetts once again invoked its colonial law of blasphemy to stem social unrest. The target was Antanas (Anthony became his anglicized name) Bimba, a much different defendant than Kneeland. Born in Lithuania and raised in the Roman Catholic faith, Bimba in 1913, when he was nineteen, followed his two older brothers to the United States and worked in a steel mill. His politics quickly moved to the left. He joined the Socialist Party and the ranks of radical trade unionism. Deciding that his church was to blame for much of the problems faced by American wage earners, he renounced his religious faith. In 1919, after the Bolshevik revolution in Russia split the radical movement in the United States, Bimba resigned from the Socialist Party to join the fledgling Communist Party.

Despite the legal dangers he faced in working for the CP, Bimba stayed clear of any trouble until he gave a speech in Brockton, Massachusetts, in January 1926. His audience was a small but militant section of the Lithuanian American working class. He spoke extemporaneously, so in the court proceedings that followed there was no transcript of the speech. However, one member of the audience took notes that he claimed represented an accurate version of Bimba's remarks, which were printed in the *Boston Globe*'s March 7, 1926, edition. Apparently the words were close enough, since neither Bimba nor his attorney denied that Bimba said what he was quoted as saying. His declarations included: "People have built churches for the last 2000 years, and we have sweated under Christian rule for 2000 years. And what have we got? The government is in the control of the priests and bishops, clerics, and capitalists. They tell us there is a God. Where is he?"

Bimba's trial in Brockton for blasphemy and criminal sedition lasted for six days and received extensive coverage in newspapers across the country. Bimba owned up to his atheism. He admitted that the goal of the Communist Party was the replacement of the existing social and economic order, though his speech made no reference to violence. To officials in Boston, those opinions made Bimba a dangerous man. They did what they could to close public forums to him when he tried to deliver a public address on the eve of his trial. They failed in that effort, for Bimba found an auditorium where he spoke to over one thousand workers. At the trial the Boston prosecutors were slightly more successful in getting what they wanted.

Able counsel represented Bimba. Prominent people spoke up in his defense, disputing the basis of the charges against him. One of them was Roger Baldwin, the leader of the American Civil Liberties Union, which had been founded in response to government prosecutions of alleged radicals in the aftermath of World War I. He likened Bimba's trial to the 1925 trial of John Scopes in Dayton, Tennessee. That "monkey trial" had become famous because of the courtroom confrontation between the religious fundamentalist William Jennings Bryan, who defended the literal truth of the Bible, and Clarence Darrow, the defense counsel who forced Bryan to admit to many inconsistencies and improbabilities in biblical stories. Scopes was convicted for the crime, under Tennessee law, of teaching Darwin's theory of natural selection to his classes. To Baldwin, both trials, only a year apart, illustrated the religious intolerance of many Americans.

Another defender of Bimba was Horace Kallen. Kallen, a former Rhodes Scholar, during the 1920s was a professor at the New School of Social Research in New York City. Boston officials threatened him with blasphemy charges two years after Bimba's trial. Kallen had made his offending remark at a memorial rally honoring the Italian anarchists Sacco and Vanzetti: "If Sacco and Vanzetti were anarchists, so was Jesus Christ." A few days later, officials backed off from their threat partly because Kallen was a prominent man who lived in another state and partly because of results in the Bimba case they regarded as disappointing.

Judge C. Carroll King, who presided over Bimba's trial without a jury, was fair-minded. In the proceedings he didn't want the case compared to the trial of Sacco and Vanzetti, whom Kallen had defended. They had been charged and convicted of murder in connection with robbery in Braintree, Massachusetts. Even people who were convinced that Sacco and Vanzetti were guilty criticized Judge Webster Thayer's conduct of the trial. The many Americans who thought that the two Italian immigrants had been railroaded accused the judicial system of bias against foreigners. According to them, it wasn't solid evidence of homicide that convicted Sacco and Vanzetti but simply their belief in anarchism and their militant atheism. Sacco and Vanzetti were friends with followers of Luigi Galleani, an Italian anarchist who advocated revolutionary violence. Galleanists had been responsible for a number of fire bombings, including an attack on the home of Attorney General A. Mitchell Palmer, who had relentlessly pursued radicals and Bolsheviks in raids conducted in 1919 and 1920. They were also suspected, though no Galleanist was ever formally charged, of masterminding the bombing of Wall Street in September 1920, an explosion that killed twelve people and left another 150 seriously injured. That incident and a number of other bombing plots, some successful and some not, left many people nervous and more than a little predisposed to believe in the guilt of the two men.

At least in the case of Sacco and Vanzetti there was an actual crime of violence. This was not true in Bimba's case. Judge King even publicly said that he regretted charges against Bimba had been brought at all. He listened patiently to the testimony of six witnesses called by the prosecuting attorney, mostly saying things that were not in dispute. The defense mounted by Bimba's attorney Harry Hoffman didn't depend on proving that Bimba believed in God or that he wasn't a communist. He followed the same line of defense mounted by Kneeland's attorney many years before. Bimba was protected by the Massachusetts Constitution to believe whatever he wanted and to express those views by shouting them from the rooftops if he so chose. In what was a novel argument for the time, Hoffman claimed that atheism was a form of religion fully protected by Massachusetts's guarantee of religious freedom. Whatever happened in the trial court, Hoffman hoped that an appellate court would declare Massachusetts's statute against blasphemy unconstitutional.

Judge King defeated Hoffman's aim in that particular, for he found Bimba not guilty of blasphemy. He did uphold the charge of sedition, but only tepidly. He fined Bimba $100, the minimum penalty under Massachusetts law, and made no comment about the attempt of the prosecuting attorney, I. Manuel Rubin, to link the two charges. According to Rubin, Bimba's atheism was indelibly connected to his radicalism. Bimba, he said, first sought to convince his hearers that there was no God and then, having disposed of the true basis of all authority, to persuade them of the necessity of overthrowing the government by force or violence. "This," he said, according to the *Boston Globe* on February 28, 1926, "is the usual procedure with revolutionists."

Bimba managed to become a naturalized American citizen a year after his trial and lived in the United States until he died in 1982 at the age of eighty-eight. But in 1963, during the Cold War, the State Department remembered his efforts on behalf of the Communist Party and tried to deport him. It claimed that Bimba had concealed his 1926 trial at the time of his naturalization proceedings. The government didn't succeed in its effort to kick Bimba out of the country but not for want of trying. Its proceedings against Bimba continued for four years. The Cold War crusade against communism reiterated the argument that prosecutor Rubin used at Bimba's trial: atheism was the root cause of revolutionary aspirations to overthrow the government.

Rubin's point of view failed to send Bimba to jail, and Massachusetts never again tried anyone for blasphemy. At the same time, what Rubin argued remained strongly rooted in American public opinion. In 1929 textile workers in Gastonia, North Carolina, struck the Loray Mill, then the largest mill in the world under one roof. The southern textile industry was ripe for labor strife. Northern mill owners had moved their capital south to take advantage of cheaper and non-unionized labor. The National Textile Workers Union, affiliated with the Communist Party, led the strike in a determined effort to break the antiunion policies of the textile mill owners. In response to the strike, management evicted the families of the strikers from their mill-owned homes. The workers erected a tent city where a series of violent confrontations erupted between the strikers and the police. In one of them, Gastonia's chief of police, O. F. Anderholt, was shot and killed. Two other police officers were wounded, as were several of the striking workers. Seven of the workers faced trial on charges of murder.

North Carolina law required witnesses to swear that they believed in life after death. It rarely came up because most witnesses in North Carolina had no problem with the oath. However, one of the key defense witnesses, Edith Saunders Miller, who had come from New York to aid the striking families, and her husband, one of the defendants, did. She freely admitted that she was a communist and an atheist. The prosecuting attorney leaped upon both admissions to block her testimony, saying the law required it. The judge refused the prosecution's motion and allowed Miller to take the stand. However, he upheld a second motion of the prosecution and instructed the jurors that they could take her religious and political views into consideration in weighing the truthfulness of her testimony. He told them that Miller's communist views might "impeach" her credibility. As for her atheism, the judge stated, "If I believed that life ended with death and there is no punishment after death, I would be less inclined to tell the truth."

Miller testified that the defendants were not near the scene when the shots that killed Anderholt were fired. The jury, all but one of whom said during the jury selection process that they went to church, didn't believe her. It convicted the defendants of second-degree murder, and the appeals court found nothing amiss in the judge's ruling. He had followed the law of North Carolina. It's perhaps understandable that jurors in trials involving allegations of violence might look suspiciously at the testimony of people committed to overthrowing the judicial system. What matters in our story is how events conspired to keep nonbelievers under the same cloud of suspicion. Was it credible in the twentieth century that people who did not believe in an afterlife and divine judgment were more likely to lie than people who still believed in hell? The truth is that most perjurers in American history have happily professed religion and have freely taken an oath to tell the truth.

Nonetheless, many Americans had come to regard atheists, even when they were utterly detached from any association with social radicalism, as dangerous people and unworthy citizens. A constant chant in the media proclaimed it so. In the two decades that preceded American's entry into World War II, the Daughters of the American Revolution, the American Legion, and various Catholic youth organizations launched campaigns to "wage war" against the spreading danger of atheism. Throughout the early twentieth century, Catholic bishops along with Protestants of every denomination made their concern over atheism a crusade. At a time when American Protestants and American Catholics rarely united in common causes (anti-Catholicism remained strong among the Protestant clergy, and Catholic clerics regarded contact with Protestants almost as contagion), atheism was one issue that sometimes joined them in a united front.

A few examples of the strong language employed: the *Washington Post* on September 28, 1909, recorded a call for religious unity from

Reverend A. H. Thompson, the pastor of Washington's Waugh Methodist Church. In a sermon attacking Pierre-Joseph Proudhon, a leading theorist of anarchism, and Karl Marx, author of *The Communist Manifesto*, he warned, "We are face to face with open and avowed atheism. . . . If the evil continues, what will result? Nothing but the destruction of all that is desirable in life." On March 8, 1932, the same paper covered an interfaith meeting of Catholic, Jewish, and Protestant leaders at Washington's Willard Hotel. The Episcopal bishop James E. Freeman sounded the theme for this gathering, calling for unified action against the forces of atheism "now seeking to destroy the American nation and its institutions." On January 15, 1939, the *Post* covered the launching of Church Unity Week at Catholic University. The Right Reverend Patrick J. McCormick called for an eight-day crusade to form "a solid front against their common enemy—the unbeliever." His words defined a "life and death struggle between those who believe in God and those who deny his existence."

Based on any reasonable assessment of the national mood, atheism was not winning the hearts of many people in the United States. Church membership, which stood at somewhere around 40 percent of the population at the beginning of the twentieth century, grew during the decade after World War I. It dipped slightly in the 1930s, but not to any degree suggestive of a spike in the number of Americans who didn't believe in God. That number had never measured more than a few percentage points, and immigrants to the United States, who often were assigned the blame for radical political activity, were if anything even more godly than native-born Americans. In a new and confusing country, the churches of recent arrivals who had passed through Ellis Island or other points of entry became the center of their community life. Freedom to practice their religion was their way of becoming American.

Nonetheless, the fear of rampaging atheism guaranteed that an organization founded in 1925 by Charles Lee Smith got more than its fair share of publicity. The American Association for the Advancement of Atheism announced its goal as the complete secularization of American government. Smith and his followers wanted to "stop the boot-legging of religion into the public schools," and to remove the motto "In God We Trust" from American coins. A judge of the New York Supreme Court initially denied Smith's organization a certificate of incorporation. The *New York Times* on December 27, 1925, reported his ruling that its aims were "purely destructive . . . operating as a wrecking company." Smith found another judge who granted incorporation to the AAAA, but Smith made little progress in achieving any of his "secular" goals.

Smith then went to Arkansas and tried to win approval for the teaching of Darwinism in the state's public schools. He knew that was impossible. Despite the bad publicity heaped upon Arkansas during the Scopes trial, Darwinian theory had not made it into the curriculum of the state's public schools, and an atheist from the North was not going to change matters. On the other hand, any trouble he managed to stir up might get his organization sympathetic attention in the national press. So he counted it a success when he got arrested on charges of blasphemy because he posted in a storefront window in Little Rock a sign reading, "Evolution is true. The Bible's a lie. God's a Ghost." Unamused city officials hauled him into court, where another Arkansas law, one that prohibited atheists from testifying at all, prevented him from speaking in his own behalf. The judge changed the charge from blasphemy to distributing scurrilous literature, and sentenced him to a short jail time. Once out of prison, Smith resumed his activities and was again charged with blasphemy. This time the original charge stuck, and Smith served more jail time. The national press did take note of Smith's activity, but even if an editorial supported his defense of Darwin, it didn't support his atheism.

Smith's atheist activism was uncommon for his day, but as a native-born citizen with nonradical political views, he was more typical of nonbelievers in the United States than the socialist and anarchist radicals to whom they had been linked in the public mind. Science and secularism were his causes, not the replacement of capitalism. In many unfortunate ways he was just an ordinary white American steeped in prejudices common to his culture. He was an anti-Semite, a virulent anti-Catholic, and an enthusiastic subscriber to the doctrine of scientific racism. Like some scientists in the 1920s, Smith twisted Darwin's idea of natural selection into theoretical proof that some races had evolved more than others. Smith hardly qualifies as an American hero, though he was the last person in American history to be jailed for blasphemy.

Even so, some states refused to repeal laws making blasphemy a crime. No appellate court ever declared such laws unconstitutional, and the spirit of blasphemy lingered for many years in cases involving the censorship of books, of theater, and of student publications. The famous Hollywood code, the Hays Code, enacted in the early 1930s, tried to "clean up" the movies by specifying that the words "God," "Lord," Jesus," and "Christ" were forbidden unless they were used reverently in connection with "proper religious ceremonies." The Code declared that films could not "ridicule the clergy." Clergy of course meant Christian clergy.

But what about our fallen hero, Thomas Paine, who began this chapter? Changes in the treatment of freethinkers over the course of the nineteenth century might be roughly measured by the change in Thomas Paine's reputation. At the beginning of the twentieth century, Paine stood higher in American historical memory than when he died. Much of the credit belongs to the determined efforts of Moncure Conway, a southern-born abolitionist who was prominent in progressive circles in both the United States and England. A graduate of the Harvard Divinity School in 1854, he moved through a spectrum of religious commitments. He began as a Methodist, serving for a time as a Methodist circuit rider, switched to Unitarianism, and ended in Free Thought, which was really an attitude more than a set of fixed dogmas. His views about Christianity approximated closely enough Thomas Paine's deism.

In 1892 Conway published a two-volume biography of Paine, which he followed with a four-volume edition of Paine's works. These were the first assessments of Paine's career approaching the standards of modern scholarship. Conway proceeded in 1894 to found the Thomas Paine Historical Society in New Rochelle, New York, where Paine had lived for several years at the end of his life. The Society restored and preserved Paine's home, and in 1905 erected a bronze bust of Paine on Paine Avenue.

Conway died in 1907, but not before challenging Theodore Roosevelt's "blunder" in calling Paine a "filthy little atheist." Roosevelt's remark had appeared in his 1888 biography of Gouvernour Morris. In a letter to the *New York Times* on October 21, 1899, Conway noted that Paine was never filthy (he was "scrupulously neat and elegant in his attire") and that Paine believed in God. He quoted Paine: "religion has two principal enemies: fanaticism and infidelity; or that which is called atheism." For good measure, another Paine booster added that he wasn't "little" either, for he stood close to six feet in height. In 1925, New Rochelle authorized a new building for a Paine museum. To add respectability to the occasion, Thomas Edison, who from his boyhood admired Paine's writings, showed up to turn the first shovel of earth to mark the beginning of construction. In a long interview with a *New York Times* reporter (June 7, 1925), Edison praised all of Paine's writings, including *The Age of Reason*, and deplored the fact that Paine's "teachings have been debarred from schools everywhere."

However, the testimony of Thomas Edison was unable to undo the damage of the long clerical campaign to vilify Paine and bury his name. The efforts of Conway failed to lift Paine into the circle of America's most esteemed forefathers. His reputation hit a ceiling and it was a relatively low one. To be sure, if Paine had taken Jefferson's advice and not published his scathing attack on religion, his authorship of *Common Sense*—despite the fact that the book has become America's all-time best-seller—would not have won Paine the same level of historical admiration accorded to Washington, Franklin, Jefferson, and Madison. But publish he did, and the burden of his association with the wrong religion, equated with atheism, and the wrong revolution, the one in France, dragged down his reputation.

In 1942 the Fairmount Park Commission of Philadelphia rejected a request to place a statue of Paine in Fairmount Park because of his religious ideas. The same rejection happened in Providence, Rhode Island, in 1955 because of opposition from the Catholic Church; and in 2007 legislation designating a Thomas Paine Day failed in Arkansas after a member of the state House of Representatives protested Paine's criticism of religion. New Rochelle's Thomas Paine Historical Society campaigned hard for a statue of its hero in Washington, D.C., a city filled with monuments and statues erected to honor historical figures, both famous and forgotten. The directors thought they had succeeded when Congress authorized a memorial to Paine in 1992, but from there the effort fell flat. No site or design was ever selected; private money necessary for the memorial didn't materialize; and approval of the authorization expired in 2003. Excluding a seated wax figure of Paine in New Rochelle, there are only two full-sized statues of Paine in the United States, one of them in Bordentown, New Jersey, and the other in Morristown, New Jersey.

Paine's name is no longer anathema in American public life. Franklin Roosevelt opened one of his fireside chats by quoting from *American Crisis*, a series of pamphlets Paine wrote between 1776 and 1783. The line chosen by FDR, "These are the times that try men's souls," was read to Washington's troops before they crossed the frozen Delaware River in December, 1776—at night and in a blizzard—and won a great victory at Trenton. At the other end of the political spectrum, Ronald Reagan cited a passage from *Common Sense* ("We have it in our power to begin the world over again") when he accepted the Republican nomination in 1980. But selective quotations from Paine have not extended to *The Age of Reason*. As the Harvard historian Jill Lepore has noted, that book continues to be "willfully excluded from memory."

Perhaps then it's not surprising that the only capital city that has honored Paine with a statue is Paris. In France the charge of atheism doesn't stir much public interest. Thus, the French have been able to appreciate better than Americans the close connection Paine saw between "a revolution in the system of government" and a "revolution in the system of religion." For Paine no disparity existed between his celebrated revolutionary tract *Common Sense* and his despised attack on religion. The same common sense that challenged the tyranny of monarchs worked to challenge the tyranny of clerical dogma.

3

★

The Political Cost of Nonbelief
in Nineteenth-Century America

ON OCTOBER 5, 1893, a reporter for the *Boston Globe* summarized a debate between Miles Grant, an Adventist preacher, and J. Spencer Ellis, the editor of a Canadian journal, *Secular Thought*. Elder Grant's church "was crowded to its utmost capacity with attentive hearers, who seemed to be about equally divided in their sympathies. . . . The occasion was especially noteworthy since it is said to be the first time an atheist occupied a Christian pulpit and proclaimed doctrines subversive of Christian doctrine. It was certainly the first time when such doctrines were so enthusiastically applauded in such a place."

In light of the dislike Americans had showered upon atheists, any public acclaim accorded to one at the end of the nineteenth century might seem to be an altogether rare event. It was and it wasn't. Without question, the progressive-minded Supreme Court Justice David Brewer had a point when he famously observed in the 1892 case *Church of the Holy Trinity v. United States* that "this is a Christian nation." Brewer wasn't citing any congressional act declaring America a Christian country. There wasn't one. He was referring to what he thought was a thick veneer of Christian culture that informed daily life in most American communities. He had salient facts on his side. The first hundred years of the American republic marked a steady rise in Christian church membership. The increase in church attendance was accompanied by an explosive increase in the amount of money spent to construct houses of religious worship. The largest private organizations in the United States, the Young Men's Christian Association, the Woman's Christian Temperance Union, and the Chautauqua Assembly, all rested on strong Protestant religious sponsorship. Catholics also formed clubs as centers of their communal life. In the minds of American Christians Sunday remained a day set aside for Christian worship with rules about operating businesses that applied to everyone.

As is usually the case in describing America's pluralist society, every observation can elicit a contrary observation. If the nineteenth and first half of the twentieth centuries were a golden age of traditional denominational religion, they also marked a golden age of religious questioning and of religious inventiveness. Nineteenth-century Americans took religion seriously. They went to church and bothered to learn the tenets of their respective denominations. Baptists knew why they were different from Presbyterians, and both kept their distance from Methodists and Episcopalians. A very high wall of ritual and belief separated all Protestants from all Catholics. Splinter groups were endlessly breaking away from large denominations because of disagreements over fine points of doctrine, because of geography and ethnic difference, or because of what often looked like just plain orneriness. Slavery drove denominational divisions that persisted a century after the Civil War ended. In a lecture delivered in 1854, the Swiss-born and German-educated Philip Schaff termed the American religious landscape "a motley sampler of all church history." Although he didn't entirely approve of such unrestrained religious diversity, he found America's religious enthusiasm impressive all the same.

Because nineteenth-century Americans took religion seriously, they loved to argue about it. They read the reports of sermons printed in American newspapers. They shelled out hard cash to attend public lectures on religious subjects and especially relished debates between partisans of rival religious positions. Contrary to what one might expect, they often flocked to hear what nonbelievers had to say. No one seemed to have a monopoly on truth, and that fact gave birth to new religions as well as to doubts about the truth of all religions. The nineteenth century made room for Joseph Smith's Mormonism and Mary Baker Eddy's Christian Science. It also made room for Robert Ingersoll and Elizabeth Cady Stanton, two famous Americans whose work received a great deal of public acclaim but who paid a heavy price for their nonbelief.

Robert Ingersoll is no longer the household name he was through-out much of the United States at the end of the nineteenth century. It would be different had he succeeded in his early ambition of being elected to high office. Many of his peers expected that to happen, at least at the beginning of Ingersoll's career. When he died in 1899, eulo-gists praised Ingersoll for what he might have been rather than for what he was. An obituary published by the *Chicago Tribune* on July 22, 1899, repeated a commonly held opinion that "he could have won great dis-tinction in the field of politics had he so chosen. But he was determined to enlighten the world concerning the 'Mistakes of Moses.' That threw him out of the race. The Republican leaders were more than delighted to have his services on the stump, but they would have shuddered at the thought of running him for office. . . . The religious element would not tolerate him."

The *Washington Post* delivered the same judgment on the same day: "With his splendid gifts of oratory, his magnetic manners, his genial humor . . . there was no position of honor to which he might have aspired with an almost assured certainty of success but for his . . . agnosticism." Ingersoll loved his country. He spoke with earnest patri-otic flourish about the success of American democracy. Yet he was determined to prove to his fellow Americans that God had nothing to do with America's greatness or with anything else. You can't become president of the United States running on that platform.

Ingersoll was born in 1833 in Dresden, New York, a very small town on the western shore of Seneca Lake. His father, Reverend John Inger-soll, was a Congregationalist minister who got bounced from pulpit to pulpit, not because of any unorthodox views on Christ's divinity or the reality of hell, but because of his strong abolitionist stance. Many of his parishioners viewed his opposition to the 1850 Fugitive Slave Law, which required the return to their owners of slaves who had escaped to a nonslave state, as too militant a political stance for a man of the cloth. Young Robert's allegiance to his father's religious faith faded quickly as he moved beyond boyhood, but he admired his father's stance on slavery. The lesson he took from his father was that standing up for one's beliefs often meant standing against the majority.

Ingersoll's schoolhouse education was spotty, as it was for many young Americans in antebellum America. He read voraciously, however, and high on the list of his favorite authors were Voltaire and Thomas Paine. He became a lawyer, his lifetime vocation, and with one of his brothers set up a law practice in Peoria, Illinois. An ambitious young man, he started looking for a way to satisfy his developing political ambition. In 1860 he was soundly defeated when he ran for Congress as a Democrat. The Civil War interrupted his career, but when he returned home from his stint in the Union Army he switched his party allegiance to the Republicans and looked for an opportunity. In 1867 the governor of Illinois appointed him the attorney general of the state, a position of influence that in 1868 prompted him to set his sights on the governorship. Already recognized as a powerful orator, he just might have succeeded in attaining that office had it not been for his opposition to all religion. When his views became known, some of his supporters backed off.

An apocryphal story recounted by one of his biographers tells that a group of delegates to the nominating convention approached Ingersoll and advised him to renounce his unorthodox beliefs if he wanted to be considered. Allegedly, Ingersoll refused the advice and asked the delegates to read a statement to the convention: "I have in my composition that which I have declared to the world as my views upon religion. My position I would not, under any circumstances, not even for my life, seem to renounce. I would rather refuse to be President of the United States than to do so. My religious belief is my own. It belongs to me, not to the State of Illinois. I would not smother one sentiment of my heart to be the Emperor of the round globe."

Although nothing quite so dramatic happened, Ingersoll's reported words capture well enough a decision that the young man of thirty-six had to make. His religious opinions were well known in local Illinois politics, but he hadn't yet published them. In 1868 he still had time to reverse himself on religious questions and start going to church. Or he might have chosen the strategy undoubtedly followed by many politicians over the course of American history and kept his doubts about God's existence to himself. Instead, Ingersoll opted to proselytize for nonbelief. Eight years after Ingersoll's unsuccessful bid for governor, Thomas Henry Huxley, the English natural philosopher and champion of Darwin's views on natural selection, would coin the term "agnostic," the position of someone who doubts God until his existence can be proved. By then, Ingersoll had already adopted Huxley's position, but he relished the new word. He called himself an agnostic for the rest of his life.

His published essays about religion began to appear in the 1870s. An early piece held up Thomas Paine as his model. Paine was a man "who for the sake of truth, accepted hatred and reproach for his portion. . . . He lost the respect of what is called society, but kept his own." Ingersoll knew that vehement opposition to his religious views sent Paine to a lonely grave, but Ingersoll did not on that account soften his words attacking Christianity. In an 1872 polemic entitled "The Gods," Ingersoll wrote that "the notion that faith in Christ is to be rewarded by an eternity of bliss, while a dependence upon reason, observation, and experience merits everlasting pain is too absurd for refutation, and can be relieved only by that unhappy mixture of insanity and ignorance called 'faith.'" He dismissed the Bible as a book of purely human invention, and a badly flawed one at that. With notable success, Ingersoll began to say the same things on the lecture circuit.

Even at this point, the political fallout wasn't clear. At the 1876 Republican Convention Ingersoll was picked to nominate for the presidency James G. Blaine, a seasoned politician from Maine who was elected to the Senate following his congressional career as Speaker of the House of Representatives. Blaine and Ingersoll held in common a strong belief in the separation of church and state, though Blaine's view owed to his aversion to Roman Catholicism rather than to agnosticism. While in Congress Blaine sponsored an amendment to the federal Constitution that would have made the religious clauses of the First Amendment incumbent on the states. Its primary intention was to prohibit states from making any expenditure of public funds for parochial schools. The amendment failed, and it wasn't until 1940 that the Supreme Court made the First Amendment binding on states. But in the late nineteenth century the idea of denying tax money to Catholic schools was popular, and a number of states passed versions of the Blaine amendment.

Ingersoll's nominating speech electrified the convention. He dubbed Blaine "the Plumed Knight," a nickname that stuck with Blaine and that even today helps students identify him when they take Advanced Placement tests in American history. Even though the convention passed over Blaine and nominated Rutherford B. Hayes, Ingersoll had been the star of the convention. He was enlisted to campaign for Hayes in what was one of the bitterest elections in American history. Neither Hayes nor his Democratic opponent Samuel J. Tilden won a clear victory in the Electoral College, and the decision went to the House of Representatives. The ensuing Compromise of 1877, brokered by congressmen, put Hayes in the White House but came at the cost of ending Reconstruction efforts in the former Confederate states. Once in office, President Hayes, who was grateful to Ingersoll for campaign work, considered appointing him the American ambassador to Germany; but Ingersoll withdrew his name. The *New York Times*, in its obituary of Ingersoll on July 22, 1899, pinpointed the reason: "The suggestion that a declared and boasting unbeliever should be chosen to represent a Christian country brought a storm of indignation."

Ingersoll's political future looked bleak. In 1880 he campaigned hard for James Garfield, the Republican Party's successful nominee, but then for a few years he took a vacation from politics, returning to his lucrative legal practice and his steadily increasing popularity as a lecturer debunking religion. When Blaine became the party's nominee in 1884, he no longer sought help from Ingersoll. In a delicious irony, Blaine's narrow defeat in the general election was attributable to the overeager support he got from Reverend Samuel D. Burchard, who attacked the Democratic Party as the party of "rum, Romanism, and rebellion." That remark enraged Catholic voters in New York City, who turned out in large numbers to vote against Blaine. Losing the electoral votes of New York cost Blaine the victory. Religious politics cut in more than one direction. They ruled out the infidel Ingersoll, but they also defeated the overzealous Protestant Blaine.

In 1894, Reverend A. C. Dixon, a Baptist pastor with a church in Brooklyn, addressed two thousand listeners assembled in a New York City Broadway theater. Devoting his lecture to the errors of "Ingersollism," he proclaimed that any politician who sought Ingersoll's support would go down in flames. He mentioned Ingersoll's unsuccessful nomination of Blaine in 1876, and then largely fabricated a story about a later aspirant for the Republican nomination, Walter Q. Gresham. According to Dixon, Ingersoll was supposed to nominate Gresham at the 1888 Republican Convention until an unknown man in a crowd protested that "no man nominated by an infidel has ever been or could be elected president" (*New York Times,* April 23, 1894). Ingersoll had supported Gresham's unsuccessful bid for the nomination, but he was never slated to nominate him. Nonetheless, Reverend Dixon's fabrication contained a large measure of truth. The well-known Presbyterian minister Thomas DeWitt Talmadge, who was a persistent critic of Ingersoll, apparently remarked that "Christianity must be true because an infidel cannot be elected to office." Ingersoll made fun of Talmadge's logic, but the second part of his statement was true enough.

Ingersoll had a few clerical friends, most notably Henry Ward Beecher, the liberal Protestant preacher with a devoted following at Brooklyn's Plymouth Church and a national audience. Beecher was the son of Lyman Beecher, perhaps America's premier Protestant preacher in the early nineteenth century, and the brother of Harriet Beecher Stowe, the author of *Uncle Tom's Cabin.* He and Ingersoll sparred on the subject of religion, but shared a willingness to provoke controversy. Beecher had almost as many clerical critics as Ingersoll, and not just because the newspaper editor Theodore Tilton accused Beecher of seducing his wife. Dixon and Talmadge were more typical among American ministers in attacking Ingersoll. In a rare burst of pique, Ingersoll threatened to sue Dixon for libel because of Dixon's claim that Ingersoll was the leader and friend of some of the most "notorious dealers in indecent literature in New York." The only truth in this charge was that Ingersoll opposed the eponymous Comstock Law that Congress enacted in 1873 to forbid the circulation and distribution of obscene material, which included information about birth control.

From the mid-1870s until his death in 1899, Ingersoll lectured in every state except Mississippi, North Carolina, and Oklahoma. His speaking repertory was not limited to religion. He drew large audiences to hear him talk about artists, writers, and thinkers he admired. These included the Scottish poet Robert Burns, the German composer Richard Wagner, and the writer Ingersoll had worshipped from an early age, William Shakespeare. He named Walt Whitman as his favorite American poet and counted him as a friend. Whitman had his own problems with the clergy. He was a religious freethinker but called himself a pantheist rather than an agnostic. Whitman's religious views were responsible for a relatively minor part of the hostility he received from his "genteel" critics. They were much more upset by the explicit evocation of sexual pleasure in his poetry. Whitman's sensuality didn't bother Ingersoll. He was an honorary pallbearer at Whitman's funeral and delivered the concluding eulogy. What he said of the great poet, he doubtlessly thought about himself: Whitman was "maligned and slandered simply because he had the candor of nature. . . . He gave to us the gospel of humanity—the greatest gospel that can be preached."

Despite the variety of his repertory, Ingersoll's most popular lectures were the ones that attacked Christianity, the Bible, and clerics. He filled the biggest auditoriums in America's major cities. When he spoke in towns with no large arenas, his supporters constructed tents. The price of admission was one dollar, a large sum of money at the time, and "speculators," what we now call "scalpers," at many of the sold-out events collected whatever price they asked for the tickets they had had the foresight to amass in advance. Public oratory in the nineteenth century was a major form of entertainment. All American newspapers gave extensive coverage to Ingersoll, because he was the best of all the orators. He could speak without notes for over two hours, and newspaper accounts emphasized the frequent applause and laughter that greeted his remarks. Ingersoll's lectures might have been humorous and good-natured, both traits of his personality, but they contained stinging critiques of religion.

Consider the following remarks culled from newspaper accounts of Ingersoll's speeches in the 1880s and 1890s: "Christ never did anything to better the world. He never encouraged education, home, or marriage. He was a wanderer, and his disciples had no business." "I hate this Bible, because it has driven men to insanity: I hate it because it has always been the enemy of human liberty and the bulwark of slavery." "What is real blasphemy? . . . To prevent the growth of the human mind; to pollute children's minds with the dogma of eternal punishment; . . . to excite the prejudice of ignorance and superstition." "Where do we get our ministers? A young man, without constitution enough to be wicked, without health enough to enjoy the things of the world, naturally fixes his gaze on high. . . . Every pulpit is a pillory in which stands a convict; every member of the Church stands over him with a club called a creed." Ingersoll's critics called him a blasphemer, but he never faced charges.

Observers disagreed about the composition of Ingersoll's audiences. Hostile ministers predictably described his hearers as mostly men who wished to be entertained with "intellectual flippancy" and "boisterous mirth" directed at "high and sacred themes." Others judged the people in the crowds "intelligent and respectable," noting that Ingersoll's wife and daughters regularly attended his lectures along with many other women. We can't be sure, but all the evidence suggests that Ingersoll reached a cross section of the American population that behaved not like an ill-mannered mob but like people attending a serious entertainment. In all likelihood, the men and women who sat for several hours listening to Ingersoll's attacks on Christianity included churchgoers who enjoyed arguing about church doctrine and laughing at jokes they told to themselves about their beliefs and their ministers. They were, that is, very much like the Republicans who flocked to hear Ingersoll address political rallies. Although his religious views disqualified him for elected office, his skills as an orator gave him celebrity status in Republican electoral politics.

Ingersoll's political views sometimes veered toward progressivism but had nothing in common with the sorts of radicalism linked to atheism discussed in the preceding chapter. After the Civil War and Reconstruction ended, he continued the stance he had taken as an abolitionist and championed the rights of the freed slaves. He vigorously protested the Supreme Court decision in 1883 that effectively rendered the post–Civil War civil rights acts useless in protecting the rights of black American citizens. Ingersoll was also a vigorous advocate of equal rights for women—their right to vote, their right to plan their families, their right to divorce. In 1886 he supported Henry George, author of the best-selling *Progress and Poverty*, when he ran for mayor of New York City. George proposed a single tax on property that in effect would have confiscated the wealth that accrued to men simply by their holding title to land that they never put to any use. George lost the race, held in the same year as the Haymarket Affair, but he split the Republican vote, defeating the party candidate Theodore Roosevelt, who finished an embarrassing third in the race.

It's easy to misread Ingersoll's support for George. It didn't reflect a radical position but a deeply conservative one. Ingersoll explained himself to a *New York Times* reporter on November 5, 1886: American workers didn't need strikes or unions or socialism. They needed faith in democratic politics. Ingersoll supported George hoping that his campaign would convince workers that they had a stake in democracy. They would look to the ballot as a way to better their position. He took the same tack with respect to the convicted Haymarket anarchists. He said publicly that they hadn't received a fair trial and asked the Republican governor of Illinois, Richard Oglesby, to commute their sentences from execution to life imprisonment. He had no sympathy for anarchism, but the working class needed to believe that American law treated everyone equally. He told the *Chicago Tribune* on November 4, 1886, much the same thing: "In this country," Ingersoll argued, "there is no excuse for Nihilism or Socialism." In a longer interview about Haymarket, given to the New York *Mail and Express*, and included in his *Collected Works*, Ingersoll pointed out what he considered an unproblematic truism: "The source of power here is the people. . . . If the laws are oppressive it is the fault of the oppressed. If the laws touch the poor, leave the poor without redress, it is the fault of the poor. They are in a majority . . . and have the power to make every law that is made in the United States. There is no excuse for any resort to violence in this country." Ingersoll hoped workers would come to believe that the vote was the only tool they needed to resolve their disputes with management and to promote their self-interest. His faith in democracy was absolute, and his own vote usually went to support the comfortable and the rich.

Ingersoll lived through decades of political corruption, especially in the Republican Party, which was the usual party in power, and abusive practices of unregulated American corporations. Those matters never became the subjects of his speeches. In one of his most celebrated legal victories, he successfully defended high-ranking officials who were charged with fraud in the "Star Route scandal" of the 1880s. They were accused of taking bribes in awarding postal delivery contracts to private interests. The scandal embarrassed the Republican administration and led to calls for civil service reform. The Pendleton Civil Service Reform Act of 1883 was a modest step in that direction. Ingersoll was not a supporter of that act. He sided with his close friend Roscoe Conklin, the powerful New York senator who led the "Stalwart" faction of the Republican Party. Conklin, by dint of his office, controlled the patronage of the New York Customs House, a position threatened by civil service reform. In 1888, Conklin died and Ingersoll delivered what the *Chicago Tribune* on May 10, 1888, termed a "matchless eulogy" at Albany's Academy of Music attended by 3,500 people. Its theme was Conklin's absolute honesty: "His hand was never touched by any bribe, and on his soul, there was never a sordid stain."

Such were the limits of Ingersoll's skepticism. It extended to religion, but not to the operations of American democracy. In the last decade of his life he remained in high demand as a Republican orator who effectively attacked William Jennings Bryan's Populism, defended the gold standard, and championed William McKinley and his politics of expanding the territory of the United States beyond its borders. It came late in his life, but he never doubted for a minute the wisdom of the Spanish-American War.

Clarence Darrow admired Ingersoll's agnosticism and that affinity drew them together in friendship. Darrow's famous cross-examination of William Jennings Bryan at the trial of John Scopes followed a legal script that might have been lifted from Ingersoll's shredding of biblical stories recounted in both the Old and New Testaments. On the other hand, as a lawyer Darrow took on unpopular causes, often involving labor radicals, that never figured in Ingersoll's legal practice. Despite his theological differences with Bryan, Darrow supported his Populist reform ideas. Ingersoll was on the other side of the political fence. At a memorial meeting in Chicago held to honor Ingersoll, Darrow struck a discordant note: "Ingersoll believed in liberty so far as the church was concerned, but on political questions he seemingly was colorblind. The older and more venerable a political superstition was, the more he would cling to it" (*Chicago Tribune*, August 27, 1900).

At the service, Ingersoll's admirers hissed and booed Darrow's remark, but Darrow was correct about Ingersoll's basic conservative outlook. Ingersoll's politics were unexceptional in Republican circles and might have made him a powerful Republican candidate for high office. Ingersoll was a passionate defender of the goodness of the United States. He was a great orator, who could make complex issues seem simple and clear to voters. He held the attention of a crowd better than any public figure in his time. He was a man with a great capacity for friendship, and a deep and abiding love for his wife and daughters. He might have become president—except he didn't believe in God.

Ingersoll spent thirty years moving in high political circles, but in the end the course he had set for himself in 1868 left him without a significant place in the history of American politics.

If Ingersoll had regrets, he didn't record them. He couldn't understand why Americans didn't applaud Thomas Paine's statement that "any system of religion that has anything in it that shocks the mind of a child cannot be a true system." His own religious upbringing had made him miserable as a youth. He recalled: "When I was a boy Sunday was considered altogether too holy to be happy in. . . . Nobody said a pleasant word; nobody laughed, nobody smiled; the child that looked the sickest was regarded as the most pious. . . . No matter how cold the weather was, there was no fire in the church. It was thought to be a kind of sin to be comfortable while you were thanking God." That unhappiness or illness could be interpreted as piety made no sense to Ingersoll.

Ingersoll's childhood anguish caused by Christian instruction bears a striking parallel to the early years of Elizabeth Cady Stanton, arguably the most important American in the nineteenth-century struggle for women's rights. Stanton was twenty years older than Ingersoll and grew up in privileged circumstances in Johnstown, New York, a city that lay in the Mohawk Valley of upstate New York. The winters of Johnstown were cold, as cold as the doctrines of Stanton's Presbyterian church that were steeped in strict Calvinist views about the hell that awaited most of humankind. In her autobiography *Eighty Years and More*, Stanton recalled: "So when the thermometer was twenty degrees below zero on the Johnstown Hill, . . . we trudged along through the snow . . . to the cold hospitalities of the 'Lord's House,' there to be chilled to the very core by listening to sermons on 'predestination,' 'justification by faith,' and 'eternal damnation.'"

Daniel Cady, Stanton's father, was a prominent landowner and attorney who served one term in the United States House of Representatives. Later he was a justice on the New York Supreme Court. His conservative views on social and political matters extended to his acceptance of traditional gender roles. Women's sphere lay primarily in the home. His daughter's academic quickness posed a problem for his conventional viewpoint, especially after the early death of the last of his male heirs. "Ah," he sighed to her when she brought home a prize attesting to her academic excellence, "you should have been a boy." The remark "devastated" the young Elizabeth, but Cady at least made certain that his daughter was educated. She studied Latin, Greek, mathematics, and science until she was sixteen. Then, unable to enter the all-male Union College where her brother Eleazar had gone, she enrolled at the Troy Female Academy founded by Emma Willard.

Fears about eternal damnation haunted Stanton into her late teen years. Charles Grandison Finney, the most famous evangelical preacher of his generation and later the president of Oberlin College, held a protracted revival meeting in Troy while Elizabeth was a student there. Sadly, she recalled in her autobiography, she was one of the "first victims" of "this terrifier of human souls." Finney's dramatic stress on "the total depravity of human nature" made "the most innocent girl" believe herself "a monster of iniquity" poised on the brink of hell. "Visions of the lost [souls] haunted my dreams. Mental anguish protracted my health. Dethronement of my reason was apprehended by friends." Nineteenth-century autobiographies often tell of the solace that men and women found in religion. Elizabeth Cady's case, like Ingersoll's, was different.

Conversations she had with her brother-in-law Edward Bayard and with her cousin, the radical abolitionist Gerrit Smith, were critical in helping Elizabeth find new intellectual horizons. Bayard introduced her to phrenology and homeopathy, two causes that Elizabeth embraced as founded on science and reason as they were then thought to be. Smith's views challenging the ideology of slavery led Elizabeth to question the ideas of justice held by her father. He owned a slave until slavery was abolished in New York in 1827. Clear thinking, unencumbered by religion, made it plain to her that women endured a form of slavery. "After many months of weary wandering, . . . I found my way out of the darkness into the clear sunlight of Truth. My religious superstition gave place to rational ideas based on scientific facts."

By the time she turned twenty, Elizabeth was no longer a Christian and didn't believe in any religion. "The memory of my own suffering has prevented me from ever showing one young soul any of the superstitions of the Christian religion." Unlike Ingersoll, however, she waited a long time before aligning her public career with attacks on religion. Another social crusade began to occupy her attention on the eve of her marriage. Gerrit Smith introduced her to Henry Brewster Stanton. Like Smith, he was a radical abolitionist, the sort who supported John Brown and was open to new forms of social order. He was content when he wed Elizabeth that she insisted on dropping the word "obey" from the marriage vows. She took her husband's name, but she never signed her name Mrs. Henry Brewster Stanton. She was Elizabeth Cady Stanton.

The marriage of Elizabeth and Henry lasted until his death in 1887. She had seven children, who all lived to adulthood. Complaints about her domestic responsibilities as wife and mother are minimal in her published writings, but then her marriage was not a conventional one. Both Stanton and her husband became activists who were called to distant places on speaking engagements. Some of the trips lasted for months. Husband and wife were as often apart as together. So often were their ideas. A harbinger of the separation that marked their married life occurred on their honeymoon. They traveled to London, where Henry was a delegate to the World Anti-Slavery Convention. Only male delegates were allowed to speak at the convention. Its rules, ones that would split the abolitionist movement, insisted that women remain silent at political meetings just as they did at church. Henry spoke and Elizabeth sat in the audience. She was outraged: "Many remarkable women . . . were all compelled to listen in silence to the masculine platitudes on women's sphere." She blamed the "clerical portion" of the convention. They "were in agony lest the women should do or say something to shock the heavenly hosts."

That was in 1840. After the convention ended, the Stantons toured France and Germany before returning to the United States to set up a household, first in New York City and then in Boston. Henry practiced law, and his wife became a mother. In the spring of 1847, concerns over Henry's health prompted the family to resettle in Seneca Falls, New York, at the northern end of Lake Cayuga. Stanton knew the town because her sister and her husband lived there. It was this unforeseen relocation of the Stantons that destined an unlikely town to become the birthplace of the women's movement. Barely a year after her move from Boston, Stanton and her friend Lucretia Mott issued a call for a Women's Rights Convention. Mott, who was a Quaker and a long-time activist in the abolitionist movement, had met Stanton at the antislavery convention in London that Stanton had attended with her husband on their honeymoon. Mott and Stanton had discussed a women's rights convention then, but it took eight years for the idea to come to fruition.

Although the announcement went out only five days before the event, the sessions held on July 19 and 20, 1848, were crowded with over three hundred attendees. Sixty-eight women and thirty-two men signed the Declaration of Sentiments that Stanton had coauthored to resemble the Declaration of Independence. An opening paragraph that mimicked Jefferson's language to declare the equality of men and women was followed by a long set of grievances. Accompanying the Declaration of Sentiments was a list of resolutions. Stanton's husband was supportive to a point and helped draft the resolution on women's property rights. However he balked at the demand for women's suffrage, warning his wife that her insistence on the vote for women would turn the convention into a "farce." He didn't attend the convention and he didn't sign the Declaration of Sentiments.

In fairness to Henry, many women at Seneca Falls agreed with him and didn't support the demand for women's suffrage. Mott was one of them. Although she later changed her mind, she placed little value on politics at the time of the Seneca Falls Convention. Stanton was not a person inclined to compromise. She was not about to put aside a demand she deemed essential just because it was unpopular and lost signatures on the Declaration. Her insistence carried the day, and in a short time the demand for women's suffrage became the most celebrated of the Seneca Falls resolutions.

Susan B. Anthony was not at Seneca Falls. She didn't meet Stanton until 1851. Yet from that moment on they worked effectively as a team, a collaboration lasting until Stanton's death in 1902. Anthony lived for another four years. The younger Anthony never married, although she frequently stayed in Stanton's house, taking care of the children while Stanton wrote. In their five decades of partnership, Stanton probably spent more time with Anthony than with her husband. The consensus among scholars is that Stanton was the better writer and the sharper thinker of the two, Anthony the better organizer and tactician. Anthony also believed, unlike Stanton, that it was sometimes wise to keep her opinions to herself if stating them made the cause of suffrage unacceptable to "fashionable" women. Both women were agnostics, but there came a time when Stanton thought it necessary to trumpet her views to those fashionable women, and Anthony demurred.

Until that time they seemed to be of one mind. Together and separately they traveled the country on speaking tours. In addition to women's suffrage, they worked for temperance laws, for divorce reforms that gave women more legal grounds to escape an abusive husband, and for laws that secured property rights for married women. Jointly they formed the first women's suffrage organization, and together they wrote a three-volume *History of Woman Suffrage*. They also made joint mistakes. One of them was their opposition to the passage of the Fifteenth Amendment, which extended voting rights to former male slaves freed by the Civil War, despite their friendship with Frederick Douglass, who was at the Seneca Falls Convention and signed the Declaration of Sentiments as one of "the gentlemen present in favor of the new movement."

Their opposition was a tactical one fueled by their disappointment that Douglass, despite their own work for the abolitionist movement, refused to insist that the vote be granted "jointly to freedmen and all women, black and white." Though Douglass strongly supported women's right to vote, he feared that the resolution insisted upon by Stanton and Anthony would spoil "The Negro's Hour." The principle that explained why Stanton and Anthony refused to support the Fifteenth

Amendment is understandable, but they unfortunately sometimes expressed their opposition in racist language. Stanton called it a mistake to "stand aside and see Sambo walk into the Kingdom [of civil rights]" before white women of "education and refinement." Stanton and Anthony's insistence on suffrage for everyone or nothing for the black male split the woman's movement into two organizations.

Into the 1880s Anthony was every bit as confrontational as Stanton. She was the one who went to jail for trying to vote. In 1885, the two women attended a service in the nation's capital officiated by Reverend William Patton, the president of Howard University. In his sermon Patton claimed that "freedom for women led to incredulity and immorality." In leaving the service, Anthony remarked to Patton, in a voice loud enough to be picked up by reporters: "Doctor, your mother, if you have one, should lay you across her knee and give you a good spanking."

Yet by 1890, when the two largest women's suffrage organizations reunited to form the National American Woman Suffrage Association, the tactics of the two women had clearly diverged. The new organization had significant support from the Woman's Christian Temperance Union. As a result, Anthony grew alarmed when her impatient friend became more outspoken in attacking religion. Because Anthony didn't want to offend the "very fashionable women" of the WCTU, she didn't endorse Stanton's claim that Christianity held women in a "condition of slavery," as Stanton argued in an article she published in the *North American Review* in May 1885. She answered the question she posed in her title "Has Christianity Benefited Woman?" with a resounding "no." "Sacred scriptures," she wrote, make "woman an afterthought in the creation, the author of sin, in collusion with the devil, sex a crime, . . . and maternity a curse . . . a just punishment for affecting the downfall of man." All these "monstrous ideas" belonged to an "exclusively masculine religion," personified in the New Testament by Peter and Paul, who falsely claimed that it represented "the word of God."

Anthony, who was reared in a radical Quaker family, held religious views almost identical to the agnosticism of Stanton. Like Stanton she had no personal use for organized religion, rejected all claims about the divine inspiration of the Bible, and had grave doubts about an afterlife. However, Anthony recognized that if the attainment of suffrage had to wait until all potential allies became agnostics, women would never vote. You could not win the support of Frances Willard, the president of the WCTU, by telling her that women didn't deserve to vote until they chased religion from their minds. Christian women had proved to Anthony's satisfaction that they could be strong supporters of women's rights.

Stanton didn't agree. Church loyalties made women their own worst enemies. A woman "would never be fit for freedom . . . until she ceased to hold to her bosom the primary cause of her degradation— her religious superstitions." Stanton was more interested in finding allies among working-class women than among church ladies. In the early 1890s she vigorously championed opening Chicago's celebrated Columbian Exposition on Sundays, despite opposition to it by most of the clergy. She supported the Populist Party and on the political spectrum moved toward socialism. In a speech she delivered in 1888 to the Women's Council in Washington, D.C., she warned: "The time is not far distant when, if men do not do justice to women, the women will strike hands with labor, with Socialists, with Anarchists, and you will have the scenes of the Revolution in France acted over again in this Republic." According to a *Chicago Tribune* reporter who covered the event on March 30, 1888, the "pronouncement was received in silence," without the slightest ripple of applause, and prompted a number of angry protests.

Anthony worked hard but mostly in vain to soothe the feathers that Stanton ruffled. She was able to use her political capital to make sure that Stanton was elected president of the newly formed NAWSA. That leadership position didn't moderate Stanton's views or incline her to compromise with prominent women she viewed as wrongheaded. She in fact took little interest in the office. Knowing that many women in the organization didn't like her, she gave up the presidency after two years and turned her full attention to a project she conceived in the 1880s. Having concluded that the mere achievement of the vote would not do enough, not nearly enough, to gain equal rights for women, she wanted to provide women with a better understanding of the reasons for their lowly place in the world. She settled on the Bible as women's biggest problem. It was not a holy book that women ought to revere. It was a man-made invention that relegated women to second-class status. The writing and publication of *The Woman's Bible* dominated Stanton's career in the last decade of her life. The first volume appeared in 1895, and the second three years later. Anthony took no part in the enterprise and warned Stanton that "it was a great waste of time . . . to descant on the barbarism of 6,500 years ago."

Stanton failed to locate many women who were eager to aid her in her labors. Some early sponsors of the project quickly backed off when they realized what Stanton had in mind. These included Frances Willard. Stanton eventually assembled a "Revising Committee" composed of American and European women. It was a hodgepodge of women who did little more than allow their names to be listed. On the list was Mrs. Robert G. Ingersoll. That was appropriate, for Stanton was a great admirer of her husband. When he died, she wrote in her diary, "No other loss, outside my own family, could have filled me with such sorrow. The future historian will rank him as one of the heroes of the nineteenth century." In addition to the Revising Committee, a much smaller group of women helped Stanton write commentaries on culled scriptural passages that Stanton believed demeaned women. They were the crucial parts of *The Woman's Bible*.

Part I of *The Woman's Bible* covered the books of the Pentateuch— Genesis, Exodus, Leviticus, Numbers, and Deuteronomy. The second part dealt with passages in other books of the Old Testament as well as some in the New Testament. According to Stanton, the project's purpose was "to revise Biblical texts relating to women, or those in which women were made prominent by exclusion." The commentaries in both volumes of *The Woman's Bible* reinterpreted biblical stories where "mistranslation" had resulted in denigrating statements about women, or simply excised male-centered passages that were beyond redemption. Most of what Saint Paul said about women fell in that second category.

But Stanton was not always of one mind with the women who helped her. Some of the latter, whatever revisions they accepted, still regarded the Bible as a holy book. They didn't share Stanton's opinion that it was essential to destroy the Bible's claim to divine inspiration and reduce its status to that of an ordinary book that was uplifting in some places but utter drivel in other places. In writing one of her commentaries Stanton noted as an aside: "Some members of the Revising Committee write me that the tone of some of my comments should be more reverent in criticizing the 'Word of God'." She dismissed the criticism without the slightest deference to their feelings. "Does anyone at this stage of civilization think the Bible was written by the finger of God?"

In fact, many members of the National American Woman Suffrage Association did. The organization played no role whatsoever in the production of *The Woman's Bible*. Stanton was no longer its president when the first volume appeared. The negative publicity that greeted its publication convinced many members of the NAWSA that they had to avoid guilt by association. Despite the fact that most of them had been part of the audience of eight thousand that gathered in New York's Metropolitan Opera House to celebrate Stanton's eightieth birthday two weeks after the publication of the first volume, they plotted to set a distance between the NAWSA and Stanton. They wanted to follow the lead of the WCTU, which had already passed a "sorrowful condemnation" of Stanton's labor. Part of the resolution read: "We accept the place given us in God's book with joy; . . . the attempt to mar the perfectness of the Holy Scripture for personal reasons or self-aggrandizement is a sin."

At its annual convention of the NAWSA in 1896, delegates were asked to vote on a resolution repudiating any "official connection with the so-called *Woman's Bible*." The resolution further stated that "the very essence of religion is equal and exact justice for all women and men; therefore, the demand for woman suffrage is in the largest sense a moral and religious movement." Anthony regarded the motion as a deliberate snub of Stanton, and whatever her disagreements with Stanton she wanted no part of it. She strongly urged the convention to reject the resolution. Her speech was a brave one, and despite her desire not to offend Christian women, she allied herself with Stanton's religious views. "I have yet to see the first editorial word from an honest soul that takes the position that the Bible was divinely inspired."

Anthony's main point was inclusiveness. "A Christian has no more right on our platform than an Atheist." She reminded delegates of Ernestine Rose, a Polish-born Jewish immigrant to the United States who even before the Seneca Falls Convention gave lectures on abolitionism and equal rights for women. She was an outspoken atheist, and on many occasions defended nonbelief at the annual birthday celebrations of Thomas Paine each January. Rose, who died in England in 1892, served as president of the fifth National Women's Rights Convention in 1854. Despite the outspoken clerical opposition to everything Rose did, she always, Anthony emphasized, "stood for justice and freedom." Anthony concluded her speech by echoing one of Stanton's favorite lines: "If women are going to do without thinking they had better do without the vote."

Anthony's appeal fell mostly on deaf ears. The resolution passed 53 to 41. Stanton's work with the NAWSA was effectively done. Anthony put the loss of the vote behind her and continued to work with the WCTU. Her strategy of inclusiveness survived and doubtlessly was an essential element in the eventual victory for women's suffrage almost two decades after her death. It guaranteed her fame. Stanton was left to grouse unfairly: "They have given Susan thousands of dollars, jewels, laces, silks, and satins, and me criticism of my radical ideas." At the end of her life, Stanton found a publisher for her autobiography, though she complained that it wasn't widely reviewed, but she failed to find financial backing to publish a collection of her speeches and papers.

When Stanton died, eulogists spoke respectfully of her work on behalf of women's rights, but almost no one referred to her agnosticism. One exception was Helen H. Gardner, who told mourners at a memorial meeting in Washington that Stanton "wished it known that she died, as she had lived, a fearless, serene agnostic." There were even fewer references to *The Woman's Bible*. The work in which Stanton had invested such hope sank into oblivion. Opponents of the women's suffrage amendment cited Stanton's disbelief as a reason to vote against the measure. Two of her children when they published excerpts of her letters and diaries in 1922 deleted her references to her struggles against religion. In 1923, with suffrage safely won, Alice Paul introduced the Equal Rights Amendment before the National Woman's Party, praising Anthony and saying not a word about Stanton. In the archives of major newspapers in the twentieth century, articles about Anthony are over ten times as numerous as references to the woman who made Seneca Falls famous and who predicted correctly that the vote by itself would not make women equal to men.

The lesson to be taken from the lives of Ingersoll and Stanton seems pretty clear. If you want to be revered in American memory, don't mix your work with an insistence that Christianity is a foolish set of superstitions that cripple the progress of reason and science. But does this caveat have anything to do with religious liberty? Ingersoll and Stanton weren't burned at the stake. They were not tarred and feathered and driven out of town. Neither of them spent a night in jail because of their religious beliefs, or paid a fine for expressing them publicly. Both of them lived comfortable lives with their families. They were influential people. Aren't these facts a testament to America's openness to all religious expression, including free thought? To tolerate a religious position doesn't mean you have to like it. Americans don't want atheists to lead them. So what? Neither Ingersoll nor Stanton was shy about expressing open contempt for Christianity. What's sauce for the goose is sauce for the gander.

We argue in a later chapter that nonbelievers in America remain legally underprivileged in important ways. But law is not the question now, but the force of public opinion. Americans in the past and in the present may choose not to vote for a declared atheist. But is that a religious test? The simple answer is "no," but a simple "no" won't settle the question about whether public opinion, as John Stuart Mill argued, can infringe on liberty, in this case religious liberty, in a way that should worry us. We need to ask another question. What's the cost of excluding qualified people from positions of leadership because they hold a minority religious position that harms no one and that, despite the associations discussed in the preceding chapter, isn't typically linked to violence or social disruption. Atheists don't go to church, but they are no more likely to commit crimes than people who claim to pray every day. History as well as contemporary events suggest pretty clearly that we have much more to fear from the consequences of religious zealotry than from the consequences of religious free thought. History also suggests that Golda Meir, Winston Churchill, and Jawaharlal Nehru were effective leaders despite their lack of theistic faith. A prejudice, and that is what we are talking about, can work as strongly to constrain belief as legal censorship or prohibition. If people must hide their religious opinions to run for public office, then do we really live in a society ruled by religious liberty? Or have we poisoned religious liberty by encouraging hypocrisy?

There is another point of equal importance. Textbooks of American history are filled with examples of how religion shaped our country. That's fine. The Puritans did what they did because they were religious. Churches of every denomination were important institutions to Americans as they settled new communities. Mormons could not have survived persecution and reached the Great Salt Lake without their faith. Slave religion proved an essential way for African Americans in the antebellum south to define their humanity, and free blacks in the north relied on black churches to build their resistance to discrimination. Catholicism provided the means for many immigrants to adapt the lives they had left in Europe to new circumstances in the United States. The question is not why religion looms so large but why textbooks say nothing about the importance of atheism to many other Americans. Schoolchildren need to learn the full range of motives that propel people to action. And they don't.

We want to be clear about this. Atheists succeed in America and are honored for their work. Albert Einstein was an agnostic like Charles Darwin, but he was celebrated as perhaps the greatest scientist of the twentieth century. So was Thomas Edison for his multiple inventions that ranged from electric lighting to recorded sound to motion pictures, although he admired Thomas Paine and in his own philosophy substituted Nature for the idea of a God who intervened in human affairs. Andrew Carnegie successfully pursued his career as a steel magnate and was praised for giving large sums of his money to endow museums, libraries, and universities, although he wrote how important it was for him that he "got rid of theology and the supernatural" and believed that "the whole scheme of Christian salvation is diabolical." Alexander Graham Bell, the man credited with the invention of the telephone, was agnostic from an early age. But American schoolchildren don't learn that these men and many other American innovators linked their ability to make creative leaps outside the box of received thought to their agnosticism. It's akin to teaching them that the Massachusetts Bay Puritans liked to work hard without mentioning their religious belief that steady work in their calling was a sign they were among the saints God had chosen for salvation.

Take one more instructive example. Luther Burbank (1849–1926) was a self-taught botanist and horticulturalist who developed more than eight hundred strains of fruits, flowers, grains, grasses, and vegetables. The Russet Burbank potato remains the most widely cultivated potato in the United States and is used by family-friendly McDonald's to make french fries. Celebrated for his modesty and benevolence, Burbank lived a noncontroversial life until just before he died. In the year he turned seventy-seven, he published an article that declared "I Am an Infidel." His decision to announce publicly views he had long held was prompted by the dismay he felt over the Scopes trial. Though he was a friend of the religious fundamentalist William Jennings Bryan, Burbank wrote in exasperation, "And to think of this great country in danger of being dominated by people ignorant enough to take a few ancient Babylonian legends as the canons of modern culture." Claiming that all religions rest on "a tottering foundation," he stated, "I am a doubter, a questioner, a skeptic." Burbank regretted that scientists like him had not spoken out sooner against religious bigotry. He praised Robert Ingersoll for his bravery in taking on the clergy and the superstitions they defended: "I do not think there is a person in the world who has not been a more ardent admirer of Ingersoll than I have been."

On January 27, 1926, the *Los Angeles Times* recorded that Burbank's remarks elicited a storm of criticism from clergy across the country. The WCTU in Santa Rosa, the city where Burbank lived, prayed that Burbank's "eyes may be opened" and that "the youth of the community may not be led astray from the religion of their fathers." Burbank was stunned by the hate mail he received in response to his article and patiently wrote back to his critics hoping that reason would lead them to change their minds. But he died before the task was nearly done.

Even so, Burbank's reputation survived the declaration made at the end of his life. Over five thousand admirers showed up for a memorial service held in Santa Rosa, California. They listened to the eulogy of Judge Ben Lindsay of Denver, another agnostic, who presided. Lindsay enjoyed a national reputation as a progressive reformer who pioneered a successful movement to create a separate court system for juvenile offenders. He was less celebrated for his religious views and for his advocacy of trial marriage for young couples before they tied the official knot. In honoring Burbank, Lindsay made no apology for Burbank's disbelief in a life after death. His immortality lay in his work. Lindsay observed that Burbank, rather than respecting the effort "of hidebound theologians, still desperately trying to chain us to the past," spoke for "a real religion that actually works for human betterment—a religion that dares to challenge the superstition, hypocrisy and sham that so often worked cruelties, inquisitions, wars, and massacres."

The outpouring of support for Burbank was impressive and came despite his declaration of unbelief. His agnosticism didn't overturn his work. A number of schools across the nation bear Burbank's name. However, how many of the students who attend those schools ever read his essay "I Am an Infidel" or hear of Burbank's fears that the United States is "dominated by people ignorant enough to take a few ancient Babylonian legends" as true? Nowhere in the curriculum will it be suggested that Burbank's creativity was owed in part to his agnosticism. Knowledge involves learning why people act as they do, and when schoolchildren aren't asked to consider connections between nonbelief and creativity when that lesson is relevant, or may learn instead that nonbelief is un-American, they are being shortchanged. The purpose of education should not be what Betsy DeVos, the secretary of education during Donald Trump's administration, claimed: advocacy of the "advance of God's kingdom."

With respect to the matter of what system of thought best benefits humanity, organized religion does have one significant advantage over the forms of nonbelief that emerged in the nineteenth century, and it needs to be acknowledged. When Robert Ingersoll died, Reverend Frank G. Tyrrell dismissed his legacy: "Like infidelity in all ages, this dead advocate . . . built nothing . . . left nothing but a memory that will soon perish." Tyrrell was right about Ingersoll leaving no institutional legacy. Elizabeth Cady Stanton, whose memory was not effaced, only whitewashed, was wrong when she predicted that future historians would rank Ingersoll as a great American hero. Historians remember Ingersoll as a secondary figure in American politics, and most other Americans don't know his name at all.

On at least one occasion, Stanton recognized why Christianity persisted as a force. In 1882, while staying in Toulouse, she confided to her diary, "What a wonderful organization the Catholic Church is! In these convents and sisterhoods, it realizes . . . the principle of cooperation. My dream of the future is of cooperation. But is there any other foundation outside of religion on which it can be based? Can a belief grounded on science, common sense and love of humanity sway the human soul as fears of the torments of hell and promises of the joys of heaven have done?" Ingersoll's career of lashing out against religion made him famous in his time, but it left no community or tangible work to keep his memory alive.

Stanton was hardly the first person to marvel at the power of religious worship to sway not just individuals but communities. In doing so, she was not falling back on theology, certainly not Catholic theology, but for her, being an unchurched American meant nothing in particular unless she used her independence to advance an important cause. No matter how many examples of the moral blindness of organized religion Stanton or Ingersoll could cite, they both recognized its power to move people to action. That power continues to challenge atheists in America. What, after all, is the good of nonbelief if it cannot promote collective actions to better the human condition and leads only to a narrow self-fulfillment? That question haunted the three agnostics who are the subject of the next chapter. Each, in different ways, tried to define a "church" that could unite nonbelievers in moral action. As we shall see in later chapters, the question they addressed remains a problem that has not been solved.

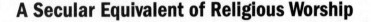

A Secular Equivalent of Religious Worship

IN HIS FAMOUS essay "The Moral Equivalent of War," the American philosopher William James weighed the truth of the following proposition: "If war had ever stopped, we should have to re-invent it . . . to redeem life from flat degeneration." The essay, James's last published utterance, appeared in the *Popular Science Monthly* in 1910, the year of his death. James was an ardent pacifist who hated war, but his essay acknowledged that in the past war and military valor generated virtues important to our collective life—a contempt for softness, intrepidity, and the surrender of private interest. If human beings managed to stop the slaughter of military combat, they would need to find an irenic equivalent to martial ideals of glory and valor to inspire self-sacrifice. It wouldn't be easy.

James might have made a similar argument about a belief in God. He was never able to convince himself that God existed. But agnosticism, a position of suspended judgment, didn't satisfy James. Sometimes people had good reasons to commit to actions and beliefs without conclusive proof of their likely efficacy. If a belief in God kept a person from falling into a debilitating pessimism, then that person should certainly and wholeheartedly choose to believe in God. The contented life that resulted was itself proof of the belief. Critics of James might say that he taught a philosophy that justified make-believe, but James thought that an optimism that worked to make a person's life constructive was better than a capitulation to the fate of Mark Twain, who also died in 1910. Remembered as America's greatest humorist, Twain was in fact an atheist who in his final years painted a bleak canvas of human life. In *The Mysterious Stranger*, an uncompleted novella published posthumously, Satan, a nephew of the fallen angel of the same name, delivers Twain's gospel message: "It is true, that which I have revealed to you, there is no God, no universe, no human race, no earthly life, no heaven, no hell. It is all a foolish dream—a grotesque and foolish dream." In 1906 Twain published some of his bleak views about the human condition but only in an anonymous essay "What Is Man?" He had a reputation to protect: "I . . . expose to the world only my trimmed and perfumed and carefully barbered public opinions, and conceal, carefully, cautiously, wisely, my private ones." But keeping his authorship a secret didn't save him from the bitterness that consumed his last years. Twain's atheism produced profound pessimism.

In different ways the trio of remarkable people discussed in this chapter searched for a surrogate for religious worship. Each of them, Felix Adler, Jane Addams, and John Dewey, came from strong religious backgrounds, but their faith foundered in their early adulthood. Their careers spanned the years of America's Progressive Era (roughly from the last decades of the nineteenth century until America's entrance into World War I in 1917), when America's class of educated leaders included fewer clergy who had once been presidents and trustees of denominational colleges and universities and more of a new breed of professional men and women trained in increasingly secularized institutions of higher education and licensed, by stricter standards than had prevailed before, by individual states to become doctors, lawyers, engineers, and teachers. At the turn of the twentieth century, Americans as measured by church membership and attendance were not abandoning religion. But the three people selected for discussion here were like some other American thinkers and activists born in the same generation searching for an alternative to religion that did not end in the fate of Mark Twain. What came out of their search provides a bridge between the two parts of our book.

Felix Adler, an American philosopher who knew and admired William James, rejected all conventional religion. In his mind the theological doctrines on which the historic churches based themselves were becoming increasingly unbelievable. They constituted a drag on people's ability to adjust to a new age based upon science. Still, he worried about what would happen in a world without any religion. What could replace churches to keep alive ideals of human justice? Was there a secular equivalent of religion that could make a democratic society work and fuel the higher ranges of our "spiritual energy?" Could a nontheistic equivalent for religion motivate people to pursue morally driven public service that required a sacrifice of selfish interests? Answering those questions became Adler's life work.

Adler was born in Germany in 1851 and came with his family to America when he was six. His father had been appointed chief rabbi of Temple Emanu-El in New York City, one of the most important centers for Reform Judaism in the country. Educated at Columbia University and then at the University of Heidelberg, Adler was groomed to succeed his father at Emanu-El. It didn't happen. His doctoral studies in Germany left him without a belief in the God of Moses necessary to accept, let alone teach, even the liberal ideas of a Reform temple. Adler never declared himself an atheist. In a lecture he delivered in New York City in 1879, titled simply "Atheism," he rejected any position that asserts "the rule of chance, the denial of the transcendent importance of morality, the blasphemy against the Ideal." However, he retained no belief in a personal God ("no 'big man' above the clouds") or the divine origins of Hebrew scripture. The very idea that people must be moral because God had commanded them to obey his laws or because they feared hell came to offend him.

In 1874, instead of taking over from his father at Temple Emanu-El, Adler became a nonresident professor of Hebrew and Oriental literature at Cornell University. Adler apparently liked the time he spent in Ithaca, but when his three-year term on the faculty ended,

Cornell didn't renew his appointment. The records do not make clear the reasons for his termination, but anti-Semitism played a role. The very Christian Henry Sage, a powerful Cornell trustee and university benefactor, had always opposed Adler's appointment. Adler was sorry to lose his title of professor and was happy when his alma mater, Columbia, appointed him Professor of Political and Social Ethics some years later. He also must have felt a certain vindication when in 1917 he delivered a convocation address at Cornell to one thousand students.

Even so, in 1876, when Adler lost his Cornell appointment, he was busy working on another project, a project that brought his career closer to what it might have been as a rabbinical leader—a career leading an organization committed not to any existing religion but to ethical practice. Already there existed in the United States several societies that promoted free religious thought and rejected any claim that the Bible was the word of God or that Jesus was the son of God. Adler was a member of both the Secular Union and the Free Religious Association, the latter founded in Boston in 1867. Its president was Octavius Brooks Frothingham, a "radical" Unitarian with "antisupernatural" views, and among its first members was Ralph Waldo Emerson. But these societies didn't satisfy Adler. In his mind they didn't provide the sort of community life that committed their members to moral action. Although they rejected religious dogma and promoted a secular America, they in no way replaced the work of America's churches.

Adler came up with an alternative. In 1877 he incorporated the New York Society for Ethical Culture. By the turn of the century the more broadly named Ethical Culture Society had branches in many American cities and ties to similar organizations in England, France, Germany, and Switzerland. Among Adler's projects were a free kindergarten and elementary school for poor members of the working class, and a home-visiting nurse service in New York City. In the first part of the twentieth century leaders in the Ethical Culture movement were variously involved in the founding of the National Association for the Advancement of Colored People (NAACP), the National Civil Liberties Bureau (later the ACLU), and virtually every organization formed

to promote world peace. The ideas of Ethical Culture were also important to the future Supreme Court Justice Louis Brandeis, the first Jewish
member of the court, who married the sister of Adler's wife.

Adler distinguished his Ethical Culture Society from sectarian
religious organizations, welcoming nonbelievers as well as believers as
members. In an address he delivered in 1900, "The Essential Difference
Between Ethical Societies and the Churches," Adler said that a secular
society that aimed to take the place of churches must bring together
a community of dedicated believers who met regularly and listened
to "inspirational lectures." Its intent had to be, as it was for churches,
to become "a powerhouse in which the electric fluid that moves the
world's charities shall be generated." On the other hand, as a school
of "moral idealism," the Ethical Culture Society, unlike churches, promoted moral idealism "without any formulated creed, with no formulas imposed, which may be accepted today and rejected tomorrow,
with no intellectual fetters of any kind." To accomplish this purpose,
while rejecting even the most liberal theologies of the day, the society
that Adler founded held weekly public meetings on Sunday, the day
most Americans celebrated as the Sabbath, meetings that, while devoid
of prayer or rituals of divine worship, solemnized marriages and conducted funeral services. He found room in his philosophy for a faith
in things that transcended human life. The Ethical Culture Society
stood on middle ground between a merely secular charitable society—
secular being too flat a word for Adler—that asked its members only
for money, and religious organizations that spurred the moral activism
of individuals by citing divine commandment.

In his effort to think through and justify the Ethical Culture Society, Adler was probably most influenced by Immanuel Kant, especially the treatise that Kant published in 1793 when he was seventy
years old, *Religion Within the Limits of Reason Alone*. Adler seized
upon Kant's effort to separate man's ethical duty from any sense of
dependence upon a divine lawgiver. According to Kant, ethical duty in
human beings grew out of an innate sense of an "ought," a primordial
understanding of a distinction between right and wrong. Moral com-

mands are recognized as "engraved upon the heart of man through reason." Kant then based morality upon "the conception of man as a free agent . . . who stands in need neither of the idea of another Being over him, for him to apprehend his duty, nor of an incentive other than the law itself, for him to do his duty. . . . Man himself must make or have made himself into whatever, in a moral sense, whether good or evil, he is or is to become."

These ideas all appear in Adler's own philosophy along with one other critical component—the need for association. Virtually every speech or essay coming from Adler reminded his audience that human beings might know their moral duty, but alone as individuals they lacked the passionate will to perform their moral duty. All kinds of daily concerns got in the way of turning a recognized duty into action. In an address he delivered in London in 1925, "Some Characteristics of the American Ethical Movement," he stressed the need for "binding ties" that were imposed not from above by the "fiat" of God, but by the vision of a "radiant" and very human future. "Binding ties" worked to curb the individual's "acquisitive instincts, and the philosophy of the unrestrained manifestation of self." The Ethical Culture Society aimed to create a community of people who worked together for "the progressive advance of mankind toward a state of things in which the light of ethical perfection shall be realized from the force of human society, that is, in which all men shall live and move and have their being in mutually promoting the highest life of each and all."

At the beginning of his work, Adler pondered whether he should call Ethical Culture a religion. It dealt with fundamental questions of meaning and the purpose of human existence. Adler certainly saw it as a society protected under the umbrella of free religious practice. The Ethical Culture Society was treated as a tax-exempt church. Yet Adler hesitated over terminology. In a November 21, 1882, letter to William Salter, the leader of Philadelphia's Ethical Culture Society who suggested that Adler call Ethical Culture a new religion, Adler was cautious: "I have repeatedly stated that a previous discipline in moral experience and comprehension of moral ideas is necessary before the meaning of an ethical religion can at all be adequately appreciated." He added that "common folk" could not hear the word "religion" without that word evoking "a wrong impression." To talk about any concept of God, however vague, prior to making moral duty the focus of discussion would quickly turn people's minds back to their notion that their primary religious role was to try to please God with rituals of worship.

Yet Adler, whatever his criticism of religious faith, never delighted in making public attacks on organized religion. Dogmatic religions might be outmoded, but they had an honorable past in bringing people together in collective assembly. No other institution had demonstrated a comparable power. On many social values taught by traditional religions, especially issues touching on sex and marriage, Adler was a staunch conservative. He believed strongly that what passed for religion even in his own day might be useful in pushing back against materialist ideas that Adler most assuredly did not like and in making people understand that the practice of virtue was a collective endeavor.

In a letter of January 12, 1885, again to Salter, Adler indicated a partial change of mind over the question of whether to identify ethical culture as a religious movement. He announced a series of lectures in which "I mean to lay more stress than I have ever done before on the religious aspect of the Ethical Movement." Adler was not ashamed to admit to a faith in things he could not prove, even if there remained a gulf between a "religion based on an impersonal idea and one based on the worship of a personal being." In the same way he rejected atheism, he rejected materialism. Feeling a connection to a "supersensible" world helped to give human life coherence and to hold human beings above a void of meaninglessness that many feared was all that would be left for human beings if their religious faith died. Writing on October 15, 1885, to Samuel Weston, a Unitarian minister and another stalwart of Philadelphia's Ethical Culture Society, Adler distinguished between claiming to "know" the "supersensible," which he believed we couldn't, and being attentive to the "effect of the supersensible in us." Like William James, he believed the effect of the supersensible was knowable by science. Also like James he was not an agnostic who was immobilized by his doubts. He didn't especially admire Robert Ingersoll, for Ingersoll didn't understand that attacks on outmoded religious beliefs by themselves led to social inertia rather than to social progress.

In 1889, a decade after the launching of Ethical Culture, Jane Addams co-founded, with her close friend Ellen Gates Starr, Hull House, a settlement house in Chicago modeled after London's Toynbee Hall. Its purpose was to aid Chicago's immigrants, not with monetary handouts but with classes, activities, and vocational training designed to help them remake their lives in the United States. Born in 1860, Addams never became as settled in her religious views as Adler. She was not a philosopher, and she did not in the same self-conscious way as Adler set out to find an alternative to traditional forms of organized religion. But as a young woman at the Rockford Theological Seminary she found that she could not subscribe to the Christian faith taught there, and for the rest of her life she never found a satisfactory religious identity. At various times she attended Protestant churches and even joined a Presbyterian one. She always found inspiration in "early Christian humanitarianism." Even so, nothing about conventional religion won her allegiance, for modern churches, she believed, were bounded by creeds that largely mucked up the simple ideas of sharing and self-sacrifice taught by Jesus. She found a solution to her problem of a meaningful community not in her church membership but in her settlement house project. She and the many young people who worked at Hull House found in their collective commitment a secular outlet for their "spiritual longings."

Addams constructed Hull House without any reference to organized religion or to the charitable work associated with organized religion. Hull House was not a missionary society or a YMCA or anything that resembled the Salvation Army. The religious services she sometimes allowed in the beginning of her settlement work disappeared as her enterprise went forward. The reputation of Hull House among Chicago's clergy was mixed. Liberal voices hailed her work as roughly Christian. Hull House showed them a way to apply the word of the gospel to social work, what many called the Social Gospel. Conservative clerics didn't like Hull House and were correct in saying that it eschewed a religious mission and aimed at "worldly results only." The British journalist William T. Stead, author of the best-selling *If Christ Came to Chicago*, spoke of the need for a "Civic Church" with a "determined worker" at its head who could "resolve that he or she . . . will never rest until the whole community is brought up to the standard of the most advanced societies." Stead praised Hull House as representing Chicago's best hope for such a civic church. It was something far better than churches steeped in religious dogma. The idea of a civic church fit nicely with the formulas of Adler, who wanted to tap into religious energy but without religion. Hull House provided Addams with a way to pursue moral action in fellowship with others.

That's a crucial point. The fellowship of Hull House was not just for the immigrants in the neighborhood of Halstead Street. Hull House served the needs of Jane Addams and "the community of university women" who lived as residents there. Dedicated involvement benefited the volunteer workers who found a way to put into practice their professional spirit that combined research and reform and provided an "outlet for the sentiment of human brotherhood." In "The Subjective Necessity for Social Settlements," an article she published in 1892, Addams wrote, "These young people . . . bear the brunt of being cultivated into unnourished, oversensitive lives. They have been shut off from the common labor . . . which is a great source of moral and physical health." In a sentence that Adler would have endorsed, she added: "The good we secure for ourselves is precarious and uncertain, is floating in mid-air, until it is secured for all of us and incorporated into our common life." Hull House found its volunteer workers among people who had cut loose from their churches but who did not wish "to retreat into unconnected private lives."

One frequent visitor to Hull House was the American philosopher John Dewey. Born in Vermont in 1859, the same year that Darwin published *On the Origin of Species,* he left behind the religion of his youth. He came to hold ideas about religion that resembled those of Adler except in one important particular. Dewey's philosophy of pragmatism had no use for supersensible worlds, and he rooted human knowledge firmly in concrete and observable experience. Adler and Dewey, while longtime colleagues at Columbia University, never became close friends. In all of Adler's papers, there are only two letters from Dewey—both of them brief acknowledgments of the gift of a book. Dewey, like Adler, worried about a world in which religion simply disappeared with nothing but science and a militant secularism to replace it. However, it took him a long time to get to the subject of religion. In *A Common Faith*, the Terry Lectures he delivered at Yale and published in 1934, he sought to answer a question posed by *The Christian Century* in 1933: "What does John Dewey think about God?"

Dewey's answer was complicated. While he believed that any religion that posited a supernatural realm was inconsistent with science and therefore unsustainable, he was also prepared to consider the question of why religion endured. It wasn't because it was true. *A Common Faith* gave short shrift to the truth claims of all forms of organized religion from fundamentalism to Protestant liberalism. He was particularly hard on the latter position since that was the persuasion of most of his Yale audience. They were the ones who needed a good talking to. They hadn't been bold enough. They were stuck in a useless enterprise of trying to prove that certain claims of supernaturalism were consistent with science. Protestant liberals had reduced the importance of dogma and tried to stay in step with scientific discovery, but they still wanted to regard religion as a separate realm of experience, distinguishable from ordinary natural phenomena. Dewey would have none of it.

Dewey followed in his remarks a strategy of giving old supernatural formulas new meanings that didn't stray beyond the bounds of our natural world. He attributes the survival of religion to "factors in experience that may be called religious" or a "religious quality of experience" or "religious elements of experience." But none of these phrases designated anything supernatural. They referred to emotions. Dewey emphasizes that the process of making sense of our collective encounter with nature is not a cold recording of facts. Science, in Dewey's mind, recognizes that meaningful advance in understanding the world is prompted by emotion, by imagination, and by desire. Human beings experience life-altering events that can restore health or provoke a sudden flash of creative insight. What Dewey finds objectionable is the attempt to "denaturalize" these moments by calling them "conversion" and explaining them by an appeal to divine intervention. Scientists had to take seriously what past ages had called "religious" experience because it mattered. "The religious," Dewey says in quoting Matthew Arnold, "is morality touched by emotion," and we cannot build a better society without harnessing that natural force to promote morally effective community action.

In an interesting passage that might have come from Adler's pen, Dewey suggests that militant atheism and supernaturalism are almost equally pernicious because both promote an "exclusive preoccupation . . . with man in isolation" from other men and also from nature. For Dewey most forms of American Protestantism, his most usual reference point when he talks about supernaturalism, are the spiritual equivalent of laissez-faire economic practice. They regard "the drama of sin and redemption enacted within the isolated and lonely soul of man as the one thing of ultimate importance." "Militant atheism" ends up with the same consequence. For its adherents "the ties binding man to nature that poets have always celebrated" are passed over lightly. The attitude taken is often that of man living in an indifferent and hostile world and issuing blasts of defiance. To think oneself into such a position was in Dewey's mind worse than useless.

From this thought Dewey moves to a tentative endorsement of the word "God," if it were stripped of any metaphysical significance. For Dewey the word has possible social utility insofar as it helps human beings to imagine their connected place in nature: "A religious attitude needs the sense of a connection of man, in the way of both dependence and support, with the enveloping world that the imagination feels is a universe. Use of the words 'God' or 'divine' to convey the union of actual with ideal may protect many from a sense of isolation and from consequent despair or defiance." Dewey's word "ideal" is not

Platonic but rather a moral goal, binding our consciences, that is projected by our imagination onto our social experience. Politically, that idea for Dewey translated into democracy and a more or less socialist economic order.

Dewey, with his particular notion of religious experience, was more than happy to see entities called churches, once released from the burden of trying to explain the supernatural, rally people, passionately, to their responsibilities toward the "continuous human community." The new churches, relieved of their need to defend dogma that even their members didn't take seriously, could take a more active interest in social affairs. The thought cheered Dewey. "Were men and women actuated throughout the length and breadth of human relations with the faith and ardor that have at times marked historic religions the consequences would be incalculable."

Although in the Terry Lectures, Dewey didn't mention Jane Addams as a person with the faith and ardor he hoped for (she died one year after Dewey gave them), he surely had her example in mind. In other contexts he cited Hull House as an institution reflecting his pragmatic philosophy. However, unlike Adler, Dewey didn't attempt to found an institutional equivalent of churches. The most concrete result of his ideas was the founding of the American Humanist Association in 1941. Following the principles of a humanist manifesto that Dewey had helped draft just before his appearance at Yale, the early work of the association was educational. By 1952, the year Dewey died at the age of ninety-three, it had helped place Dewey's concept of "secular humanism," as an alternative to theism, into the American lexicon.

As for Adler and Addams, their projects did not in the long run prove as contagious as they had originally anticipated. You can still find the handsome building of the Ethical Culture Society on Central Park West in New York City. It prospers, but some elements of its original mission have disappeared. The Workingman's School, founded in 1878, has expanded into two elite and expensive institutions: the Ethical Culture School and the Fieldston School. Though they offer scholarships, they serve primarily New York City's wealthy elite. After

Adler's death in 1933, Ethical Culture lost momentum and ceased to expand. Hull House suffered from attacks on Addams after World War I because of her pacifism and her alleged sympathy for a conquered Germany. In the antiradical fever that stirred America's first Red Scare in 1918 and 1919, Addams became another victim of the association made in the minds of many Americans between social radicalism and opposition to religion. Addams recovered her public esteem and won the Nobel Prize for Peace in 1931. Hull House carried on after her death, but its original home was displaced in the 1960s by the concrete buildings of the University of Illinois, Chicago Circle. Its shell, dwarfed by these structures, now sits as a small museum. The Jane Addams Hull House Association continued work as a nonprofit organization until it filed for bankruptcy in 2012.

A fair summary is that Dewey, Adler, and Addams failed to stem a retreat of nonbelievers away from organizations—churches and secular organizations alike. But their work was important and the story of what they attempted left an important legacy. The final chapter of our book shows that a dramatic increase in the number of American nonbelievers has encouraged atheists and agnostics to organize. The American Humanist Association has shifted its focus to support a growing atheist activism that battles in the court system to eliminate the second-class citizenship of nonbelievers. What remains uncertain is whether this "Atheist Awakening" has found ways to give positive meaning to nonbelief. Put simply, it's one thing to say that the United States doesn't have any special connection to divine favor. But how then does nonbelief that on its face is only a negative assertion do anything to promote "liberty and justice for all"? Are America's nonbelievers capable of cooperative efforts to promote the moral idealism that Adler, Dewey, and Addams, along with the founders of America, thought necessary to sustain democracy? Finding a moral equivalent of religion, like finding a moral equivalent of war, wasn't easy in the early twentieth century. It isn't easy now.

★

PART TWO

ATHEISTS IN AMERICA: THEIR PRESENT

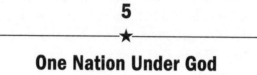

5

One Nation Under God

Every morning in most American public schools the day begins with students participating in a teacher-led Pledge of Allegiance to the flag. This ritual of schoolchildren is an adult ritual on many public occasions as well. The United States Senate begins each session collectively reciting the pledge, as do many city councils, school boards, and civic organizations. Alone among advanced democracies of the world in requiring such recurring affirmations of loyalty from schoolchildren, America also invokes God in this nationalist ritual:

> I pledge allegiance to the flag of the United States of America
> and to the Republic for which it stands, one nation, under God,
> indivisible, with liberty and justice for all.

No Founding Father authored this pledge to sustain our young republic. Its history is of a relatively more recent vintage and, alas, is permeated by more mercantile motives. The pledge was written in 1892 as part of a public relations campaign run by the respected and popular Boston-based magazine *Youth's Companion*. The magazine had launched a national initiative in the late 1880s together with the Association of Union Army Veterans to "have a flag fly over every school house" in America. Offering sales of flags with a printed order form, the periodical campaigned in 1892 to have 13 million schoolchildren participate in that October's national celebration of the four hundredth anniversary of "the discovery of America" in 1492 when "Columbus sailed the ocean blue." How better to sell flags to schools than to have the *Youth's Companion* invent a pledge to the flag that could be recited "in every school house"?

The author of this pledge was Francis Bellamy, a cousin of the famous socialist writer and activist Edward Bellamy, who had written the best-selling utopian novel *Looking Backward* in 1889. Equally radical in his politics, the thirty-five-year-old Francis had been pastor of Boston's Bethany Baptist Church for six years when in 1891 his Christian socialist preaching led to a breach with his congregation. Finding a job as a journalist with *Youth's Companion*, Bellamy never returned to the pulpit nor for that matter to socialism. For the next thirty years he was a pioneer in the new American professions of advertising and public relations.

The pledge that Bellamy wrote to help sell flags in 1892 made no reference to God, nor even to the United States. His pledge, published in *Youth's Companion* on September 8, 1892, was:

> I pledge allegiance to my flag and to the Republic for which it Stands—one Nation indivisible—with liberty and justice for all.

For Bellamy, who still was inclined toward progressive ideas, the key words were first "indivisible," because the Civil War had preserved the one federal union over the states'-rights claims of slave-holding states; and second "liberty and justice for all," an egalitarian affirmation of the rights of the poor as well as the rich. Auguring well for his future career, Bellamy's other achievement in 1892 was convincing President Benjamin Harrison to issue a proclamation declaring October 12 to be Columbus Day, a national holiday honoring Columbus, while also obtaining a congressional resolution endorsing the celebration.

Washington in 1919 became the first state to require Bellamy's

Pledge of Allegiance in public schools. By 1935 some ten states had such requirements, though it was a much more widespread practice, frequently mandated by local school boards. Indeed, by the 1950s reciting Bellamy's pledge had become a morning ritual in most American public schools with the pledge to "my flag" replaced officially by Congress in 1942 to "the flag of the United States of America," a change pushed by the American Legion and the Daughters of the American Revolution. Both organizations worried about the large number of immigrants in America and wanted them to understand that their flag was now the American flag.

But for that tiny change, Bellamy's pledge remained as he wrote it until the 1950s, when God was put into it, itself an interesting historical irony. There were serious religious critics of the pledge in the first half of the twentieth century, but their objection was to saying the pledge at all. To Mennonites and especially Jehovah's Witnesses the saluting and pledging allegiance to a flag constituted idolatry and worshipping a graven image. Their protests led to the important pair of cases, first *Minersville School District v. Gobitis* (1940) that ruled a school could compel students to recite the pledge, and then *West Virginia v. Barnette* (1943), in which the Supreme Court, famously reversing itself, held the opposite. No one could be required to recite the pledge. The second ruling, made in the middle of World War II, is still binding.

Graven image or no, the flag with an attendant godly pledge was shortly to become for many inseparable from a religious crusade. As the Cold War revved up so were religion and God more publicly embraced. The popular Reverend Billy Graham warned that Americans would perish in a nuclear attack unless they embraced Jesus Christ as their savior. President Eisenhower initiated prayer breakfasts in the White House and Congress created a prayer room in the Capitol. The deeply religious secretary of state John Foster Dulles, who was the son of a Presbyterian minister and a leading figure in the National Council of Churches in Christ, believed that the United States should oppose communism less because the Soviet Union was a totalitarian regime than because its leaders were "godless atheists." "In God We Trust" was by law made the nation's official motto, replacing "E pluribus unum," one out of many, which, despite the Civil War, had done fairly well for nearly two hundred years. "In God We Trust," placed on some currency since the Civil War, was engraved on all American money in the 1950s, and the Senate Judiciary Subcommittee held hearings on Vermont Senator Ralph Flanders's proposal to amend the Constitution in order to recognize the authority and law of Jesus Christ. To be sure, the latter proposed idea never made it to the floor of either chamber, but the fact that some took it seriously is remarkable in itself.

In such a political environment the Catholic fraternal organization, the Knights of Columbus, well aware of the historical linkage of Bellamy's Pledge of Allegiance to Columbus Day, proposed in 1951, during the Korean War, to add the words "under God" between the words "nation" and "indivisible" of the pledge. In part because it had been pushed by Catholics, such a bill, introduced in Congress in 1953, had little support, and was even publicly opposed by Bellamy's son.

But in February 1954, one sermon delivered before one important parishioner married American patriotism to godliness. That month George MacPherson Docherty, the pastor of the New York Avenue Presbyterian Church in Washington, D.C., which President Eisenhower attended, delivered a sermon with the president sitting in front of him. In it Docherty lamented that the Pledge of Allegiance could be the pledge of any country and that it needed "under God" added to it. "I could hear little Muscovites repeat a similar pledge to their hammer and sickle flag," he said. The Soviets claimed to be an indivisible republic, too, he pointed out. The Cold War, Docherty insisted, was not about political beliefs, "Thomas Jefferson's political democracy over against Lenin's communistic state," or about economic systems, "between, shall we say, Adam Smith's *Wealth of Nations* and Karl Marx's *Das Capital*." Rather, it was a "theological war. . . . Judeo-Christian civilization in mortal combat against modern, secularized, godless society."

Four days later Louis Rabaut, a Democratic congressman from Michigan and a devout Catholic, quoted Docherty's sermon at length in the House of Representatives, noting that though they were "not of the same Christian denomination," Docherty had "hit the nail right on the head." Americans' belief in God is what distinguished them from the Soviets. "From the root of atheism . . . stems the evil weed of communism and its branches of materialism and political dictatorship," Rabaut told Congress.

Docherty's sermon had ended with his ringing call for Eisenhower to help in the legislative effort to add "under God" to the pledge, in order to describe what was special about the United States as opposed to the Soviet Union. Eisenhower did. By June 1954, four months later, the law changing the pledge, putting God into it, had passed Congress and was signed by the president. Congressman after congressman claimed that by adding the two words, America, as Representative John Pillion put it, "acknowledged the dependence of our people and our government upon the Creator and denied the atheistic and materialistic concept of Communism." Representative Frances Bolton agreed. "We are officially recognizing once again this Nation's adherence to our belief in a divine spirit, and that henceforth millions of our citizens will be acknowledging this belief every time they pledge allegiance to our flag."

When he signed the legislation on June 14, 1954, Flag Day, Eisenhower said he was pleased that from "that day on, millions of our school children will daily proclaim in every city and town . . . the dedication of our nation and our people to the Almighty." He went on, "To anyone who truly loves America nothing can be more inspiring than to contemplate this rededication of our youth, on each school morning, to our country's true meaning." After the bill was signed, the sponsors of the legislation gathered before a national TV audience for what the CBS News anchor Walter Cronkite described as "a stirring event." They recited the new pledge "to our nation and the Almighty." The flag was raised and a bugle played the strains of "Onward Christian soldiers, marching as to war, with the cross of Jesus going on before."

We have seen that as early as the nineteenth century Americans had linked atheism to social radicalism. Now Congress made the linkage official. Godlessness and Russian Marxism were two sides of the same coin. But the alteration of the pledge signaled something else as well. Many Americans had certainly felt that their country was "under God" before these two words were put into the pledge in 1954. The use of those words was supposed to remind Americans that they stood under God's judgment, that the blessing of God's favor meant also God's expectation of good behavior, and that God's will was inscrutable. Seventeenth-century Puritans had made that understanding of "under God" explicit. The religiously independent president Abraham Lincoln had placed that notion at the center of American political rhetoric. His memorable usage of that phrase came in the Gettysburg Address: "We here highly resolve that these dead shall not have died in vain. That this Nation, under God, shall have a new birth of freedom." Lincoln and others meant the phrase "under God" to serve a humbling and cautionary purpose. For them being under God meant that God would judge Americans and their actions, that God would hold Americans accountable and punish them for their misdeeds. When Congress officially changed the pledge to place America under God in 1954, there was nothing humbling about the words; they were said triumphantly. It was a Cold War claim that America was a superior nation, and better than others because of its belief in God.

Whether it was understood as Lincolnesque or simply anti-Soviet, a Gallup poll indicated surprisingly that 21 percent of Americans opposed the change in the pledge, then approximately 35 million people. The words "under God" in the pledge were challenged in court for the first time three years after they were added. The Free Thinkers of America, claiming that "under God" constituted an unconstitutional establishment of religion, sought to have the New York State Commissioner of Education delete the phrase from the required public school pledge. The trial judge, ruling that the First Amendment prohibited a state religion but not "the growth and development of a religious state," declined to do so. Appeals to two higher courts by the Free Thinkers garnered no support and finally, seven years after the original suit, the United States Supreme Court in 1964 declined to review the lower-court ruling, letting it stand.

And so it would go for the next thirty years. Periodic challenges to "under God"—a 1963 ACLU case in Los Angeles, a 1964 Hawaii suit brought by the atheist crusader Madalyn Murray O'Hair, a 1968 challenge by students in Redding, California, and a 1989 federal suit brought by Illinois atheist Rob Sherman—were all rejected by the courts. Judge after judge agreed that "under God" in the pledge was not state sponsorship of religion and thus not a violation of the First Amendment.

Enter Michael Newdow, who grew up in the Bronx, New York, and Teaneck, New Jersey. A graduate of Brown University, UCLA Medical School, and the University of Michigan Law School, Newdow, who worked as an emergency-room physician in Sacramento, California, filed a federal lawsuit in March 2000. He claimed that the teacher-led daily recitation of the Pledge of Allegiance with the phrase "one nation under God" harmed him and his daughter, a student in the Elk Grove, California, Elementary School. He argued that the state-run ritual proclaimed the existence of God and was thus an unconstitutional violation of the First Amendment's prohibition of an establishment of religion, which courts have regularly interpreted to mean a prohibition of state sponsorship or endorsement of religion. Newdow and the mother of his daughter had never married and were not living together. The girl's mother described herself as a born-again Christian; Newdow was himself a Jewish atheist. Some of these familial issues would prove central in the final resolution in the case.

The District Court dismissed Newdow's case in 2001. He then appealed to the Ninth Circuit Court of Appeals, which sits in San Francisco, and whose liberal leaning has led journalists to dub it "the left coast Court of Appeals." In June 2002, to the nation's amazement, a panel of the Appeals Court ruled 2 to 1 that it was, indeed, an unconstitutional sponsorship of religion, a violation of the First Amendment, for public schools in Elk Grove to ask students to recite "under God" as part of the Pledge of Allegiance.

No sooner had the ruling been publicized than every politician in America raced to appear on television denouncing it. President Bush said the decision was "ridiculous" and that it reinforced his resolve to appoint "common sense judges who understand that our rights were derived from God." Senator Kerry, soon to be the Democratic candidate for president, said that "holding 'under God' in the Pledge unconstitutional was half-assed justice . . . the most absurd thing. . . . that's not establishment of religion." Senate majority leader Tom Daschle declared the ruling to be "just nuts." Robert Bird of West Virginia, the author of legislation declaring September 17 (the day the Constitution was signed in 1787) "Constitution Day," and the acknowledged congressional guardian of the document, was apoplectic about the decision. It came, he fumed, from "a stupid judge" and an "atheist lawyer." America, he warned, should not be "ruled by a bunch of atheists."

Almost immediately the Elk Grove School Board, supported by the Bush administration, took the case to the United States Supreme Court. Judge Alfred Goodwin, who had written the decision, a Republican appointed to the Ninth Circuit Court in 1971 by President Nixon, and known to his friends as "Tex," the very next day postponed any implementation of his ruling until the Supreme Court ruled. The United States Senate quickly passed legislation reaffirming the words "under God" by a vote of 99 to 0 and the House did the same by 416 to 3. All fifty state attorneys general filed a petition urging the Supreme Court to reverse the circuit court decision. An Associated Press poll showed nine out of every ten Americans believing the phrase "under God" should be part of the pledge, though a Gallup poll indicated that 14 percent, or 39 million Americans, agreed with the Ninth Circuit Court's decision.

Judge Goodwin's ruling was joined by Judge Stephen Reinhardt, a liberal Democrat. Although their judicial concurrence managed to bridge the political spectrum, it failed utterly to quell an ensuing firestorm. The decision strongly sided with Newdow, who had argued his own case, that "under God" failed all three tests the Supreme Court had developed over two decades to use in deciding establishment cases. It failed the *"Lemon* Test" (*Lemon v. Kurtzman*, 1971) because the words have a religious not a secular purpose. To say the United States, Goodwin writes, "is a nation under God is a profession of a religious belief, namely a belief in monotheism." The words "under God" in the pledge failed next the "endorsement test," articulated by Justice Sandra Day O'Connor in her *Lynch v. Donnelly* (1984) concurrence. Goodwin believed that the reference to God in the pledge constituted government endorsement of religion that sent a message to Newdow's daughter that as a nonbeliever she is an outsider and not a full member of the political community. And, finally, "under God" failed the "coercion test," promulgated in *Lee v. Weisman* (1992), which disallowed government actions that pressured school students to either participate in a religious ceremony or to protest it.

Worth noting, especially in light of how much attention would be paid to it in later pledge cases, is that Goodwin's surprisingly spare ruling made only a one-sentence reference to the legislative history of the 1954 congressional change in Bellamy's pledge. His finding also involved no detailed excursions into the, to be sure, inconsistent record of state and federal establishment cases. Newdow's argument that "under God" is an establishment of religion is accepted as obvious and self-evident, needing little or no judicially learned or argumentatively persuasive legitimization.

The dissenting justice, Ferdinand F. Fernandez, appointed to the Circuit Court by George H. W. Bush, was even less inclined to enter the legal thicket of establishment jurisprudence. Instead, he offered what he described as "judicial good sense," a worrisome warning that to rule against God in the pledge allows atheists like Newdow to put America on the slippery slope that would end by evicting religion from the American way of life and the triumph of irreligion itself: "Upon Newdow's theory of our Constitution, accepted by my colleagues today, we will soon find ourselves prohibited from using our album of patriotic songs in many public settings. 'God Bless America' and 'America the Beautiful' will be gone for sure, and while use of the first three stanzas of the 'Star Spangled Banner' will be permissible, we will be precluded from straying into the fourth."

In a footnote, Fernandez quotes the words of that fourth, seldom-sung stanza: "Blest with victory and peace, may the heaven-rescued land, praise the power that hath made and preserved us a nation. Then conquer we must, when our cause is just. And this be our motto: 'In God is our trust.'" Returning to his finding, Fernandez laments that judges can require the prohibition of such patriotic lyrics if they decide cases by legal "tests" as opposed to "good sense." In an unabashed defense of religion's place in American life, he cautions: "But they do so at the price of removing a vestige of the awe all of us, including our children, must feel at the immenseness of the universe and our own small place within it, as well as the wonder we must feel at the good fortune of our country. That will cool the febrile nerves of a few at the cost of removing the healthy glow conferred upon many citizens when the forbidden verse, or phrases, are uttered, read, or seen."

Fernandez argues that compared to the huge number of Americans who would be prevented from singing the National Anthem because of God in the final verse (most of whom, he fails to note, never even knew there was such a verse), the danger that "under God" in the pledge will "suppress somebody's beliefs" is so minuscule as to be "de minimis." The danger that phrase presents to our First Amendment is "picayune at most." Not unlike the majority, Fernandez's dissent eschews persuasive reasoning in the face of what he takes to be obvious and self-evident. Phrases like "under God" do not suppress the free exercise or nonexercise of religion "except," he writes, "in the fevered eye of persons who most fervently would like to drive all tincture of religion out of the public life of our polity."

When the appeal reached the Supreme Court on March 21, 2004, Newdow again argued his own case. Only eight justices heard the case on the day of oral arguments because Newdow had successfully demanded that Scalia recuse himself because of a particularly strong public speech he had given to the Knights of Columbus, criticizing Goodwin's decision. Defending the pledge and the Elk Grove School Board was Solicitor General Ted Olson, one of the most famous constitutional lawyers in the nation. But it was Newdow who impressed veteran court observers in his oral argument, with the *New York Times* reporting on March 22: "Dr. Newdow, 50, often spoke very rapidly, but never appeared to lose his footing during the 30 minutes the Court gave him. He managed a trick that far more experienced lawyers rarely accomplish, to bring the argument to a symmetrical and seemingly unhurried ending just as the red light came on."

Liberal justices David Souter and Stephen Breyer seemed unmoved, however, by Newdow's claim that "under God" made the pledge a religious exercise. It was, they told Newdow, as Olson had argued, "a civic and ceremonial acknowledgement" of the historical fact that the Framers saw God as the source of their rights, including "the right to revolt and start a new nation." That interpretation would have come as news to President Bush. In June 2002 he had signed a letter to many who had written the White House about the pending case. In it he asserted that the pledge was a way of "proclaiming our reliance on God," and of "humbly seeking the wisdom and blessing of divine providence." Bush did understand the pledge was more than a "civic and ceremonial acknowledgement" of history.

Newdow complained that "Government" was "putting her [his daughter] in a milieu where she says, "Hey the Government is saying that there is a God and my dad says no, and that's an injury to me."

Souter replied with Fernandez's de minimis argument: "Isn't in actual practice the affirmation in the midst of this civic exercise as a religious affirmation so tepid, so diluted, so far, let's say from a compulsory prayer that in fact it should be in effect beneath the constitutional radar . . . that the religious, as distinct from a civic content is lost, close to disappearing."

Newdow answered: "It's not the view I take. . . . The Government comes in here and says, 'No Newdow, your religious belief system is wrong . . . and anyone else who believes in God is right." On March 24, the libertarian columnist for the *New York Times* William Safire agreed with him with damning condescension: "The only thing this time-wasting pest Newdow has going for him is that he's right. Those of us who believe in God don't need to inject our faith into a patriotic affirmation and coerce schoolchildren into going along."

The justices never ruled on Newdow's claim that "under God" was an unconstitutional establishment of religion. On June 14, 2004, Flag Day again, exactly fifty years to the day after President Eisenhower had signed the legislation putting God in the pledge, the Supreme Court preserved God's place in it, not with booming legal arguments but with whimpering procedural sidesteps, ruling that Newdow had no standing when he brought the original case against the Elk Grove school, because, it held, he was a noncustodial parent. He was never married to his daughter's mother, who, according to her lawyer, Kenneth Starr, the former Independent Counsel leading the investigation of President Clinton, was giving her daughter a religious upbringing "and wants her to say the Pledge with 'under God.'"

Justice John Paul Stevens announced the reversal of the Court of Appeals ruling in favor of Newdow, with Justices Breyer and Souter, along with Ruth Bader Ginsburg and Anthony Kennedy, concurring. The three other justices also concurred in the reversal, not on the issue of standing, but on the constitutional issues raised. They were eager to engage them. Chief Justice William Rehnquist held that, in fact, Newdow had standing, but that the 2002 decision deserved to be reversed because reciting the pledge with "under God" in it did not violate the Establishment Clause of the First Amendment. The Circuit Court had mistakenly relied on *Lee v. Weisman*, a 1992 case. Rehnquist insisted that unlike the decision in *Lee*, which had held that prayers at high school graduations were an unconstitutional coercive establishment of religion, the pledge with "under God" was clearly a "patriotic exercise, not a religious one; participants promise fidelity to our flag and our Nation, not to any particular God, faith or church."

In her concurring opinion Justice Sandra Day O'Connor urged reversal because she saw "under God" in the pledge passing the "endorsement" test she devised in the 1984 *Lynch* case, in which she concurred with the court's majority in upholding a Nativity scene erected on public property. These words in the pledge defined no one as outsiders, or less than "full members of the political community." It is using "the (religious) idiom for essentially secular purposes." References to religion in public life and government, she held, "are the inevitable consequence of our Nation's origins," adding that religious references "in our culture serve the legitimate secular purposes of solemnizing public occasions." We mark "important occasions or pronouncements with references to God." O'Connor used a term for these acknowledgments or references "to the divine without offending the Constitution": "ceremonial deism." Her whole line of argument, even to her use of that phrase, is based on the position liberal Justice William Brennan developed twenty years earlier in *Lynch*. Ceremonial invocations of God, as in the pledge, she concludes, again using Brennan, are permissible because they have "lost through rote repetition any significant religious content."

Justice Clarence Thomas, insisting, too, that Newdow had standing, concurred with reversal while urging an unexpected and important root-and-branch rethinking of the Establishment Clause. He disagreed with Rehnquist's claim that "under God" does not fall within the *Lee* precedent because it "is not a religious exercise." Agreeing with Newdow, without saying so, he writes of the phrase "one Nation under God" that "it is difficult to see how this does not entail an affirmation that God exists." Whether or not we classify affirming the existence of God, he adds, as a "formal religious exercise akin to prayer, it must present the same or similar constitutional problems." This led Thomas to repudiate the *Lee* precedent altogether, for "adherence to *Lee* would require us to strike down the Pledge." The *Lee* case was wrongly decided because, as the recused Scalia had urged in his "originalist" *Lee* dissent, the Establishment Clause neither "created or protected any individual rights"; it only "precludes the Federal Government from establishing a national religion. . . . States and only States were the direct beneficiaries."

Thomas stood alone here, but the Supreme Court's decision, rendered on Flag Day, was a boon to Republicans in general during the ensuing months of the 2004 presidential election. President Bush remembered well how his father had exploited pledge politics in the campaign of 1988 by denouncing the veto that his Democratic opponent Governor Dukakis had cast in 1979 of a bill requiring Massachusetts teachers to lead their classes in the pledge. Billboards appeared across America in the fall of 2004 with just two large words "UNDER GOD" and below them, in slightly smaller print, "BUSH-CHENEY."

Meanwhile, the House of Representatives, still angry at both the Ninth Circuit's 2002 decision and the Supreme Court's 2004 decision, only based on Newdow not having standing, passed the Pledge Protection Act, which would deny jurisdiction to any federal court "to hear or decide any question pertaining to the interpretation of the Pledge of Allegiance or its validity under the Constitution." Many in the House were clearly worried about this blatant assault on the separation of powers, accounting for the surprising vote of only 260 in favor to 167 opposed. All the other congressional votes on matters touching "under God" were virtually unanimous.

But the indefatigable Newdow was not silenced. In September 2005 he brought a new case on behalf of himself and three other unnamed parents and their children in the nearby Rio Linda Union School District to the same California District Court he had tried in 2000. District Court Judge Lawrence Karlton in January 2006 ruled in Newdow's favor, holding that the pledge's "under God" violated the First Amendment. He, too, stayed the carrying out of his ruling, pending appeals by the Rio Linda school board. The case was, indeed, appealed to the Ninth Circuit Court of Appeals with arguments heard on December 4, 2007.

Newdow once again acted as his own attorney, contending that the pledge's words "under God" violated the Establishment Clause. It was by now a familiar argument for him. In November 2005 he had filed a suit to have "In God We Trust" removed from United States currency as a violation of the First Amendment, a claim rejected in June 2006 by U.S. District Court Judge Frank Damrell, Jr., who ruled that the national motto was a "secular national slogan," lacking any "theological or ritualistic impact." Undaunted, Newdow reiterated his case against God in the pledge in December 2007 before a new three-judge panel of the Ninth Circuit.

Unlike the first Newdow case heard by the Ninth Circuit, which attracted no attention until Goodwin's surprising decision and the firestorm it created, Newdow's 2007 case was major news. There were long lists of amicus curiae briefs on both sides. Opposing Karlton's ruling in favor of Newdow were, among many others, the Knights of Columbus, the American Legion, and the attorneys general for all fifty states. On Newdow's side were the American Atheists, the Freedom From Religion Foundation, the Secular Coalition for America, and the American Humanist Association. Most importantly, this time a phalanx of lawyers representing the Rio Linda school board, the State of California, and the United States Department of Justice, were arrayed against the lone Newdow. Pride of place in the legal team defending the pledge before the panel were those from the Becket Fund for Religious Liberty, founded in 1994 in Washington, D.C., which by 2007 had emerged as the most important nonprofit law firm defending God in the pledge.

It took over two years, until March 2010, for the panel to decide the Rio Linda case, during which time Newdow, ever vigilant on establishment infringements, had unsuccessfully sought an injunction to prevent Chief Justice John Roberts from saying "so help me God" at the end of President Obama's inauguration oath in January 2008, words not found in the Constitution's prescribed presidential oath. Exactly ten years after Newdow brought his first and ill-fated suit on behalf of his daughter, the Ninth Circuit finally and definitively resolved the legal status of the phrase "under God" in the pledge by holding that the two words were not state sponsorship of religion, thus overturning the 2006 ruling of District Court Judge Karlton.

The court's fifty-eight-page ruling was written by Carlos T. Bea, a 2003 George Bush appointee who was born in Spain, grew up in Cuba, and was educated at Stanford. He was joined in the majority by Justice Dorothy Nelson, who had been the first woman law professor at the University of Southern California and was appointed to the Appeals Court by President Carter. The pledge, Bea wrote, was "of allegiance to our Republic, not of allegiance to God or to any religion." Congress's purpose in 1954 (and in its reaffirmation in 2002) in adding God "was patriotic not religious." Once this was acknowledged, the rewording of the pledge easily passed all three tests the courts had used to decide if a practice violated the Establishment Clause. Bea held that adding the words had a secular political purpose and did not endorse, favor, or promote religion, did not endorse one religion over another, nor did it coerce students into participating in a religious exercise.

The tests were all passed, Bea held, because "under God" in the pledge had no religious significance, but was merely a secular political statement. It is not a prayer, but patriotism. It was added to the pledge to make the political point that America has a limited government, unlike the Soviet's all-powerful government that provided for and dominated the people. It represented the American political belief that government was not supreme, but that a power greater than government, God, gave the American people their rights. Putting God into the pledge, Bea argued, was merely to restate the political philosophy of the Founding Fathers who saw God granting, as Jefferson put it, certain "inalienable Rights" to the people, which government cannot take away. Students reciting "one nation under God" are thus referring to the historical traditions of America, not making a personal affirmation, through prayer or invocation, that the speaker believes in God or that God exists. The pledge, then, the court concluded, is a patriotic exercise designed to foster national unity and pride. It is not turned into a religious activity because it includes words with a religious meaning. The use of God, the court was saying, has no genuine current religious content.

The court went on to argue that citing God in the pledge is merely rhetorical and stylistic. Using the older arguments of Justice Brennan and the more recent 2004 concurrence of Justice O'Connor, Bea contended that mentioning God merely gives "a note of importance, which a pledge to our nation ought to have and which ceremonial references to God invoke in our culture." Reference to God simply adds a solemn and inspiring note to pledging loyalty to the flag. It shows how seriously Americans take their pride in being American. Such a ceremonial invocation of God to indicate seriousness is not religious but a general cultural reflex. "Under God" in the pledge, then, the court concluded, is unrelated to religious belief; it "has the predominant purpose and effect of only adding a solemn and inspiring note to what should be a solemn and inspiring promise—a promise of allegiance to the Republic."

To all of this the dissenting Circuit Court justice responded "pure poppycock." The self-proclaimed legal gadfly, Stephen Reinhardt, who had sided with Goodwin in the original Newdow case heard by the Ninth Circuit, wrote the dissent in *Rio Linda*. Appointed to the court by President Carter, he was considered the most liberal of all the Circuit Court justices. Indeed, he was the justice whose decisions were more often reversed by the Supreme Court than those of any other judge. His dissent, twice as long as Bea's majority opinion, is exasperated, unbelieving, and utterly dismissive of the ruling, which he describes by turns as "muddled" and "self contradictory." Reinhardt goes so far as to suggest that no other judge "familiar with the history of the Pledge could in good conscience" agree with Bea and Nelson's "absurd" finding that "under God" was "inserted into the Pledge for any purpose other than an explicitly and predominantly religious one."

Reinhardt devotes much more attention than Bea did to the legislative history of the congressional debates leading to the 1954 change in the wording of the pledge. Nowhere in those debates does he find any suggestion that adding "under God" implies a theory of "limited government." It is an argument "fabricated by the members of the majority." The two words were, in fact, added, according to Reinhardt "for the purpose of indoctrinating public school children with a religious belief . . . that God exists."

The post 1954 pledge thus fails all three establishment tests for Reinhardt. It violates the *Lemon* test because Congress amended the pledge "with the express purpose of promoting a state-sponsored belief in God." It fails the endorsement test because "how could atheist, agnostic, Hindu, or Buddhist children . . . feel anything but that they are outsiders" when asked to recite the pledge? Finally, it fails the coercion test because students "must either remain silent or leave the classroom, neither of which option avoids the injury they suffer or cures the constitutional violation to which they have been subjected."

The Ninth Circuit majority ruling saw it otherwise. "Under God" in the pledge was not an unconstitutional endorsement of religion because the reference to God is understood to be religiously meaningless. Stripped of spiritual significance, God is secularized and performs political, patriotic, and rhetorical service. Citing God reminds Americans of the historical truth that the founders saw a divine source for inalienable rights, and citing God stylistically adds solemnity and importance to certain utterances and commitments. Citing God has nothing to do with religion.

Justice Bea in 2010, like Brennan in 1984 and O'Connor in 2004, was pleased to label religious language and actions that were "protected from Establishment Clause scrutiny" as "ceremonial deism." Actually, the phrase was first used in 1962 by Eugene V. Rostow, then dean of Yale Law School, to describe references to God repeated so often and so reflexively that the "rote repetition" removed all religious significance from them. Like saying "God bless you" after a sneeze, reciting "under God" in the pledge has only secular, not spiritual, meaning. It was similar to the argument used by some educators in late-nineteenth-century America to justify daily Bible reading in public schools; they claimed that a few Bible verses read to students at the beginning of the school day calmed them down and put them in the right frame of mind to learn. And so, too, in 2010, the Supreme Court heard the argument that a giant cross on federal land in the Mojave Desert on a national war memorial honoring World War I veterans was not a religious symbol but a secular marker of death and "in the context of a veteran's memorial the cross is a symbol of the ultimate sacrifice made for one's country."

However, the God under whom America was supposed to exist and in whom it trusts is utterly unlike the deist god who was supposed to set the world operating and then removed itself from human affairs. No surprise then that many religious observers of the Ninth Circuit court, while approving the majority ruling, were just as critical of Bea's argument about the pledge's lack of religious content, his relegation of God to a nonreligious term, as were Newdow and Reinhardt. Father Richard John Neuhaus, the respected founder of the religious journal *First Things*, announced that "most Americans agree . . . with Mr. Newdow . . . that a reference to God is a reference to God, the government's brief notwithstanding." Have we come to the point, he asks, when "references to God in public are permissible because nobody really believes what they say?" If so, he concludes, "Maybe the Court will next rule that pigs can fly." Neuhaus is particularly repelled by the Court's deist implication that God was uninvolved and aloof from the present world as opposed to a living and responsive God. America, like all nations, he contends, is "under divine judgment" and through prayer "we may be under Providential care." President Bush in 2002, as we have seen, had similarly depicted an America "under God" as "humbly seeking the wisdom and blessing of Divine Providence."

Other contemporary religious figures echoed the 1954 legislators who originally put God into the pledge, as one said, to prove that America is "uniquely favored by the divine and uniquely in touch with God's will." Garry Bauer, former vice president of Focus on the Family and Republican presidential hopeful in 2000, saw the pledge as honoring God because "America cannot find the way forward . . . without the protection of divine Providence." His comment reprises the claim of Representative Peter Rodino in 1954 that "the new phrase under God recognizes the guidance of God in our national affairs."

Bea's insistence that "under God" was added to the pledge simply to make the political point that America had a limited government was roundly repudiated by Thomas Berg, professor of law and codirector of the Center of Catholic Thought, Law, and Public Policy at the University of St. Thomas School of Law in Minnesota. In a restatement of Catholic natural law theory, he argued that "one nation under God" sees American government, properly, as subject "to transcendent moral standards." Yes, government "is a limited institution," but it is "subject to standards of authority higher than itself" from God who is the source of human rights. Berg is distraught at the court's "emptying religious phrases of their religious meaning. If that is the price of upholding religious elements in government ceremonies," he laments, "it is not worth paying."

Similarly, Grace Y. Kao, professor of religious studies at Virginia

Polytechnic Institute, concluded in her *Journal of the Society of Christian Ethics* essay that "if keeping under God in the Pledge of Allegiance requires us to controvert the plain meaning of the text and accordingly suppress its religious significance, the cost is too high." Moreover, she noted provocatively, if the affirmation "I pledge allegiance . . . to one nation under God is not to be taken as seriously religious," as the court holds, it is "essentially encouraging young school children to break one of the Ten Commandments by taking the Lord's name in vain."

Those like Justice Bea, for whom the post-1954 pledge has a political, "predominantly patriotic purpose," and those like Newdow, Justice Reinhardt, Father Neuhaus, and professors Berg and Kao, for whom it has an "indisputably religious purpose," are all correct. What the Ninth Circuit Court of Appeals did in 2010 was codify and legitimize the intimate linkage of Americanism and religiosity, which had been a drumbeat during the Cold War. Congress and Eisenhower may have been less interested in 1954 in indoctrinating schoolchildren with monotheistic beliefs, as Reinhardt argues, but they fervently wanted to identify America as God-fearing and thus as different from and better than the atheistic Soviet Union. But changing the pledge was an establishment and sponsorship of religion because it married religion to citizenship. Being religious, believing in God, is declared to be central to what it means to be an American and becomes a litmus test for citizenship. It is the creedal core of an American civil religion, a merging of the political and the spiritual.

As the last congressman to speak in the 1954 debate, Representative Hugh Addonizio, put it, "Our citizenship is of no real value to us unless we can open our souls before God and before Him conscientiously say, I am an American." Or, as Reverend Docherty preached that Sunday with Eisenhower seated before him, "An atheistic American is a contradiction in terms." The descriptive claim that Americans are believers has become the prescriptive, normative insistence that to be an American one must be a believer. Thus Bea's finding that the pledge doesn't privilege a particular god or a particular religion makes it acceptable and inoffensive. That religion itself is privileged is so fundamentally American as to be unassailable.

As the historic differences between and among religions in America declined in the second half of the twentieth century, the chasm between believers and nonbelievers increased. Affirming a religious identity is taken as the sign of being a good American. Studies show that large majorities of Americans assume that all good Americans have some sort of spiritual life and that to be irreligious is to be "un-American." Referring to efforts to remove "under God" from the pledge, a roadside Pennsylvania billboard depicted a young child pledging allegiance to the flag with the printed message, "Why do atheists hate America?" Another, in West Virginia, reads, "Anti-God is Anti-American." If, as many scholars contend, communities achieve solidarity and identity only when they imagine an "other" who does not share the values of those legitimately within the community, then in America the nonbeliever is the "other," unworthy of citizenship.

What we label American civil religion, and identify as an affront to the wall of separation between church and state, is different from what others have meant when using that term. Robert Bellah, a sociologist of religion who had a distinguished career at the University of California, Berkeley, popularized the concept of an American civil religion. Writing in a 1967 issue of *Daedalus* during the most divisive season of the Vietnamese War, Bellah argued that Americans had over the course of their history used a variety of nondenominational religious tropes and metaphors, such as Exodus, chosen people, covenants, and rebirth, to describe and interpret their experience. Sanford Levinson, a professor of politics and of law at the University of Texas, in his *Constitutional Faith*, wrote of a secular civil religion, a "web of understandings, myths, symbols, and documents," which are "worshipped" by Americans, such as the flag, the Declaration of Independence, the Constitution, and the Statue of Liberty—things Americans hold sacred because they embody the abstraction that is Americanism. For us, the authors, American civil religion is a mistaken and dangerous literal coupling of political citizenship with religious belief as trumpeted in the Pledge of Allegiance, legitimized in spirit by the Supreme Court in 2004 and as definitive judicial precedent in 2010 by Justice Bea. The political scientist Samuel Huntington best articulated this troublesome notion of civil religion. He wrote: "Civil religion enables Americans to bring together their secular politics and their religious society, to marry God and country, so as to give religious sanctity to their patriotism and then to merge what could be conflicting loyalties into loyalty to a religiously endowed country."

Reciting the Pledge of Allegiance, the last ritualized act in the naturalization ceremony for new citizens, makes clear that affirming loyalty to America requires asserting a belief in God, even if "God" is so allied with the United States that the courts could see God as secular. It signifies that what defines an American is being a believer and that nonbelievers are unwelcome in the American political community. Some years ago the respected scholar of American religion William "Will" Herberg observed that "Not to identify oneself and be identified as either a Protestant, a Catholic, or a Jew is somehow not to be American." Or as the politician Newt Gingrich put it, when as Speaker of the House he introduced his proposal for an amendment to the Constitution to allow school prayer, the amendment "would produce an America in which a belief in God is once again the center of being an American." More recently, in 2011 Gingrich worried that America would soon be "a secular atheist country . . . with no understanding of what it once meant to be an American."

Surprisingly, the ostensibly more secular of the Presidents Bush, George H. W., was an avid apostle of this American civil religion. When asked at a press conference by Rob Sherman, then a correspondent for an atheist news organization, if he would reach out to atheist citizens in the campaign of 1988, he replied, "I don't know that atheists should be considered as citizens, nor should they be considered patriots. This is one nation under God." No wonder Professor Douglas Laycock, then of the University of Texas Law School and now of the University of Virginia Law School, in a 2004 Supreme Court amicus curiae brief opposing "under God" in the pledge, noted that its message is that "if you are doubtful about the existence of God, you are of doubtful loyalty to the Nation."

Children know what is happening, however, even if they don't know labels like "civil religion" with which to characterize their experience. A study asking what the daily patriotic pledge to the American flag meant to grade-school children found that they make sense of the pledge by focusing on a word they understand, which leads them to such conclusions as "the most important part is talking about God" or "we better be good cause God is watching us even if he is invisible." The early architects of American civil religion, the members of Congress who put America "under God" into the pledge in 1954, had succeeded. Children's understanding of the pledge was exactly what they had sought. "Each time," Alexander Wiley from Wisconsin told the U.S. Senate, "the children pledge allegiance to Old Glory, they will reassert their belief . . . in the all-present, all-knowing, all-seeing, all-powerful Creator."

Newdow's decade-long atheist crusade against God in the Pledge of Allegiance had produced by 2010 an unintended outcome in the federal court system, reiterated soon thereafter in state-court pledge cases, as we shall discuss in the next chapter—the judicial doctrine of civil religion, the assumption that one has to be religious, i.e., believe in God, to be a good American. This linkage is assumed in the courts even as paradoxically they insist they are not affirming or establishing religion and, even more paradoxically, as the number of self-proclaimed nonbelieving Americans grows dramatically, as we shall also see.

Meanwhile, the late iconoclastic comedian Robin Williams remained unpersuaded about America's dependence on divine guidance. If he could, he told audiences, he would yet again rewrite the pledge; this time with less attention to religion and more to geography. He offered as his new pledge: "I pledge allegiance to the flag of the United States of America and to the Republic for which it stands, one Nation, under Canada and above Mexico, indivisible, with liberty and justice for all."

6

Fifty States Under God

UNDER GOD OR under Canada, the debate over the pledge heated up after the September 11, 2001, attack on the World Trade Center. New Hampshire, for example, passed a law in 2002 that required all public schools to begin classes with a salute to the flag. The practice had been widespread for decades, but it rested on custom, not law. The New Hampshire Patriot Act mandated that on each school morning teachers lead a voluntary recitation of the Pledge of Allegiance. As for students who chose not to participate, the act provided that they could "silently stand or remain seated." That escape clause was not good enough for an atheist couple, dubbed by the court Jan and Pat Doe, who brought suit against the Hanover School District on Halloween, 2007, on behalf of their three children, one in middle school, the other two in elementary school. They claimed that the act violated their children's First Amendment rights since the required phrase "under God" was an unconstitutional establishment of religion, as well as a denial of their children's Fourteenth Amendment right to "the equal protection of the laws."

The Hanover case opened a second front in the war over the pledge, one that directs our attention to state laws and their constitutions. As discussed later in this chapter, God plays a much more prominent role in the fifty state constitutions than in the national Constitution. But we begin with state cases that tried to achieve in individual states the ban on "under God" that Newdow had sought for the nation in his appearances before federal courts. Helping to fund the battle in New Hampshire was a pesky atheist activist organization based in Madison, Wisconsin, the Freedom From Religion Foundation (FFRF). Not surprisingly, it enlisted as leader of Jan and Pat Doe's fight Michael Newdow—the champion of the national effort to end the nation being "under God." Aid and encouragement on the other side came from the Becket Fund and the American Center for Law and Justice, both major pro bono law firms defending religious groups from what they perceive as secularist assaults, whether legislative or judicial.

Both sides reached beyond the New Hampshire courtroom in making their cases. "The Constitution doesn't ban the word God from public discourse in California or New Hampshire in the Pledge or anywhere else," Seamus Hasson, the founder and president emeritus of the Becket Fund argued for the school district, while the FFRF's copresident Annie Laurie Gaylor and Newdow reported that "the FFRF continues to receive so many requests by our members to restore the original Pledge, and by parents of school children and students in public schools around the nation who are offended, stigmatized, embarrassed or even disciplined for not wishing to recite a religious pledge."

The Hanover case would take three years to run its course. In 2008 United States District Judge Steven A. McAuliffe ruled against the "Doe" couple, and Newdow appealed to the U.S. First Circuit Court of Appeals. In vain it turned out. A three-judge panel in November 2010 unanimously held for the Hanover School District against the plaintiffs and upheld the constitutionality of the New Hampshire Patriot Act and of the pledge. This defeat for Newdow came eight months after Justice Carlos Bea, writing for the Ninth Circuit three thousand miles away from New Hampshire, had ruled against him.

Still Newdow might have taken some solace from the skepticism with which the First Circuit Court considered the argument that God talk is empty of religious content. Chief Judge Sandra L. Lynch, appointed by President Clinton, and the first woman to serve on the First Circuit, spoke for the three-judge panel. Though making no reference to Bea's decision, Lynch dismissed the claim that the Pledge violated the Establishment Clause with a similar finding that the pledge with "under God" passes the three tests: *Lemon*, endorsement, and coercion. Her reasoning as she traversed the three tests is not novel, but it is less interested in emphasizing the patriotic and the political. Indeed she is more nuanced and thoughtful than Bea. She acknowledges, for example, that the phrase "under God" has some religious content and that "mere repetition of the phrase in secular ceremonies does not by itself deplete the phrase of all religious content." She notes that "it is demeaning to persons of any faith to assert that the words 'under God' contain no religious significance."

Nevertheless, even with their religious meaning, the words are constitutional and allowable because they "are not themselves prayers, nor are they readings from or recitations of a sacred text of a religion." The New Hampshire law in 2002, Judge Lynch held, did not seek to advance, establish, or support religion, because "it takes more than the presence of words with religious content to have the effect of advancing religion." The claim of the FFRF and Newdow that the Doe children were rendered "outsiders, not full members" of the school community was irrelevant because they had voluntarily chosen not to recite the pledge.

Most of the relatively short seven-page decision deals with the Establishment Clause, and, almost as an afterthought, only its last paragraph addresses Equal Protection, which parallels the balancing of the two claims made by Newdow. In an underdeveloped part of his argument, he had asserted that the law treated the Doe children differently and without equal respect because it "created a social environment that perpetuated prejudice against atheists." Lynch dismissed the claim; the New Hampshire law did not involve different or preferential treatment "to any class of persons" because of any "particular religious beliefs." Newdow, with the financial backing of the FFRF, appealed Justice Lynch's November 2010 decision to the United States Supreme Court, which in June 2011 refused to hear the case.

The Supreme Court may have declined to hear the case, but the justices had not ended it. There was life yet in the argument against God in the pledge. The battle in the states continued because nonbelieving plaintiffs made a dramatic change in their argument, henceforth shifting their primary complaint from Establishment Clause claims to one based primarily on the Fourteenth Amendment's Equal Protection clauses. What had been a subordinate argument before now came to the center of the briefs. The shift was intellectually informed by law review articles written in response to the often contradictory District, Circuit, and Supreme Court rulings in Establishment Clause violation claims, not only in pledge cases but in others. The Supreme Court, for example, in 2005 held in *McCreary County v. American Civil Liberties Union* that exhibiting the Ten Commandments in a Kentucky courthouse violated the Establishment Clause (though a vigorous dissent from Justice Scalia called the principle that "government cannot favor religion over irreligion . . . demonstrably false") while holding in *Van Orden v. Perry* that same day that a statue commemorating the Ten Commandments on the Texas State Capitol grounds did not.

"Thou Shalt Use the Equal Protection Clause for Religion Cases (Not Just the Establishment Clause)" was the hortatory title of a 2008 piece by Susan Gellman and Susan Looper-Friedman in the University of Pennsylvania *Journal of Constitutional Law*. It's more honest and easier to prove, they argue, that atheist schoolchildren who decline to recite "under God" suffer harm because they are treated differently and are discriminated against by government rather than that they are encouraged or coerced into monotheistic religious belief.

As the argument goes, like racial minorities nonbelieving children are marginalized as a class in a country where the vast majority are believers. A governmental embrace and use of religious expression makes atheists feel "that they are outsiders, almost second-class citizens, and not equally American." Quite appropriately, Gellman and Looper-Friedman enlist Justice O'Connor's repeated concern that "school sponsorship of a religious message is impermissible," if it "sends the message to nonadherents that they are outsiders, not full members of the political community." Although Justice O'Connor raised equal-protection fears, she usually dismissed them, leaving Gellman and Looper-Friedman to make the argument that nonbelieving students who stand silently during the pledge are rendered marginal as they are daily reminded "who the 'real' citizens are." If governmental statements, practices, or displays convey the message that "non-Christians are not welcome" or that "atheists are immoral" or "unpatriotic, even if they are not primarily sacred, coercive, or interfering," they are discriminatory all the same.

Meanwhile, other law-review articles were exploring how to label the harm done to individuals who were not treated with equal concern by governmental religious speech or practices. A school of legal scholarship, using what it labeled an "expressivist" theory about the social meaning of words, contended that individuals are denied equal protection not only when they are substantively treated differently by government, but also by "the message conveyed by the state action," whatever its intent or its measurable practical effect. As one law-review piece put it, "An expressive harm . . . results from the ideas or attitudes expressed through a governmental action, rather than from the more tangible or material consequences the action brings about." Not just by deeds, but by words, the expressivists argued, can the state show that it values some more than others.

Caroline Corbin, professor at the University of Miami School of Law, made a strong expressivist case in a 2012 article in the *Iowa Law Review*, insisting that including God in the national pledge "like segregation sends a message of inequality." Like race and sex, religious beliefs are a protected characteristic under the Equal Protection Clause because, she argues, they too, are "deeply constitutive of identity." Even if the state does not denigrate nonbelievers, it announces in the pledge that it favors believers, which clashes with its obligation to treat everyone equally.

Corbin, for good measure, contends that government religious speech, whether it's God in the pledge or God in the national motto and on money, causes material harm as well. It reinforces stereotypes of atheists as immoral and unpatriotic, which, she claims, contributes to the ever-present risk of discrimination that atheists face in all aspects of American life. Government religious speech, usually the affirmation of God, Corbin concludes, "sends a message that non-believers are not worthy of equal regard."

The new president of the Washington, D.C.–based American Humanist Association, David Niose, was coming to similar conclusions in 2012. In his book *Nonbeliever Nation* Niose urged the secular movement to shift its legal strategy from the Establishment Clause to the more identity-oriented focus of equal-protection cases. Atheists, he argued, would fare better when they prove membership in a "suspect class," like racial minorities, "who are understood to be frequent targets of discrimination." A lawyer by profession, Niose practiced what he preached, filing and arguing in Massachusetts a lawsuit, *Doe v. Acton-Boxborough Regional School District,* accusing the school district of violating his plaintiffs' equal-protection rights under the Massachusetts Constitution by requiring daily recitation of the Pledge of Allegiance containing the words "under God." The American Legion and Jay Alan Sekulow representing the American Center for Law and Justice filed amicus curiae briefs that supported the school district.

The suit on behalf of an atheist couple and their three children, aged ten, twelve, and fourteen, was originally rejected by a Middlesex Superior Court judge. It was then heard on appeal in 2013 by the Massachusetts Supreme Court, which rendered its decision in May 2014. Niose told the court that the plaintiffs and their children did not believe that the United States or any country is "under God" and that the pledge "suggests that all good Americans believe in God" and that others like them "who do not believe in God, aren't as good as others who do believe." The effect of the pledge ritual was to marginalize the plaintiffs and their children, reinforcing "general public prejudice against atheists and humanists," and "classifying them as outsiders and second-class citizens." This perception could, Niose argued, possibly lead "to unwanted attention, criticism, and potential bullying."

Writing for a unanimous seven-person court in May 2014, Chief

Justice Roderick Ireland rejected the claim that the plaintiffs' equal-protection rights were violated. There is "no evidence, nothing empirical or even anecdotal" indicating that the three children "have in fact been treated . . . differently from other children . . . because of their religious beliefs or because of how they participate in the Pledge." There was no tangible harm, he notes; they have not "been punished, bullied, criticized, ostracized, or otherwise mistreated by anyone as a result of their decision to decline to recite some (or all) of the Pledge." More importantly, Ireland rejected the expressivist claim that the children have felt themselves "stigmatized," or been made to feel "that they do not belong" or "that they are unpatriotic outsiders." Only objective evidence of mistreatment counts, not subjective feelings, he argues. "The feeling of 'stigma' is not legally cognizable for purposes of the equal rights amendment."

To drive home his point that a voluntary school program (reciting "under God"), which may leave some feeling stigmatized or excluded, does not necessarily violate equal-protection principles, Ireland cites the practice of Massachusetts schools that made condoms available to students. Accepting the claims of Niose and the plaintiffs would allow, he suggests, religious critics to claim that "condom vending machines in the restrooms—sends a daily message to them that the school accepts and even promotes values that do not comport with their religious views, and therefore publicly renders them 'outsiders' based on their religious beliefs." Should courts, he concludes, accept the plaintiff's subjective expressivist theory, "numerous programs and activities that are otherwise constitutional would be scuttled under the rubric of equal protection."

It wasn't a bad argument, and it kept Justice Barbara Lenk, a Harvard-trained jurist, on his side. However, her interesting concurring opinion left room for future litigation. In it, she suggests that the presence of the phrase "under God" in the Pledge of Allegiance "creates a classification that is potentially cognizable under the Equal Rights Amendment of the Massachusetts Constitution." A reference to a supreme being, does distinguish, she notes, "between those who believe such a being exists and those" who do not. "Theists are acknowledged in the text of the pledge, whereas nontheists like the plaintiffs are excluded from that text, and are, therefore implicitly differentiated."

She then notes that the plaintiffs did not argue that their children actually received tangible negative treatment because they chose not to say "under God." But, surprisingly, she added, "Our holding today should not be construed to bar other claims that might rely on sufficient indicia of harm. Should future plaintiffs demonstrate that the distinction created by the pledge as currently written has engendered bullying or differential treatment, I would leave open the possibility that the equal rights amendment might provide a remedy." With these words the judicial door is left open, if not necessarily to subjective feelings of not being treated equally, certainly to objective evidence of it.

Nine months later, in February 2015, the Superior Court of New Jersey closed the door. Niose and the American Humanist Association had filed a suit on behalf of an atheist family and their son, a student in a Monmouth County school, claiming that the required flag salute violated his equal-protection rights guaranteed by the New Jersey Constitution. The case, *American Humanist Association v. Matawan-Aberdeen Regional School District*, captured national attention in November 2014, when Judge David Bauman allowed the plea of Samantha Jones, a senior at a nearby school, to be read to the court, "that kids like me shouldn't be silenced just because some people object to timeless American values. . . . Ever since I was little I've recited the Pledge of Allegiance because it sums up the values that make our country great." Jones, supported by the Becket Fund, the Knights of Columbus, and the American Legion, became an instant media star, interviewed and featured on Fox News throughout the early winter of 2014–15.

Justice Bauman rejected the equal-protection claim; no discriminatory classification existed because the pledge recitation was "entirely voluntary." No evidence was presented that the atheist student "was punished or mistreated for not participating." Bauman acknowledged, on the other hand, that "the Court is not insensitive" to the Doe child's claim to feel marginalized by the presence of the words "under God" in the pledge. "Subjective feelings, however, do not and cannot serve as a constitutional litmus test for equal protection in the absence of some invidious classification, because potentially anything offensive to one's subjective sensibilities could be struck down as unconstitutional."

Bauman, though he granted Samantha Jones "leave to intervene in this action," showed palpable anger in noting that the American Humanist Association had "improperly placed before this Court," in an affront to various New Jersey rules of evidence, a collection of emails from "allegedly atheist students," "hearsay statements attributed to certain avowed atheist students from around the country" describing "the discrimination they allegedly experience." His court, Bauman pointedly added, "is not the appropriate forum in which to seek redress for their concerns." Its focus is the "narrow issue" of the students in Doe's regional school.

A puzzling, if not disturbing, aspect of Bauman's ruling, given its relevance to the issue of equal treatment, is found in an extended footnote where he acknowledges that during the November oral argument the American Humanist Association had produced a printed policy statement, issued by the Matawan-Aberdeen School Board, requiring the parents of pupils refusing to salute the flag to provide the school administration "a written statement of their child's conscientious objection." Bauman's footnote points out that when pushed on this, the school's attorney "was unaware of the existence of this school board policy." The footnote ends with the terse statement that between the oral argument in November and his February ruling the school board had revised its policy, deleting the required written statement, thus acknowledging that such a requirement was "potentially problematic." The school board's action meant that "any issue raised by plaintiffs with respect to [that] board policy is now moot."

So ended in New Jersey state-based legal efforts to free America from being "under God." God would remain in the Pledge of Allegiance, even while God is notably absent from our nation's most significant and enduring document—the Constitution. It is striking that in their rulings both Judge Ireland and Judge Bauman commit the same inexcusable mistake. They both cite earlier court pronouncements offering as historical truth "the fact the Founding Fathers believed devotedly that there was a God and that the unalienable rights of man were rooted in Him is clearly evidenced in their writings from the Mayflower Compact to the Constitution itself."

They are both wrong. God is nowhere to be found in the American Constitution and that omission infuriated many at the time. The Constitution, drafted in 1787 and ratified in 1788, is a godless document. It was self-consciously designed to be an instrument with which to structure the secular politics of individual interest and happiness, to protect property rights from radical state legislatures and leveling mobs like the farmers who participated in Shays' Rebellion during the winter of 1776–77 and tried to seize the arsenal in Springfield, Massachusetts, protesting what they regarded as an unfair tax structure. The Constitution was bitterly attacked for its failure to mention God or Christianity and was called by its critics "the Godless Constitution."

The absence of any reference to God (except in the date given at the end of the document as "the seventeenth day of September in the year of our Lord, One thousand Seven Hundred and eighty-seven") in the text led to bitter fights in several state ratifying conventions in 1788. Those who labeled it a "Godless Constitution" urged, as in Connecticut, the insertion into the Preamble after "We the people of the United States" the words "in a firm belief of the Being and perfection of the one living and true God, the creator and Supreme Governor of the world, in His universal providence and the authority of His laws." The delegates in Connecticut rejected the change.

During the Civil War the great Protestant preacher Horace Bushnell, who led the North Congregational Church in Hartford, Connecticut, until 1859, urged that something be done about God's absence from the Constitution, "this atheistic error in our prime conceptions of government" from which flowed the general "atheistic habit of separating politics from religion." A chorus of clergymen joined the call. God was burying America in the ruinous Civil War, they claimed, because he was ignored in America's founding document. They proposed rewording the Preamble of the Constitution: "We the people of the United States, humbly acknowledging Almighty God as the source of all authority and power in civil government, the Lord Jesus Christ as the Governor among the Nations, and His revealed will as of supreme authority, in order to constitute a Christian government . . . do ordain and establish this Constitution for the United States of America."

This so-called Christian Amendment failed, as would four more efforts, in 1894, 1910, 1947, and 1954, to put God into the Constitution. The Constitution erected a federal system, however, and the idea of a secular state has not prevailed in the fifty states. God is prominent in every single one of their constitutions, evoked in the preambles of forty-six of them, and found a place in the body of the remaining four. A typical example is the preamble to the New Jersey state constitution: "We the people of the state of New Jersey, grateful to Almighty God for the civil and religious liberty which He hath so long permitted us to enjoy and looking to Him for a blessing upon our endeavors to secure and transmit to succeeding generations, do ordain and establish this Constitution." Justice David Bauman of New Jersey cited those words approvingly when he rejected the equal-protection claim advanced in the Matawan Aberdeen school case to discredit the phrase "under God" in the Pledge of Allegiance.

Some preambles, like Pennsylvania's, add "humbly invoking His guidance" to their being "grateful to Almighty God" for their blessings of liberty. By far the most lyrical reference to God is in the preamble to the Montana state constitution: "We the people of Montana, grateful to God for the quiet beauty of our state, the grandeur of our mountains, the vastness of our rolling plains, and desiring to improve the quality of life, equality of opportunity and to secure the blessings of liberty for this and future generations do ordain and establish this Constitution." The four state constitutions without God in their preambles, as well as many others, have inserted God into their state Bill of Rights. Indiana's reads: "All people shall be secured in their natural right to worship Almighty God according to their own consciences."

All of these confident, often mellifluous tributes to God's bounty in state constitutions make even more striking God's absence over the states assembled together in the Constitution of the indivisible nation. The disparity reflects a profound uncertainty Americans have always felt over how much government should involve itself in moral and religious issues. For much of American history, many have shared the underlying premise of the federal Constitution that government's purpose was regulating commerce and protecting personal—especially property—rights and not furthering a moral or religious order. The Framers aimed to create a commercial republic where God, certainly important in a citizen's private life, had little public role. And, indeed, the federal government has historically concerned itself primarily with economic issues. Thus, all those tariffs, like Smoot-Hawley, we memorized for the United States History SATs.

Other Americans, probably a majority in this deeply religious country, have sided with those who have found the godless Constitution a flawed document and have wanted government to preside over a godly civic life. Under the unique American practice of federalism, their vision has found a home in the state governments, which traditionally have been the arenas for handling police, education, and family and religious issues, where moral matters are front and center.

To be sure, the secular federal government's courts, using the Fourteenth Amendment, have ruled against the practices and laws that individual states put in place by prohibiting prayer and Bible reading in state schools in the early 1960s; deeming abortion legal in all states in 1974; prohibiting antihomosexual state laws in 2008; and legalizing same-sex marriage in all states in 2015—actions that, in turn, have reenergized religious advocates. All these decisions came after 1940 when the Supreme Court "incorporated" the First Amendment into all laws made by states. Before that, the First Amendment had not applied to laws in the individual states.

The protests that accompanied the above changes and the fact that God is in all the states' constitutions remains a powerful reminder of our fundamental ambivalence about the place of religion in American

public life. America is still simultaneously a national secular commercial republic and fifty divinely ordained moral republics, a godless federal Constitution coexisting with fifty godly state constitutions. Small
wonder then that our courts deliver often contradictory opinions about
the meaning of religious establishment and of free religious practice.

There is no better nor more grievous example of American civil
religion at work, no better place to see the marriage of religion and
citizenship, than in the requirement found in eight state constitutions
today that one must believe in God to hold public office in those states.
The eight states require that to exercise the defining marker of citizenship, being a state official, one has to be religious. The states are:

Arkansas—"No person who denies the being of a God shall hold
any office in the civil departments of the state."

Maryland—"No religious test ought ever to be required for any
office of profit or trust in this state, other than a declaration of belief in
the existence of God."

Mississippi—"No person who denies the existence of a Supreme
Being shall hold any office in this state."

North Carolina—"The following persons shall be disqualified for
office; first, any person who shall deny the Being of Almighty God."

South Carolina—"No person who denies the existence of a Supreme
Being shall hold any office under this Constitution."

Tennessee—"No person who denies the Being of God, or of a future
state of rewards and punishments, shall hold any office in the civil
department of this state."

Texas—"No religious test shall ever be required as a qualification
to any office, or public trust, in this state, nor shall anyone be excluded
from holding office on account of his religious sentiments, provided he
acknowledge the existence of a Supreme Being."

The *Pennsylvania* state constitution contains even more convoluted
wording than the Texas statement: "No person who acknowledges the
Being of a God and a future state of rewards and punishments shall,
on account of his religious sentiments, be disqualified to hold any
office or place of trust or profit under this Constitution." The sentence

might baffle any court charged to declare its meaning, but apparently it was meant to imply that nonbelievers could be disqualified from holding office.

The federal Constitution as drafted in 1787 specifically declares in Article 6, "No religious test shall ever be required as a qualification to any office or public trust under the United States." At the state ratifying conventions in 1787 and 1788 this provision added to the ire of those already convinced that God's absence from the text had produced a godless Constitution. In 1787, eleven of the thirteen states (Virginia and New York excepted) had religious tests for public office in their state constitutions, all requiring officials to be Protestants or, as in Massachusetts and Maryland, Christian. Opponents of Article 6 argued that it would be "an invitation to Jews and pagans of any kind," also to Papists, to govern in the new Republic. Interestingly, in light of twenty-first-century concerns, delegates to the Massachusetts and New York ratifying conventions worried about "Mahometans [sic], who ridicule the doctrine of the Trinity."

Defenders of the "no religious test clause" recalled the discrimination in Britain experienced by the dissenting Protestant sects that had peopled colonial America. The notorious "Test and Corporation Acts" had banned them from public office and from matriculation at Oxford and Cambridge. Those acts reserved such social privileges and basic civil rights only for those who accepted the creed of the Anglican Church. Other defenders, like Oliver Ellsworth, third chief justice of the Supreme Court, saw fundamental principles at work, writing: "A test law is . . . the offspring of error and the spirit of persecution. Legislators have no right to set up an inquisition and examine into the private opinions of men."

All the efforts in the various state ratifying conventions to blunt the federal Constitution's Article 6, like the Virginia initiative to change its wording to "No other religious test shall ever be required than a belief in the one only true God, who is the rewarder of the good and the punisher of the evil," failed. The "no religious test" clause sits in the document today, just as the absence of God does.

In the nineteenth and twentieth centuries, state after state dropped their requirements that office holders be Protestant or Christian, but not all, as we have seen, dropped the need for people to believe in God. The Supreme Court in 1961 ruled that such state religious tests were unconstitutional. In *Torasco v. Maryland*, Justice Hugo Black ruled for a unanimous court that denying Torasco an appointment as notary public because he refused to declare a belief in God violated his right to religious freedom: "We repeat and again reafffirm that neither a State nor the Federal Government can constitutionally force a person 'to profess a belief or disbelief in any religion.' Neither can constitutionally pass laws or impose requirements which aid all religions as against non-believers."

That was in 1961. Since that time, amazingly enough, none of the eight states with religious tests, including Maryland, have changed such language in their constitutions. The retained words may be symbolic, but they matter. They speak to pressures that weigh upon legislatures and the mentality of those who appoint and elect people to office. They tell atheists not to apply.

Despite *Torasco*, defenders of the eight state constitutions continue to assume that religious tests are unconstitutional only if one religion is privileged over another. That is, when various state provisions were written, the common assumption was that a candidate for state office could be any sort of Christian, even, with grudging assent, Roman Catholic. Later the assumption expanded to include Jews and perhaps members of other world religions. The possibility that a nonbeliever was covered by nonreligious test clauses was never explicitly addressed. Most of the states that require a belief in God for office holders actually have a disclaimer that they are, in fact, not imposing religious tests. The Maryland Constitution still reads "No religious test ought ever to be required as a qualification for any office of profit or trust in this State, other than a declaration of belief in the existence of God."

The argument is that a religious test is acceptable so long as no particular religion is named. In other words, a requirement that a state official be religious, believe in God, is not a religious test. One state, and only one, of the fifty provides specifically in its constitution that no test for public office shall be required "on account of religious belief or *the absence thereof*" (our italics), and it is not one of the states thought to harbor large populations of atheists or secular humanists. It is Utah, once denied membership in the Union because of an alleged failure to separate its politics from the control of the Mormon Church. Historically the most persecuted of all religious groups in the United States, Mormons in Utah exert political power as a majority but with unusually explicit recognition of the fact that people's religious convictions are not predictive of their ability to wisely handle state affairs. When Roger Williams, a fervent Calvinist, said the same in the seventeenth century and found himself way ahead of his fellow Calvinists in Massachusetts Bay, he was exiled to Rhode Island. Arguably Roger Williams is still in advance of most Americans.

So too is Thomas Jefferson, whose reference in the Declaration of Independence to men's unalienable rights endowed by their Creator is lovingly quoted by the defenders of the post-1954 Pledge of Allegiance in the debate about "under God." Forgotten is Jefferson's observation in his *Notes on Virginia* that "the legitimate powers of government extend to such acts only as are injurious to others, but it does me no injury for my neighbor to say there are twenty gods or no god. It neither breaks my leg, nor picks my pocket."

Though rarely enforced, to be sure, these state religious tests do sometimes capture public attention. In 2004 an atheist in Tennessee, a computer programmer, was nominated but not appointed to a state commission on education. He then wrote his state representative and state senator urging them to address the Tennessee constitutional requirement that office holders believe in God. His letters were never answered. In 2009 when an atheist was elected to the City Council in Asheville, North Carolina, his critics wanted him barred from office because his denial of "the Being of Almighty God" violated North Carolina's Constitution. The effort was unsuccessful and he was sworn in.

The most important incident when public attention was brought to a state constitutional religious test occurred earlier, in 1990, when

Herb Silverman, an atheist mathematics professor at the College of Charleston ran for governor of South Carolina, specifically to challenge the state's constitutional requirement that its officials cannot be a "person who denies the existence of a Supreme Being." Parallel to Silverman's gubernatorial campaign on the United Citizens Party, his ACLU lawyer filed a lawsuit against the state and its religious test. The story, picked up by the Associated Press, USA Today, and Rush Limbaugh, became national news. Silverman had to respond to accusations that his not believing in God meant he "must feel free to rape, murder, and commit any atrocity he can get away with." He received no sympathy from South Carolina's then governor Carroll Campbell, who observed that the atheist's candidacy and legal challenge were misguided because "the South Carolina Constitution was founded on God's principles."

Seven days before the election the state trial judge dismissed Silverman's case against the state constitution because it was "not ripe," meaning it would be premature for him to rule on the merits of the case until Silverman won the election. Silverman, one of four candidates and the self-described "candidate without a prayer," knew that outcome was unlikely. "I'm an atheist, not a fool." When he lost badly, Silverman remained undaunted, and the next year applied for a license as a notary public. He paid his $25 fee and crossed out the words "So help me God" from the required oath in the application, writing on the form that the United States Constitution prohibited religious tests as a qualification for public office. The governor's office, which routinely approves all such applications, rejected Silverman's, giving no explanation. Silverman sued the reelected Governor Campbell. In a deposition his ACLU lawyers discovered that 33,471 notary applications were approved from 1991 to 1993 and that Silverman's was the only one denied.

Silverman's case, Silverman v. Campbell, moved slowly, but in the summer of 1995 the South Carolina Circuit Court held that his application met all the legal requirements and that the new governor, David Beasley, should approve the application. A born-again Christian, Beasley appealed the decision to the South Carolina Supreme Court. In May 1997, the state's Supreme Court unanimously affirmed the Circuit Court's holding that the South Carolina Constitution's requirement of belief in a Supreme Being in order to hold public office violated the First Amendment's protection of the free exercise of religion and Article 6's ban on the use of religious tests for office holders. Silverman became a notary public on August 8, 1997.

Today, over twenty years after its dramatic repudiation by the state's highest court, the South Carolina Constitution still maintains the requirement that state officials must believe in God, as the other seven state constitutions still do. Not that some people aren't working hard to change that. Todd Stiefel, a wealthy patron of atheist activism, and his organization, the Openly Secular Coalition, founded in 2014, are lobbying legislators in those eight states to get rid of what the Coalition considers the "naked bigotry" of the discriminatory requirements, a daunting task given the need for rarely convened state constitutional conventions to change the wording, let alone the difficulty of finding the political will to drop proreligious language, however unenforceable it might be.

Stiefel is still trying. "If it was on the books," he told the *New York Times*, on December 7, 2014, "that Jews couldn't hold public office, or that African-Americans or women couldn't vote, that would be a no brainer. You'd have politicians falling all over themselves to get it repealed. Even if it was still unenforceable, it would still be disgraceful and be removed. So why are we different?"

A spokesperson for the American Atheists, David Muscato, who sees it as highly unlikely that the need-to-believe-in-God requirements will ever be removed from the eight state constitutions, still finds a silver lining in that unfortunate outcome. In July 2014 he told Fox News, whose libertarian leanings sometimes provide atheists a platform, that the retention of these requirements will serve an important history lesson for future generations of Americans. "Having them on the books," he suggests, "even though they aren't enforceable is a stark reminder that our country once considered an atheist unfit for office."

Muscato's thinking wasn't enough for Herb Silverman. In 2002, five years after he received his notary's license from the state of South Carolina, he became the leading force in launching the Secular Coalition for America, a lobbying group based in Washington, D.C., whose mission is to speak for "the growing non-theistic community in the United States." Among its priorities is the elimination of religious-test requirements. However anachronistic they might be in practice, they remain an affront to the idea of free religious practice guaranteed by a secular state. As discussed in chapter eight, Silverman's organization is only one of many that have given a new direction to atheist activism since the beginning of the twenty-first century, all convinced that these state religious tests, just like the recitation of "under God" in the Pledge of Allegiance, render the ground on which the "wall of separation" is built if not shaky, then certainly unstable.

7

Unequal Citizens Under God

EVEN IF FEDERAL and state court justices are right in thinking that the phrases "one nation under God" and "in God we trust" aren't usually intended as bullying cries to coerce nontheists into conformity with a theist majority, all laws that seem to endorse the principle that the United States is a religious nation effectively exclude nonbelievers from equal participation in many public ceremonies. The fiction of a religious nation has other consequences as well. In this chapter we trace the way in which it has allowed beliefs and actions based on the supposed commands of an Almighty God to carry more weight than the beliefs and actions based on nontheistic moral principles. The specific legal question is whether a constitutional interpretation of free religious practice may justify for theists, but not for others, an exemption from general laws that on their face have nothing to do with religion.

In the past fifty years, no issue has led to more division on the Supreme Court than the issue of what protection extends to a religious practice when it is not specifically part of a religious service but tied to how people conduct their nonchurch life in a quotidian world ruled by general laws passed not by religious bodies but by secular legislatures. The protection of free religious practice does not permit all behavior that might be religiously motivated. But the lines aren't clear. A man who claims that God has ordered him to drive one hundred miles per hour on an interstate highway is not likely to get very far in court. But the same man who says that God has forbidden him to prepare a cake for a gay wedding, even though a state law prohibits a business from discrimination based on sexual orientation, may do better. Such a case involving a Colorado baker has made its way to the Supreme Court.

The idea of a "religious" exemption extends back to colonial America. As we saw in chapter one, colonial legislatures, acting in accord with then prevalent notions of religious "toleration," exempted "religious dissenters" from the obligation to support the legally established church. The exemption allowed them to set up their own churches and to divert tax money collected to maintain the "established" religion to benefit their own institutions. There were other sorts of exemptions. One allowed Quakers to testify in court proceedings without swearing an oath. Another exempted Baptists from paying religious taxes altogether.

In the beginning none of these measures rested on a constitutional guarantee of free religious practice but on legislative enactments. The exemptions were quite particular about what was allowed and what was not allowed. The rights that a legislature granted could be taken away and sometimes were. By the late eighteenth century, most colonies had constitutions guaranteeing free religious practice, but again, as we saw in chapter one, the scope of free religious practice didn't create a level playing field even for all religious denominations, let alone for nonbelievers. Members of minority religious sects often relied on legislative bodies to accord them the same legal rights as members of larger denominations. Today few of us would argue that these exemptions were unjustified, for without them, dissenters had no religious freedom. Even so, an atheist asking for relief from paying any religious taxes would have gotten nowhere in a colonial court.

The American Constitution opened a new religious era. But in the nineteenth century neither it nor state laws extending rights and exemptions to members of minority churches directly addressed the question of whether notions of free religious practice might explicitly and on the same terms apply to nonbelievers. It took the world wars of the twentieth century to open a proper legal debate on that subject. In 1917, when the United States declared war against Germany, Congress passed the country's first compulsory draft law. It made all young men potential soldiers. However, the law provided an "exemption" for young men who for religious reasons objected to fighting in any war under any circumstances. It wasn't a new idea. James Madison had proposed writing into the Constitution's Second Amendment, the one granting citizens the right to keep and bear arms, the proviso that "no person religiously scrupulous of bearing arms shall be compelled to render military service in person." It was rejected. Madison's intention was to raise to the level of a constitutional right a legislative exemption that allowed pacifists, usually Quakers, to hire a substitute to do their fighting. That was a privilege that all young men on the Union side, whether pacifist or not, enjoyed during the Civil War.

Congress in 1917 hedged the exemption for conscientious objectors with a very specific definition of whose religious scruples mattered. Conscientious-objector status was available only to members of a "well-recognized religious sect or organization . . . whose existing creed or principles forbid its members to participate in war in any form." In practice, only members of a relatively small group of so-called Historic Peace Churches—the Mennonites, the Quakers, and the Brethren—qualified. In doing so, Congress did not follow the English example. England had been fighting the Germans since August of 1914. It had suffered far more grievous losses than the Americans would in their relatively brief commitment to the trench warfare of Europe. Yet England's Military Service Bill extended the right of conscientious objector status not only to draftees with religious objections but to those who on any other strong moral grounds thought it wrong in all circumstances to kill. Some prominent religious leaders in America urged Congress to use the same language. But Congress in carving out the grounds for draft exemption not only ignored humanists whose conscience made them pacifists but most religious Americans.

Not even Jehovah's Witnesses got a pass. Their church, while it forbade its members to fight in any human war, made an exception for the final Battle of Armageddon. According to the strict language of the Selective Service Act, a citizen who was willing to fight in some ultimate showdown between God and Satan had to fight in the lesser conflict pitting the good American democratic state against the autocratic regime of the German Kaiser. Conscientious Jehovah's Witnesses who refused to fight went to jail.

So did some members of the radical left who viewed the war as a conflict among European imperialists who cared nothing about the cause of democracy but who saw the war as a good opportunity to extend their colonial ambitions in Africa, the Middle East, and Asia. Louis Fraina, who later changed his name to Lewis Corey, was an American socialist leader when the United States declared war on Germany. A few years later he would help found the American Communist Party. In September 1917 he addressed a meeting in New York City protesting the draft law. In a fiery speech he urged young men to refuse enlistment on the grounds of political conscience. "Since when," he asked, "must a man necessarily belong to a church . . . before he can have a conscience?" His question was pertinent, along with his observation that "the government, in making conscientious objection to war a part of religion or creed, is placing a premium upon religion." Yet Fraina's objections to the rules of conscription weren't treated as healthy democratic debate but as "seditious speech" designed to encourage evasion of the Selective Service Act. Fraina, a nonbeliever who called religion a "superstition," joined the religiously scrupulous Jehovah's Witnesses in prison.

Two decades later another armed conflict loomed. Shortly before the United States declared war on Japan and Germany in World War II, Congress passed a new Selective Service bill. This time, when defining grounds for conscientious objectors, it dropped the requirement that a young man had to belong to a particular church. He rather had to demonstrate that he "by reason of religious training or belief was conscientiously opposed to participation in war in any form." Important religious voices, including leaders of the Historic Peace Churches, welcomed the broader grounds for granting c.o. classification. At the same time they urged Congress, as they had in World War I, not to draw a line between objections to war based on religion and ones based on philosophical grounds. Congress refused to follow that advice. Some congressmen suggested that dropping the religious test would open a loophole for Communists to shirk their military responsibilities. As we have seen, many Americans had for a long time equated atheism with communism. America's alliance with the Soviet Union in World War II didn't change that.

The intention of Congress's language limiting c.o. status to draftees with objections to war based on religious training and belief seemed perfectly clear to General Lewis Hershey. He became the director of Selective Service in July 1941, a post he held until 1970. According to Hershey, a young man seeking c. o. classification had to recognize the "Divine because it is the Source of all things." However, the cases of a few young men threw that clarity into doubt. Scholars have never agreed on a definition of religion. Why should draft boards and judges do any better? A member of the Ethical Culture Society who denied any theistic convictions received c.o. classification from his local draft board. Mathias Kauten, Randolph Phillips, and Herman Berman had less luck. Denied c.o. classification by their draft boards because they refused to base their opposition to war on religious training and belief, they appealed. What happened to them depended on which federal appeals court heard their separate cases.

Kauten had long been a pacifist when he refused induction and was at the time a commercial artist living in New Rochelle, New York. He sold his illustrations to pulp magazines. Phillips was a graduate of Columbia who in 1944 and 1945 made his living as a writer and directed the committee for conscientious objectors of the ACLU. The appeals of these two landed on the docket of the Second Circuit Court of Appeals. Justice Augustus Hand, who had in an earlier, famous ruling declared that James Joyce's novel *Ulysses* was not obscene and could not therefore be banned from import into the United States, wrote the opinion in *United States v. Kauten*. He ruled against Kauten on a technical matter. He hadn't followed proper procedures. The law required him to appear for induction before filing an appeal, which he hadn't done. However, Hand opened up grounds for the appeal of other young men by stating that the phrase "religious training and beliefs" didn't necessarily require a belief in God. He reasoned that Congress in broadening the provision of the 1917 Selective Service Act that had granted c.o. status only to members of specific peace churches meant to take account of the "characteristics of a skeptical generation." Hand's 1943 decision held that a young man's objection to participation "in any war under any circumstances . . . may justly be regarded as a response of an individual to an inward mentor, call it conscience or God, that is for many persons at the present the equivalent of what has always been thought a religious impulse."

The novel notion that "conscience" and "God" might be roughly equivalent terms didn't help Kauten, but it worked for Phillips. Phillips, who followed proper procedures in making his appeal, located the source of his pacifism not in religious training or a conception of the "divine" but on his reading of "philosophers, historians and poets from Plato to Shaw." He presented the text of a play he wrote that was antiwar but not religious to support his claim for exemption. The arguments he offered satisfied two of the judges of the three-court panel. According to the majority opinion in *United States v. Downer*, also rendered in 1943, the position taken by Phillips' conscience might not reflect the command of a God, but was "equivalent" to a "religious impulse."

The third man, Herman Berman, was Jewish and a supporter of socialist principles, who had founded a successful company in Los Angeles that specialized in engraving. In deciding his fate, the Ninth Circuit Court of Appeals took a different view of congressional intent than Judge Hand. In its 1946 decision, *Berman v. United States*, it agreed with General Hershey and linked "religious training and belief" to a "belief related more or less definitely to deity." Therefore the judges of the Ninth Circuit, although convinced that Berman was a sincere man who was strongly opposed to war, turned down his appeal. The judges found that Congress had "the specific purpose of distinguishing between a conscientious social belief, or a sincere devotion to a high moralistic philosophy, and one based upon an individual's belief in his responsibility to an authority higher and beyond any worldly one." In delivering the bad news to Berman, Judge Albert Stephens noted that Congress in drafting the Selective Service Act had ignored the advice of religious leaders that c.o. status should not be limited to religious belief.

The Supreme Court refused to take the cases on appeal, leaving as precedent the decisions of two courts with different readings of what the congressional language of the Selective Service law meant. The Ninth Circuit without doubt had a more accurate understanding of what was on the collective mind of Congress. In 1948, when it had another chance to draft a Selective Service Act, it moved to eliminate any ambiguity. The new law stated that "religious training and belief" involved an "individual's belief in a relation to a Supreme Being, involving duties superior to those arising from any human relation, and does not include essentially political, sociological, or philosophical views or a merely personal moral code." C.o. status was limited to theists. Nontheists, however high-minded and sincere their moral philosophy, needn't apply. Even so, ambiguity is a hard thing to destroy. All the judicial opinions rendered during World War II made clear that justices were uncomfortable trying to define religion. Justice Stephens of the Ninth Circuit, in deciding against Berman, conceded that religion was not static and that "manifestations, now understood through scientific law, were once attributed to the direct interposition of deity." A dissenting judge in the Berman case noted that some of the world's religions had no concept of God. Even with the revised language Congress used in 1948, future courts found room for creative interpretation.

Moreover, aside from the question of what religion was all about, there loomed another question about the c.o. provisions of the Selective Service Act. In 1947, a year before Congress revised the act's language, the Supreme Court handed down a landmark ruling regarding religion in *Everson v. Board of Education*. The case dealt with state-funded school busing programs that included Catholic students who attended parochial schools. The opinion written by Associate Justice Hugo Black held that neither Congress nor state legislatures "can pass laws which aid one religion, aid all religions, or prefer one religion over another." Any law that favored religion over nonreligion was unconstitutional. The legal formula had broad implications. When in the 1960s the United States plunged into the Vietnam War, an unpopular war that many of its supporters had trouble characterizing as a "good" or "just" one, the Supreme Court was forced to wrestle with both the congressional definition of religious training and belief as enunciated by Congress and the question of whether the Selective Service Act might constitute a religious establishment (banned by the First Amendment) by blatantly favoring religion over nonreligion.

In 1965 the Supreme Court decided the fate of three young men who had been denied c.o. classification, Daniel Andrew Seeger, Arno Sasha Jakobson, and Forest Britt Peter. To the casual observer of legal matters, the three copetitioners didn't have a chance in hell, at least based on the provisions of the Selective Service Act. The reasoning of the Second Circuit Court of Appeals in the World War II cases of Mathias Kauten and Randolph Phillips might have given them grounds for hope. But Congress had seemingly moved to block any further application of the Second Circuit's reasoning by insisting that religious belief depended on a "relation to a Supreme Being." While none of the appellants claimed to be an atheist, none of them based his case on such a relationship to God. Seeger had been raised as a Roman Catholic and was strongly influenced by Quakerism, yet in filling out the questionnaire required of applicants for c.o. status, he cited no religious tradition, left the question of his belief in a Supreme Being "open," and listed Plato, Aristotle, and Spinoza as inspirations for his "purely ethical creed." Although Jakobson believed in a "supreme reality" and Peter felt there was "an unspecified universal power beyond mankind," neither claimed that those notions affected their opposition to war.

The casual legal observer proved to be wrong. In *United States v. Seeger*, Associate Justice Tom Clark, writing for a unanimous court, ruled in favor of the appellants. Clark found legal elbowroom in the congressional use of the word "Supreme Being" as opposed to "God." A Supreme Being was a vague entity endorsed even by deists. A Supreme Being didn't necessarily try to rule the behavior of human beings with a host of commandments. Even if a young man might acknowledge the possible existence of a Supreme Being, he still had to figure out moral rules for himself. The relevant question, Clark said, is "whether a given belief that is sincere and meaningful occupies a place in the life of the possessor parallel to that filled by the orthodox belief in God." In the case of Seeger and his coappellants the answer was yes, even though they didn't base their morals on any conventional theistic notions, didn't believe in the authority of the Holy Bible, and attended no place of worship. They received their c.o. classification.

In a concurring opinion, Associate Justice William Douglas suggested the decision was a close call for him. If the Selective Service Act in fact favored religion over nonreligion, it was unconstitutional because it established religion in a way forbidden by the First Amendment. It would also violate the principle of equal protection of the law guaranteed to all citizens by the Fourteenth Amendment. Yet Douglas, perhaps leaning on the principle that it was always best to avoid the constitutional flaws of a piece of legislation if at all possible, decided that Congress gave the term "'Supreme Being' no narrow technical meaning in the field of religion." Attributing "tolerance and sophistication to the Congress, commensurate with the religious complexities of our communities," he was willing to say that the views of all of the defendants qualified as based on a relation, however vague, to a superior power. It was a creatively subjective view, and one that was more than a little disingenuous in its characterization of Congress.

Four years later the creative subjectivity of the justices faced another stiff challenge. In 1969, the case of Elliott Ashton Welsh landed in its docket. Welsh, like Seeger and his coplaintiffs, had been denied c.o. classification for flunking the test of religious training and belief. His mother had read the Bible to him as a child and sent him to a Christian Science Sunday School. But reading Bertrand Russell in high school trumped what he learned in Sunday School and turned him into a nonbeliever. In college he was a conservative who joined the Young Americans for Freedom. Then the sixties put him in the company of civil rights and peace activists. He married one of them. The difference between Welsh and the defendants in the Seeger case was that Welsh was much more definitive in declaring his agnosticism and in labeling his views as "nonreligious." He told his draft board that he didn't believe in a Supreme Being. To make his point absolutely clear, he crossed out the phrase "religious training" in the questionnaire he was required to fill out. What else did he have to do to show he didn't fit the requirements of the Selective Service Act? His case seemed to demand that the court either deny him c.o. status because his objections had nothing to do with God, or declare Selective Service Act unconstitutional on the grounds that it favored religion over nonreligion.

The majority of the justices once again avoided doing either thing, but the ruling in *Welsh v. United States* was not unanimous. Associate Justice Hugo Black wrote for the majority that ruled for Welsh. As the author of the *Everson* opinion, he had given himself strong grounds to declare that the Selective Service Act violated the Establishment Clause of the First Amendment. Yet he chose another route to get the decision he wanted. He argued that Welsh's appeals board had placed "undue emphasis on the registrant's interpretation of his own belief." Whether he knew it or not, and despite his explicit disclaimer that his views didn't rest on religious training, let alone a Supreme Being, Welsh was really like Seeger. His deeply felt objections to war occupied in his life "a place parallel to that filled by God in a traditionally religious person."

That was too much for Justice John Marshall Harlan, even though he wound up concurring in the decision. Harlan was a Republican appointee to the court, a justice regarded as a conservative, who had a sharp legal mind that he often used to dissent from the court's majority opinion. In the *Welsh* case, he wrote that Justice Black had performed a "lobotomy" on the statute that "cannot be justified in the name of the familiar doctrine of construing federal statutes in a manner that will avoid possible constitutional infirmities in them." The Selective Service Act clearly violated the Establishment Clause by making religious belief a state-endorsed source of privilege. Not assigning to Congress the sophistication that Douglas had been willing to see in it, Harlan said that the clear intention of the act, as rewritten in 1948, was to exclude men with views similar to Welsh from conscientious-objector-exemption classification. Congress, according to Harlan, had no obligation to grant c.o. status to anyone. The First Amendment's guarantee of free religious exercise did not excuse a young man from fighting for his country. However, if Congress chose to create an exemption, it could not accord "a preference to a religious conscience over the conscience of a non-believer" and that also "disadvantaged religious people who did not worship a Supreme Being."

Having taken a forceful position, Harlan swallowed hard and looked for a way that avoided striking down the Selective Service Act as unconstitutional and thereby eliminating all statutory exemptions for conscientious objection, religious or otherwise. Since no one wanted that outcome, Harlan said that it was sometimes allowable for the court to cure a constitutional defect by "patchwork" repair, in this case by including a category of young men who had been invalidly excluded because of their nonbelief in a Supreme Being. Harlan did not try to make the nonbeliever Welsh religious. But he was willing to countenance a court-made "salvaging" of a long-standing congressional policy by including nonbelievers within the "administrative framework of the statute." Harlan's complicated concurrence didn't change the majority ruling that had, without explicitly saying so, made the conscience of the nonbeliever, for purposes of c.o. classification, equivalent to the conscience of someone who professed belief in God. Even so, the court still chose to leave standing an act that on its face favored theism over nontheism.

It was an unsteady compromise, rendered more problematic by the three dissenting justices who voted against Welsh. Justice Byron White wrote for them. He reasoned that even if the Selective Service Act had a constitutional defect, that didn't help Welsh's petition. Congress still meant to exclude him from c.o. status. He went further to suggest that it didn't matter that the act seemed intended to limit c.o. classification to theists. He posed a pertinent question: "If it is favoritism and not 'neutrality' to exempt religious believers from the draft, is it 'neutrality' and not 'inhibition' of religion to compel religious believers to fight when they have special reasons to which the Constitution gives particular recognition?"

The divided opinions in the Welsh case revealed that the question of whether the Constitution allowed grounds for a religious exemption that wasn't available to nonbelievers was far from settled. Even if as a practical matter the grounds for c.o. classification applied to all young men of strong conscience, theist or nontheist, other cases decided by the Supreme Court suggested that the constitutional guarantee of free religious practice might confer something close to a privilege on members of religious organizations that didn't extend to atheists. In 1963 the settlement of a dispute involving Adell Sherbert led to a series of cases and legislative acts that raised fundamental questions about the meaning of free religious practice. These, at least in the majority opinion controlling precedent, consistently left out of the discussion any consideration of nonbelievers.

Sherbert worked in a textile mill in South Carolina. Two years after she became a Seventh-day Adventist, the mill that employed her, along with all the other mills in the area, changed its work schedule from a five- to a six-day week, the sixth day being Saturday. Seventh-day Adventists regard Saturday as their Sabbath day, and Sherbert, following her religious conscience, refused to work on that day. The mill fired her, and because she was fired for a cause, and not simply laid off, South Carolina refused her application for unemployment benefits. Sherbert sued the state, claiming that it had placed an unconstitutional burden on her religious practice.

The state of South Carolina argued that its law had not been aimed to disadvantage anyone's religion. It had not forbidden Sherbert to worship on Saturday nor required her to work on Saturday. The state had taken no position at all on Sherbert's religious beliefs or the practices that flowed from them. Its law on unemployment benefits had not been intended to discriminate against Seventh-day Adventists or any other religious group. The state had merely made the neutral ruling that if Sherbert chose to work, she had to follow the same rules as all other employees. The fact that the implementation of the law might pose an "incidental" or even substantial burden on her religious practice was not grounds for an exemption. It wouldn't be fair to other employees who might not want to work on Saturday for a wide variety of reasons, because they could not find a babysitter, for example, but who did so in order to keep their jobs.

None of the Supreme Court justices disputed the facts presented by South Carolina's legal team. Even so, Associate Justice William Brennan, writing for a divided court in the 1964 case *Sherbert v. Verner*, ruled in favor of Sherbert. Conceding that the burden on her religious practice was an indirect one and unintended by the state, Brennan argued that the court could not ignore the fact that the "effect" of the law impeded the observance of her religious belief. Its indirect effect imposed a financial burden on Sherbert even heavier than if the state had with deliberate intention imposed a fine on her for attending Saturday worship. She couldn't work and at the same time obey the religious teachings of her church. Unless South Carolina could show a compelling reason why the state had to impose the burden—and the Supreme Court ruled the state had not done that—Sherbert was entitled to unemployment benefits.

Underlying the Sherbert decision was a question that the majority decision didn't pose directly: would a victory for the plaintiff really harm anyone? Sherbert belonged to a small religious group. True, the exemption granted to her did not extend to members of far larger religious denominations or to people who claimed no religion but who might in the best of all possible worlds like to watch football games on Saturday. But that was a large reason why a ruling in Sherbert's favor, by Brennan's reasoning, didn't rise to the level of a religious establishment. The implication was that if the plaintiff had been a Southern Baptist or a member of an equally large denomination, the decision would have been different. If South Carolina had to shell out unemployment benefits to every Southern Baptist who might claim that work on Saturday interfered with his or her desire to attend special religious services on that day, the cost to the state might be substantial. Brennan wrote somewhat irrelevantly but in order to quell fears that the court's decision opened a floodgate: "Nor do we, by our decision today, declare the existence of a constitutional right to unemployment benefits of all persons whose religious convictions are a cause of their unemployment."

Numbers and minority status clearly weighed on the justices in reaching their decision. The Sherbert Rule in this sense did not demand a rule of strict equality among possible plaintiffs—exemptions never do—but it satisfied an almost innate sense of equity or fairness.

Associate Justice Potter Stewart's concurring opinion in the Sherbert case pointed to the position he would take in the Welsh case. He argued that the court should back away from what he called its "insensitive," "positively wooden," "mechanistic" readings of the Establishment Clause that threatened to turn almost any law that favored a religious practice over a secular practice into a religious establishment. The majority opinion, according to Stewart, had found for Sherbert only by ignoring the precedent of its earlier decision in *Everson v. Board of Education*. The stark fact was that the majority opinion granted to Sherbert a financial benefit not available to everyone and in doing so favored one religion over all others and over nonreligion. Stewart agreed with the result in the Sherbert case but not with the reasoning. In his mind, free religious practice was a constitutional guarantee that sometimes demanded exemptions for religious believers, and the unavailability of the exemptions to others did not constitute an establishment of religion.

Associate Justice Harlan was the naysayer who remained unmoved by Sherbert's complaint that her piety had cost her several months of unemployment compensation. His dissenting opinion held that Sherbert's decision not to work on Saturday, however religiously inspired, was a personal decision. Constitutionally speaking, it was equivalent to a choice not to work on Saturday because the lawn needed mowing. States and the federal government cannot interfere with what people do in their places of worship. That sort of religious practice is almost totally sacrosanct. So is religious belief. At the same time courts are not "constitutionally compelled to carve out an exception—and to provide benefits—for those whose unavailability [for work] is due to their religious convictions." In the public sphere a religious practice is no different from a secular practice. Harlan believed that the Sherbert decision illegitimately forced South Carolina to single out for financial benefit those whose behavior is religiously motivated and deny such assistance to "others whose identical behavior is not religiously motivated."

Harlan indicated that there was "enough flexibility in the Constitution" to permit the legislature to write "an unemployment compensation law to accommodate the religious beliefs of the appellant," though he qualified that concession with the statement that reasons to justify such legislative exceptions were "few and far between." But on the matter of whether Sherbert had a constitutional right to an exemption, he made no concession. He had a narrower concept of what counted as free religious practice than that defended in the majority opinion and a stricter view about what constituted an unconstitutional religious establishment.

Despite Harlan's dissent, the Sherbert Rule remained an accepted judicial precedent for almost thirty years. Every law student learned to cite it as a firm principle of constitutional law. Laws that substantially burdened someone's religious practice, however indirect the burden, could be challenged in court on the ground that the government lacked a compelling interest in refusing an exemption to the law. But the rule hardly resulted in easy victories for religious plaintiffs. In applying it, the Supreme Court decided for the states as often, indeed more often, as it decided for the religious complainants. While it permitted Jonas Yoder and Wallace Miller, members of the Old Order Amish religion, to take their children out of Wisconsin's public school system before they were sixteen, the required age for everyone else (*Wisconsin v. Yoder*, 1972), it upheld an Air Force dress code regulation that prevented Simcha Goldman, an Orthodox Jewish officer, from wearing a yarmulke when in uniform (*Goldman v. Weinberger*, 1986). It also permitted the federal government to build a road on public land to harvest timber, despite the claim of several American Indian tribes that the road violated sacred burial grounds used for religious worship (*Lyng v. Northwest Indian Cemetery Protective Association*, 1988).

Every case required a balancing act between the claims of a burden on religious practice and the countervailing claim, noted by Justice Sandra Day O'Connor in the *Lyng* case, that "government simply could not operate if it were required to satisfy every citizen's religious needs and desires." A religious plaintiff might prevail if the government lost nothing more than bureaucratic convenience by providing an exemption, but a strong presumption favored the state. The very fact that it enacted a law suggested a compelling interest. The first case the Supreme Court heard dealing with the claim of a burden on religious practice dated back to the late nineteenth century, when the federal government outlawed polygamy in the territories it controlled, including Utah. Though the law made no reference to the Church of Latter-day Saints, no one doubted that the law was aimed directly at Mormon religious practice. The burden on the religious practice was both substantial and intentional. Yet in 1872 the Supreme Court upheld the law. It declared that the right to hold any religious belief was absolute, but not the right to act on those beliefs. A public interest in monogamous marriage outweighed the religious duty of Mormon men to take more than one wife. The decision in *Reynolds v. the United States* was arguably modified by the Sherbert case, but it was not overruled.

The real problem with the Sherbert Rule, aside from the fact that it said nothing about how the protection of free religious practice might apply to nontheists, was not that it produced bad results, or turned every religious complaint into a privileged exemption. It was that the standard—the balancing act required to weigh a religious claim against the claim of the government—was subjective. In 1990 the Supreme Court in *Employment Division v. Smith* opted for a more objective rule that made it much more difficult for religious plaintiffs to gain exemptions. The case began when Alfred Smith and Galen Black, residents of the state of Oregon and members of the Native American Church, were fired from their jobs at a private drug rehabilitation organization because they had ingested peyote during a sacramental ceremony at their church. Holding that they were dismissed from their job because of work-related misconduct, the state of Oregon denied the pair unemployment benefits. The counterclaim of the plaintiffs followed the script of the Sherbert Rule. Oregon's action placed a severe burden on the plaintiffs' religious practice, and Oregon had failed to show a compelling reason to apply the law to them. The Native American Church carefully supervised the use of peyote in ceremonial rituals and allowed no one to leave a religious meeting until the hallucinatory effects of the drug had worn off.

Because they thought they had to, the legal counsels for Oregon presented a case for its compelling interest in regulating an illegal drug. But the majority opinion, written by Associate Justice Antonin Scalia, made their time and trouble in that effort largely unnecessary. He found another way to side with Oregon, a way that effectively trashed the Sherbert Rule. A relatively recent appointment to the court nominated by Ronald Reagan, Scalia seemed to follow the legal reasoning used by John Marshall Harlan in his dissenting opinion in the Sherbert case.

Scalia's opinion pointed to an obvious difference between the peyote case and the Sherbert ruling. When Smith and Black ingested peyote, they violated a criminal law, something Adell Sherbert had not done. Her refusal to work on Saturday was not a crime. Scalia insisted that "we have never held that an individual's religious beliefs excuse him from compliance with an otherwise valid law prohibiting conduct that the state is free to regulate." That was not really true since the court had accepted the religious beliefs of Amish farmers as a reason to allow them to take their children out of school before the legally mandated age. In any case, Scalia's decision went beyond the fact that ingesting peyote was a criminal act. It effectively relieved the state of the requirement that it present a compelling interest to justify enforc-

ing any general law that might incidentally burden someone's religious practice. To permit the intrusion of a religious objection would,
according to Scalia, citing language used in *Reynolds*, "make the professed doctrines of a religious belief superior to the law of the land and,
in effect, to permit every citizen to become a law unto himself."

Scalia raised the question of whether state legislative bodies might
create an exemption for the Native American Church without violating the Establishment Clause. A few states other than Oregon had done
that, and Scalia left that option open for Oregon. But in the absence of
legislation judges had no constitutional obligation to protect religious
minorities from the force of neutral legislation not aimed at religion.
"It may fairly be said," Scalia wrote, that "leaving accommodation to
the political process will place at a relative disadvantage those religious
practices that are not widely engaged in." Such are the vicissitudes of
democracy. There is no hint in *Employment Division v. Smith* of Scalia's
later reputation as a champion of religious liberty and the claims of a
burdened religious conscience.

Smith and Black gained a lot of public sympathy. After all, they
were not asking for license to flout Oregon's law against narcotics
by taking their belief in the efficacy of peyote onto the streets. They
were asking for the right to practice a sacrament within their church
worship service in the same way that the Catholic Church had been
allowed to offer wine to communicants during the era of national
prohibition. Associate Justice Sandra Day O'Connor concurred in the
Employment Division case but only after she applied the Sherbert Rule
and decided that Oregon had met its obligation to show a compelling
public interest in uniformly enforcing its drug laws. Directing alarm
at Scalia's language, she wrote: "The First Amendment was enacted
precisely to protect the rights of those whose religious practices are
not shared by the majority and may be viewed with hostility. . . . The
very purpose of a Bill of Rights was to withdraw certain subjects from
the vicissitudes of political controversy . . . and to establish them as
legal principles to be applied by the courts." The implication of her
judicial aside was that Scalia, by persuading the court to reject the

Sherbert Rule, had seriously undermined the protection of free religious practice.

A political response to the Supreme Court's ruling in *Employment Division v. Smith* developed, and it was surprisingly strong and bipartisan. A chorus of voices denounced it as putting religion under siege. Conservative groups, the National Association of Evangelicals, for example, along with the liberal-leaning American Civil Liberties Union, labeled the decision a threat to religious liberty. They were joined in their protest by the Mormon Church, the Southern Baptist Convention, the Union of American Hebrew Congregations, and the American Muslim Council. In 1993, following the election of Bill Clinton, Congress passed the Religious Freedom Restoration Act. Charles Schumer, a liberal Democrat from New York, introduced the bill in the House, and Edward Kennedy, a liberal Democrat from Massachusetts, sponsored it in the upper chamber. For them, RFRA (Rhee-fra), while it protected religious liberty, was a civil rights bill. It sailed through the House on a unanimous vote. In the Senate only three, southern, senators cast negative votes. Jesse Helms of North Carolina was one of them. He was easily the most conservative voice in Congress and a vociferous foe of any legislation that might be construed as a civil rights bill.

The goal of RFRA was to "restore" religious freedom by "restoring" the principles of case law used by the Supreme Court before *Employment Division v. Smith*. The act, which explicitly referred to the Sherbert case and to the Amish school cases, meant to turn the judicial principle of the Sherbert case into legislation. RFRA stated that "government shall not substantially burden a person's exercise of religion even if the burden results from a rule of general applicability" unless it proved two things: (1) The burden was necessary for the fulfillment of a compelling government interest, and (2) The offending rule was the least restrictive way in which to further the government interest.

Matters did not proceed according to everybody's plan. In 1997, in *City of Boerne v. Flores,* the Supreme Court held that RFRA was unconstitutional, at least as it applied to state actions. In reaction to that ruling, a number of states passed their own RFRA laws. In 2000,

Congress, with the same bipartisan vote that enacted RFRA, enacted the Religious Land Use and Institutionalized Persons Act (RLUIPA). The intention of the 2000 law was to protect the religious practice of prison inmates and the use of land owned by churches. In doing so, it defined "religious practice" as "any exercise of religion, whether or not compelled by or central to a system of religious belief." That language proved to be a key element in the controversial 2014 case *Burwell v. Hobby Lobby Stores, Inc.*, which changed the rules of the judicial game.

Hobby Lobby is an American chain store that sells arts-and-crafts materials. Based in Oklahoma City, it has outlets across the country. The owners of this for-profit corporation, along with an affiliated business of Christian bookstores, are evangelical Christians. They and the Mennonite owners of Conestoga Wood Company, a furniture store, filed suit claiming that "regulations promulgated by the Department of Health and Human Services under the Patient Protection and Affordable Care Act of 2010" (Obamacare) posed a substantial burden on their religious practice. The regulations required that they make financial contributions to health insurance that included payments for contraceptive coverage of their female employees. The coverage included methods that the owners of Hobby Lobby and Conestoga Wood Company regarded as abortifacients. The regulations of the Department of Health and Human Services did not require the owners to use contraceptives, to encourage their female employees to use them, or to pay attention to what their employees chose to do with the money provided by the coverage. Their female employees might or might not use the morning-after pill. Even so, the religious appellants maintained that they were forced to violate their religious beliefs by participating in a plan that might, however indirectly, lead to what they regarded as an abortion.

Over a stinging dissent written by Associate Justice Ruth Bader Ginsburg, Associate Justice Samuel Alito penned a majority opinion that gave the victory to the appellants. The decision did not challenge the government's compelling interest in protecting women's health and linking that interest to providing insurance coverage for all legal contraceptive methods. The decision rested instead on the majority's belief that the government had not used the least restrictive way to advance that interest.

Alito had a point. Health and Human Services had on its own initiative instituted an alternative plan for nonprofit religious institutions tied to churches that accommodated the ones with religious objections to contraception. In those cases, the insurance issuers excluded contraceptive coverage from the employer's plan and arranged separate payments to women employees for contraception. Justice Ginsburg's dissent vigorously disputed Alito's reasoning that put nonprofit religious institutions and for-profit corporations in the same category. But she found a much more serious problem in the almost casual way the decision accepted the plaintiffs' claim that their contribution to a health plan that might permit someone else to do something they regarded as sinful amounted to "conduct that seriously violates their religious beliefs." The Hobby Lobby decision validated judicial reasoning that widened the grounds, and by quite a lot, for securing a religious exemption from a general law. What had been before RFRA a narrow and cumbersome path to a religious exemption became a major thoroughfare with no apparent speed limit.

In all previous cases heard by the Supreme Court, the burden on the religious practice of the plaintiff was indisputable. Adell Sherbert couldn't work in the mills of South Carolina if she followed her religion. The Amish people faced possible destruction of their way of life if compelled to keep their children in public schools after the age of sixteen. Even in cases where the court found for the government, it did not question the seriousness of the religious burden placed on the plaintiff. Denying to members of the Native American Church access to the ritual smoking of peyote destroyed a central sacrament of the worship service. No such burden even remotely pressed upon the plaintiffs in the Hobby Lobby case. The businessmen who sued for relief could practice every single tenet of their religious beliefs without financial hardship. To be sure, people don't forfeit their right to free religious practice just because they have money. But in the matter of exemptions for religious conscience, or for any sort of conscience, cases that involve tangible sacrifice should have the strongest claim. The dissenting justices in the Hobby Lobby case thought that the plaintiffs in seeking to avoid a rule that had no real bearing on how they practiced their religion were using their conscience to try to influence someone else's behavior. The hardship they claimed was abstract and didn't merit accommodation.

The Hobby Lobby decision explicitly accorded to for-profit corporations the right to claim free religious practice. General Motors apparently can have a religious conscience. Justice Alito insisted that since the corporations involved in the Hobby Lobby case were closely held, with company stock owned by family members and company employees, the purpose of the decision was not to protect the corporate entity but the people who ran it. To demonstrate that a for-profit business had standing to challenge an alleged burden on its religious practices, Alito cited *Braunfeld v. Brown*, a 1961 case involving the complaint of several orthodox Jewish merchants against a Pennsylvania law forbidding them to do business on Sunday. Since their religion kept them from opening their stores on Saturday, the law imposed what was equivalent to a high tax on them for following their faith. What Alito didn't note, aside from the fact that none of the merchants was incorporated, was that the court upheld Pennsylvania's law and denied relief to the merchants. Nor did Alito cite the reasoning that led the court to reject the petition of an Amish businessman who had a "sincere" religious objection to paying social security taxes for his employees: "When followers of a particular sect enter into commercial activity as a matter of choice, the limits they accept on their own conduct as a matter of conscience and faith are not to be superimposed on the statutory schemes which are binding on others in the same activity" (*United States v. Lee*, 1982).

Alito insisted that RFRA intended to do more than "restore" the legal grounds for a valid religious objection that had applied before its passage—the Sherbert Rule—but to expand those grounds. To reach that dubious conclusion, he ignored the language of RFRA and seized instead on the language of the Religious Land Use and Institutionalized Persons Act that specified that the "exercise of religion" need not be something "compelled by or central to a system of religious belief." That language, he thought, relieved the court of making even the simplest inquiry into the centrality of a religious belief to a claim for exemption. Earlier court cases involved plaintiffs who belonged to minority churches with tenets that made clear what it was that offended their religious conscience. Even agnostics who received c.o. classification had to fill out a lengthy questionnaire explaining how their objection to war was central to principles they held that were equivalent to religion. The easy uncoupling of religious belief from any particular creed would have been unthinkable in an earlier America when a denominational commitment meant something. Church members knew what their denomination stood for and how its beliefs differed from those of other denominations. In our present age the churches that can remember what Calvinism was all about or why John Wesley distinguished Methodism from Anglicanism have been eclipsed in numbers by large independent churches with minimalist creeds. In this climate of theological indifference, under the ruling in Hobby Lobby we risk making almost anything count as protected religious practice and almost nothing as religious establishment.

However, if Hobby Lobby replaced a narrow path with a thoroughfare, it also opened the question of whether atheists might travel down it and seek exemption from a law that offended their moral conscience. Douglas Laycock, a respected legal scholar who helped draft the RFRA bill and who has ably defended it, has suggested that they might: "Religion is an answer to questions about God, about whether there is a God, about whether there is anything after death. A negative answer to those questions is as much a religion for constitutional purposes as an affirmative answer." In December 2016 President Obama took a step in the same direction when he signed into law a new version of the International Religious Freedom Act that Congress endorsed with bipartisan support. The act for the first time stated that the "freedom of thought, conscience, and religion" protected "theistic and non-theistic belief." Religious freedom included the right "not to profess or practice any religion."

Although the Supreme Court has not yet heard a case that puts this inclusive view of religious protection to a definitive test, one significant case that reached the Ninth Circuit Court of Appeals in 2005 did. It evolved from an unlikely site—a prison in Wisconsin. James Kaufman, while a prisoner in the Waupun Correctional Facility, was denied permission to form an inmate group to study "humanism, atheism, and free speaking." The court in *Kaufman v. McCaughtry* accepted the plaintiff's complaint as a legitimate First Amendment issue. An atheist has the right to complain of a burden on his free religious practice. Although the court decided that Kaufman had failed to demonstrate any substantial burden on that practice, it ruled in his favor on establishment grounds. Prison officials, "by accommodating some religious views" but not Kaufman's, "had promoted the favored ones."

Now imagine a case brought by an atheist with objections to abortion just as adamantly held as the ones maintained by the owners of Hobby Lobby and the other plaintiffs in that case. Running a small business with fifty employees, this atheist regards any procedure to end a pregnancy after conception as murder. He sues the federal government for forcing him, under a federal health care plan, to contribute to the contraceptive coverage of his female workers. He quotes Laycock, stating that a negative answer to the question of God's existence is "as much a religion for constitutional purposes as an affirmative one." Can this businessman prevail in court, either under the legislative terms of RFRA or simply by the First Amendment's guarantee of free religious practice?

Two cases heard by different federal courts leave the answer to that question uncertain. Both of them involve not-for-profit organizations that are secular but also adamantly opposed to abortion. Like Hobby Lobby, though without claiming a religious motive, the groups sought an exemption from the Affordable Care Act's contraceptive mandate. The United States District Court in Washington, D.C., ruled in favor of one of them, March for Life, and the Third Circuit Court of Appeals ruled against the other, Real Alternatives. Taken together the cases don't suggest a clear outcome of our hypothetical one. But the important question is not whether our hypothetical atheist businessman might prevail but whether a favorable outcome for him would constitute constitutional progress. Even if the court ruled that his conscience counted as much as the consciences of the owners of Hobby Lobby, the Hobby Lobby decision set a bad precedent. It got away from the reason that sometimes made exemptions from general laws serve the causes of equity and fair treatment. Whether or not the Supreme Court decides against the Colorado baker who refused to make a wedding cake for a gay couple, it has still come close to creating the curious moral anomaly of allowing claims for religious freedom to become a sanctioned way to discriminate against innocent people otherwise protected by laws. The atheist businessman should lose, just as the owners of Hobby Lobby should have lost.

The intention of RFRA was not to open a Pandora's box of endless suits filed by believers and nonbelievers that their dislike of a particular law burdened practices dictated by their religion. Areas of differentiation will remain. Unwilling churches don't have to hire women or gay people as ministers, but that shouldn't allow secular businesses of any type and many kinds of religious organizations to ignore anti-discrimination laws. Justice Harlan in his *Sherbert* dissent and Justice Scalia in *Employment Division v. Smith* laid down the best general rule against which any accommodation must be squared: there is no constitutional right under the First Amendment to an exemption from a neutral law having nothing to do with religion. In a democratic society we are free to believe what we want. We may organize religious societies and secular ethical societies according to those beliefs. However, except in unusual circumstances involving beset groups whose religious rituals are directly threatened, a belief, however strongly held, should not accord its holder a constitutional exemption from a law that everyone else must obey, unless the law provides an exemption that does not unfairly privilege one religion over another or all religions over nonreligion. This first principle of our communal democratic life in no way challenges the concept of religious liberty held by the writers of the Constitution. The principle is also compatible with the restorative intention of the Religious Freedom Restoration Act, a law that defends the free religious practice of people but not at the expense of the rights of other Americans.

8

The Atheist Awakening

EVEN AS FEDERAL and state courts and American governing institutions in general accept as given that all true Americans are believers, the number of nonbelievers in the United States steadily increases. And some of these, ordinary Americans going about their business, have been willing and visible challengers of laws that they believe treat them unequally. Very few of them in public life, however, particularly those who might want to win an election to office, have come forward to announce their nonbelief, as a matter of public pride, to a wide audience.

It was only after his retirement from the House of Representatives that the openly gay former congressman from Massachusetts, Barney Frank, came "out of the closet" a second time in 2013, publicly declaring himself a nonbeliever on Bill Maher's HBO TV show *Real Time*. A year later he appeared in one of the YouTube videos of well-known people asserting their nonbelief, a project funded by Todd Stiefel's Openly Secular Coalition. Frank, consistently chosen by the Washington press corps during his thirty-two years in the House as both the smartest and funniest member of Congress, defines himself as a "nontheist, who does not believe in God," but declines to call himself an atheist, "who is someone who assumes he knows there is no God." Frank's affirma-

tion of nonbelief was a coup for the organized atheist activism that
has roiled America since 2000. He embodied the movement's call for
atheists to go public, to copy the Lesbian, Gay, Bisexual, Transgender
movement's pride-filled coming out of the closet. Atheists insisted that
a willingness to speak openly of an unpopular identity was central to
the dramatic turn-around in American attitudes to gay people. Who
better, then, to represent atheists out of the closet than Barney Frank,
the first member of Congress to come out as gay?

While Frank need no longer worry about the electorate and its
biases, others who are interested in winning elections certainly risk
a great deal if they declare themselves to be atheists. This is true even
though the number of nonbelievers in our population is growing at
an unprecedented rate. Estimates of the number of Americans who
today identify as "nones," nonbelievers or seculars, range from 15 to
23 percent. To stick with polling data associated with the low estimate: 15 percent translates into 45–50 million nonbelieving Americans, a number, we have noted, higher than the combined total of
Methodists, Lutherans, Presbyterians, Episcopalians, Jews, and Muslims. Like Frank, who represented part of Boston and who lives now
in Maine with his husband, nonbelievers are clustered disproportion-
ally in the Northeast and the West. States with more than 25 percent of their population declaring themselves "nones" in 2014 are, in
descending order:

Vermont, 37%
New Hampshire, 36%
Massachusetts, 32%
Maine, 31%
Alaska, 31%
Oregon, 31%
Montana, 30%
Colorado, 39%
Nevada, 28%
Arizona, 27%

California, 27%
Idaho, 27%
New York, 27%.

Only four states count fewer than 15 percent identifying as "nones," and they are all in the South: Mississippi, 14%; Tennessee, 14%; Louisiana, 13%; and Alabama, 12%.

Like Frank, most "nones" are politically liberal, though there are conservative nonbelievers—for example, the libertarian followers of Ayn Rand, who died in 1982. One atheist activist estimates that maybe 20 percent of the total of nonbelievers are devotees of Rand, the author of *Atlas Shrugged* and *The Fountainhead*. Her championship of the militantly God-rejecting philosophy called Objectivism was conveniently overlooked by her acolytes in the Trump administration, like Speaker Ryan, Secretary of State Tillerson, and the president himself. Like Frank as well, more nonbelievers are men than women. Strikingly, even though Madalyn Murray O'Hair founded the American Atheists in 1963 and led it for many years, most leaders of atheist and secular organizations today are men. (An important exception is the mother-daughter team Anne and Annie Laurie Gaylor. The former in 1978 founded the Freedom from Religion Foundation, based in Madison, Wisconsin; the latter still leads it.) Frank is of white European background, a group far more represented among "nones" than Hispanics and blacks. Being highly educated, with an undergraduate and a master's degree from Harvard, he also fits the nonbeliever profile. Like many in the movement, he is culturally, but not religiously, Jewish.

Frank does deviate from the profile of the typical nonbeliever in his age. The "Atheist Awakening" is being driven dramatically by the young. One 2016 Pew Research Center study has 35 percent of millennials saying they identify as atheist, agnostic, or have no religion in particular. The political scientist Robert Putnam reports that between 2005 and 2011, among eighteen- to twenty-nine-year-olds, the "nones" rose from 25 to 33 percent, and within that cohort the number of atheists or agnostics rose from 15 to 24 percent. Compared to the latter figure, older Americans like Frank, who saw themselves as atheists or agnostics, rose only from 9 to 12 percent. Frank also deviates from the nonbeliever norm in that many of the most visible nonbelievers are scientists. They include Bill Nye, the popular "Science Guy" on TV and lecture circuits, and evolutionary biologist Richard Dawkins, author of the 2006 book *The God Delusion*, which rose to number one on the nonfiction best-seller list. Nonbelievers today see astronomer Carl Sagan and science fiction writer Isaac Asimov, who actively served as president of the American Humanist Association from 1985 to 1992, as early visionaries of the secular movement. As the magazine *Nature* in a 1998 article, "Leading Scientists Still Reject God," claimed, "over 90% of the scientists in the National Academy of Sciences are nonbelievers." And much is still made in the secular movement of the moment in 2001 when the *New York Times* science writer Natalie Angier outed herself as an atheist in a January 14, 2001, *New York Times Magazine* article, "Confessions of a Lonely Atheist."

Not all atheists are in the sciences, but they tend to have a great respect for them. Speaking on the issue of the diversity among nonbelievers, the atheist intellectual the late Christopher Hitchens told a reporter for the *Washington Post* in May 2007: "We're not a unified group. But we're of one mind on this: the only thing that counts is free inquiry, science, research, the testing of evidence, the use of reason, irony, humor, and literature, things of this kind."

What unifies and infuriates most nonbelievers is having to participate in or just acknowledge the omnipresent rituals of American civil religion. The constant invocations of God may have deep roots in American history, but, as we saw, they were given new and top-down legislative force during the Cold War years. The issues have not always divided liberal judges from conservative judges. One legendary liberal on the Supreme Court, William Douglas, referred to God's central place in American public life in making decisions about what kinds of state support of religion were constitutional. In 1952, writing for a majority in *Zorach v. Clauson*, a decision that allowed a release time program for schoolchildren to receive religious instruction outside of school, Justice Douglas noted that the First Amendment did not insist on a total separation of church and state, or otherwise: "Prayers in the legislative halls; the appeal to the Almighty in the messages of the Chief Executive, the proclamations making Thanksgiving a holiday; 'so help me God' in our courtroom oaths—these and all other references to the Almighty that run through our laws, our public rituals, our ceremonies would be flouting the First Amendment. A fastidious atheist or agnostic could even object to the supplication with which the Court opens each session: 'God save the United States and this Honorable Court.'"

Douglas concluded his list of practices exempted from religious establishment claims with the bold assertion that Americans "are a religious people whose institutions presuppose a Supreme Being." Eleven years later, Justice William Brennan, another revered liberal, while concurring in the court's finding that Bible reading in public schools violated the Establishment Clause, nonetheless noted that the national motto "In God We Trust" was constitutionally permissible, because "we have simply interwoven the motto so deeply into the fabric of our civil polity."

More predictably, the conservative Chief Justice Warren Burger in 1989 gave the Supreme Court's seal of approval to the embrace of God in a case involving Christian symbolism. In *Lynch v. Donnelly*, a 5–4 split decision that upheld the constitutionality of a Nativity scene on town property in Pawtucket, Rhode Island, Burger described approvingly "an unbroken history of official acknowledgement by all three branches of government of the role of religion in American life." Moreover, "our history is replete," he insisted, "with official references to the value and invocation of Divine Guidance in deliberations and pronouncements of the Founding Fathers and contemporary leaders." Burger then energetically affirmed the constitutionality of a bundle of practices, in addition to the Pledge of Allegiance, at the core of official American civil religion, mentioning in turn Christmas and Thanksgiving as national holidays; congressional and military chaplains; the congressional prayer room; the national motto; and the presidential proclamation of a National Day of Prayer.

One could easily add to Burger's list. Professor Steven Epstein, in a brilliant 1996 *Columbia Law Review* article, "Rethinking the Constitutionality of Ceremonial Deism," offers many more governmental entanglements with religion that are unquestioned and accepted as reflexively as those in Burger's list: prayers at presidential inaugurations; presidential addresses that invoke the name of God; the cry "God Save the United States and This Honorable Court" prior to judicial proceedings cited by Justice Douglas; required oaths for public officers, witnesses, and jurors; the use of Bibles with which to administer those oaths; and, finally, using "in the year of our Lord" (A.D.) to date public documents. Unlike Burger and the judges who concurred with him in the Nativity case, Epstein deems all of these practices unconstitutional endorsements of religion.

The nonbeliever in America is never free of the seemingly unstoppable associations drawn between the American government and God, or between citizenship and religion. Some of them have to do with the words presidents and other public officials use on solemn public occasions that all Americans are supposed to share. Many others are more than mere conventions but have the force of law. Congress made Christmas a national holiday in 1894 and Thanksgiving in 1941. In 1952, at the urging of Reverend Billy Graham, Congress passed legislation requiring an annual National Day of Prayer, which in 1988 was given the specific date of the first Thursday of May. And we have seen how in 1954, at the urging of Reverend George Docherty and the Knights of Columbus, Congress put God in the Pledge of Allegiance.

There are, to be sure, efforts of resistance by nonbelievers, from the "fastidious atheist or agnostic," to borrow Justice Douglas's phrase. Some are personal and symbolic. Barney Frank, who after his retirement wanted Massachusetts governor Deval Patrick to appoint him to fill the few months left in Ted Kennedy's Senate term after his death, publicly stated that if this happened he would take the oath with his hand placed on a copy of the United States Constitution rather than the Bible. He didn't get the appointment. Most efforts at resistance are public and, as we have seen and will see more of below, usually involve lawsuits against governing bodies claiming the unconstitutionality of the particular entanglement of government and God. More often than not this resistance is repelled and repudiated by courts which insist that government invocation of God is not state sponsorship of religion but the solemnization of public occasions, as if there were no secular ways to give solemnity and gravitas—like taking the oath of office with a hand laid on the Constitution. The courts' other defense of the governmental invocation of God is to maintain that through repeated use, "rote repetition," religious language loses its religious significance and is merely and only "ceremonial." Lost sight of here is the inherent contradiction; how can religious language both give solemnity and also be insignificant?

The practices of American civil religion, the examples of "ceremonial deism" listed by Justice Burger and Professor Epstein, are strong and resilient because most Americans do, indeed, take their religious content seriously, "rote repetition" notwithstanding. Imagine the public furor if the Supreme Court were to rule that the national motto "In God We Trust" was unconstitutional, even though it was in national history a late addition, a Cold War replacement of the motto "E pluribus unum." Despite their growth in numbers, nonbelievers face a perhaps insurmountable task in overthrowing American civil religion, especially if, as is likely, courts start using Justice Steven Breyer's reasoning in *Van Orden v. Perry* (2005). Breyer usually sides with the liberals, but in this case his quiet but well-noticed concurrence allowed a statue commemorating the Ten Commandments to remain standing on the Texas State Capitol grounds. Arguing that the First Amendment's purpose was to avoid "religiously based divisiveness," he observed that the monument had been challenged only once in forty years and that "as a practical matter of degree this display is unlikely to prove divisive," whereas a court decision to remove it, he noted, "might well encourage disputes." Courts, he is suggesting, should in matters of religion that many regard as inconsequential leave things as they are and not encourage the religious divisiveness that would emerge among Americans if cornerstones of its civic religion were removed. We agree with the philosopher Martha Nussbaum's rejection of Breyer's argument that courts should allow government sponsorship of God in order to avoid national crises as "unfortunately ad hoc, favoring majority beliefs and making a virtue of convenience."

Unable to chip away at the omnipresence of God in official political discourse, nonbelievers are marginalized, even stigmatized, as well, by their fellow citizens. This was true in the past and it remains true. No surprise then that candidates for public office would be silent about nonbelief. Atheists remain the most disliked religious minority in America. Of the respondents to a Pew Research Center survey question on attitudes to specified religious groups in 2009, 49 percent scored atheists negatively, while the unfavorable response to other groups was dramatically lower: Muslims, 32%; Mormons, 26%; Hindus, 21%; Buddhists, 20%; Evangelical Christians, 17%; Jews, 11%; Catholics, 11%. A 2011 Gallup poll that asked, "If your party nominated a generally well-qualified person for president who happened to be atheist would you vote for that person?" found that only 49 percent of Americans said yes. Responses for other similarly well-qualified nominees: black, 94%; women, 93%; Catholic, 92%; Jewish, 89%; and Mormon, 76%. An earlier iteration of the "willingness to vote for your party's nominee" in 1999, which included homosexuals among the choices, ranked them at 59 percent, higher than atheists at 49 percent.

Nor would a self-declared atheist fare well as a suitor asking for parental approval before reaching the altar. When asked into what group they would least like their children to marry, nearly half of Americans list atheists first, significantly higher than Muslims, African Americans, and Jews. So, too, when asked to name "the group that does not at all agree with my vision of American society," 40 percent of responders put atheists on top, followed by Muslims, 26%; homosexuals, 22%; conservative Christians, 13%; recent immigrants, 12%; Jews, 7%; African Americans, 5%. (All this data showing atheists as unlike other Americans and disliked significantly more than Muslims was assembled well after 9/11, but before Trump's election.)

The aversion bears questioning. We suggest that undergirding this dislike and distrust of nonbelievers are three foundational features of American sociocultural belief. First, is the conviction that one can't be a good person if one is not a believer. Nearly half of Americans believe "morality and atheism are mutually exclusive," and that "it is necessary to believe in God to be moral and have good values." True, many of the founders believed that as well, but that opinion no longer stands up. The stereotype of the immoral atheist is belied in numerous cross-national studies that show murder rates are lower in more secular nations than in more religious nations, as well as studies showing that on a personal level atheists and secular people are, as sociologist Phil Zuckerman notes, "markedly less nationalistic; less prejudiced, less anti-Semitic, less racist, less dogmatic, less ethnocentric, less close-minded, and less authoritarian." It persists even in the face of evidence that horrible deeds are often done in God's name and despite the reassurance of Pope Francis, who noted in 2013 that "even the atheists. Everyone" who does "good to others" is "redeemed by God." And in 2017 suggested "that it was better to be an atheist than a hypocritical Catholic."

The second pervasive belief is that one can't be a good American if one is not a believer, the central tenet, as we have seen, of American civil religion. Thirty-nine percent of Americans in 2008 agreed "that not believing in God was very unpatriotic" and that 'to be irreligious . . . is to be un-American."

The third foundation of persistent dislike and distrust of nonbelievers is due to American anti-intellectualism. Many see atheists as cultural elitists—philosophers, scientists, and artists, who threaten the beliefs of ordinary people in, for example, life after death, because nonbelievers "think they know better than everyone else." Nonbelievers often fuel this elitist reading of themselves, as when Richard Dawkins and Daniel Dennett suggested renaming them "the Brights."

A long list of overt officially sanctioned historical discrimination against atheists and nonbelievers has resulted from their being so unliked and mistrusted. Well into the twentieth century some localities have prohibited them from testifying in court, since it was assumed that their lack of fear of eternal damnation diminished their ability to tell the truth. In other cases atheists have been prohibited from serving on juries. A Pennsylvania court in 1987, a South Carolina court in 1998, and a Mississippi court in 2005 all made child-custody decisions specifically to the detriment of the nonbelieving parent. Numerous examples of discrimination against nonbelievers have been exposed in the military: one soldier claimed, as reported in the *New York Times* of April 26, 2008, that he was discharged for his atheism. And like the eight state constitutions that still insist that state officials believe in God, most of these scattered acts are clearly unconstitutional, but they happen all the same.

Private discrimination against nonbelievers has flourished as well. During the Cold War 1960s, 59 percent of Americans held that anyone who did not believe in God should not be able to teach in public schools and 24 percent still believed that in the 1980s. In 2003 and 2009 news stories appeared of employers terminating atheist employees. But nowhere is the private discrimination against atheists more blatant than in the Boy Scouts of America, where the Scout oath includes the promise "to do my duty to God and my country and to obey the Scout law." The Girl Scouts have welcomed nonbelievers as members and volunteer leaders, but the Boy Scouts still is closed to nonbelievers, insisting that "no boy can grow in the best kind of citizenship without recognizing his obligation to God." When a nineteen-year-old Eagle Scout from Seattle, Darrell Lambert, was recently found to be a nonbeliever, he was summarily expelled from the Boy Scouts of America. A Scout leader commented on this with words epitomizing America's attitudes to nonbelievers: "It's not discrimination, it's policy. Anybody who doesn't believe in God isn't a good citizen. . . . If an atheist found a wallet on the ground they would pick it up, plunder the money, and throw the wallet back on the ground."

Openly and brazenly stigmatized and discriminated against by religious Americans, nonbelievers have increasingly seen themselves as a besieged and oppressed minority. That consciousness has in recent years generated a widespread resistance movement. Atheist activists are increasingly demanding recognition, acceptance, and validation. They self-consciously copy the identity politics strategies of the civil rights and feminist movements with their "black is beautiful" and "consciousness raising" themes. They especially mimic the more recently successful LGBT movement with its tactical insistence that nonbelievers must in solidarity come out of the closet both to show their numbers and to counter the stereotypes that generate Americans' negative views of them.

Atheist activism is, to be sure, not totally new. We noted above that the American Association for the Advancement of Atheism, founded in 1925, after the Scopes trial, waged a crusade on behalf of science for ten years, sponsoring debates in many states, where its spokespeople attacked religious opposition to Darwin's theory of natural selection. And several of the free-thinking, nonbeliever groups we look at below were founded in the latter half of the twentieth century. But the "wake-up call to many secular Americans," according to activist David Niose, occurred in 2000 with the election of George W. Bush, the culmination of thirty years of the Christian right's successful infiltration of American politics. There was now in the White House a president who put his 1985 conversion from a wayward sinner to a believer in Christ as the defining mark of his identity. The *Guardian* newspaper records Bush pointing to his faith as the reason for embarking on war: "I am driven with a mission from God. God would tell me, 'George, go and fight these terrorists in Afghanistan.' And I did. And then God would tell me, 'George, go and end the tyranny in Iraq.' And I did."

Since that "wake-up call" many nonbelievers have united in a collective identity, dramatically facilitated by aggressive organizational activity and by the internet and social media, which have provided a new way for seculars "to come out, speak out, and meet up." The new atheist activism has many of the features that social scientists, like Charles Tilly, characterize as "social movements," involving "a sustained series of interactions between power holders and persons successfully claiming to speak on behalf of a constituency lacking formal representation."

Some scholars, most notably Richard Cimino and Christopher

Smith, with tongue in cheek, have labeled this recent social movement of nonbelievers the "Atheist Awakening," borrowing ironically from the terminology of American religious history. The Great Awakening, a movement that swept through the American colonies in the 1730s and epitomized by the preaching of Jonathan Edwards, successfully challenged the ritualistic and doctrinal focus of the leadership in the Protestant churches by emphasizing the deep emotional relationship of the individual believer with God. It was followed by a Second Great Awakening in the early nineteenth century that made revivals a staple of American Protestant preaching. The Atheist Awakening, on the other hand, describes individual nonbelievers coming together in an increasingly collective and public assault on a godly America, an assault which the users of the label hope is in its own very different way as successful as its historical namesake. At the core of the Atheist Awakening since 2000 has been the activism generated by the rich tapestry of organizations, some of them new, some of them old but with a redefined mission, that speak to and for the nonbeliever. What follows is an organizational ethnography of the major institutional players in the Atheist Awakening, offered in alphabetical order.

American Atheists (AA) was founded by Madalyn Murray O'Hair in 1963, the year she won her landmark case, *Murray v. Curlett* (a decision also referred to as *Abington School District v. Schempp*, a co-suit filed by a nonatheist plaintiff) removing school-sponsored Bible reading from public schools. O'Hair led the AA until 1986, presiding over much unrest and dissent within the group. Her son Jon served as president until 1995 when Jon, she, and her granddaughter were kidnapped and murdered in Texas by a former employee of American Atheists in a botched robbery plot. In 2010 David Silverman became president of AA and has since steered its 5,000 members zealously and combatively from a nondescript small building anonymously tucked into the warehouse district of Cranford, New Jersey.

Silverman proudly describes himself as the "bad boy" and AA as the "hard-core marines" of the movement, as opposed to the "nice guys" and the "diplomats" who are willing to work with religious believers.

These "good atheists" call themselves humanists or nonbelievers. Silverman, the "bad atheist," is a self-proclaimed "firebrand" who often wears a sweatshirt emblazoned "atheist" and drives a car with the license plate "Atheist." In his book, *Fighting God*, he writes, "I seethe with hatred for religion," and he likens himself to Malcolm X, who made Martin Luther King look moderate.

The *American Humanist Association* (AHA) embodies for militant Silverman the "nice guys," the more diplomatic face of the movement. It emerged in 1941 out of disparate factions ranging from former Unitarians and Quakers to intellectuals like John Dewey, who eschewed theism or supernatural beliefs and referred to themselves as secular humanists. The oldest, most venerable of the national secular groups and probably the largest, with some 50,000 members, the AHA, headquartered in Washington, D.C., took a decidedly radical turn in recent decades, especially after 2003 under the direction of a new president, Mel Lipman, and then his successor, David Niose, who served from 2009 to 2012. From being primarily an organization of secular nontheists committed to liberal causes like human rights, international peace, church-state separation, and reproduction rights, it has become an activist, identity-focused group, deeply committed to the rights of nontheists.

It was David Niose's arrival as the AHA's legal director and president that made the organization a major player, as we have seen, in the judicial battles over "under God" in the Pledge of Allegiance. The litigious turn was facilitated by a gift to the AHA from one of the secular movement's financial angels, the businessman Louis J. Appignani, a Catholic from the Bronx, who became a nonbeliever while a student at City College of New York when he read the writings of the English philosopher and Cambridge don Bertrand Russell. President and chairman of the modeling school Barbizon International, his generosity created the Appignani Humanist Legal Center, a judicial dynamo for secularism. Even the annual winners of the AHA's "Humanist of the Year" award, given every year since 1953, have become more noticeably outspoken nonbelievers, moving from people like Margaret Atwood and Kurt Vonnegut, who were honored more for their literary accomplishments than for outspoken nonbelief, to the openly atheistic Richard Dawkins, Daniel Dennett, Bill Nye, Michael Newdow, and, in 2014, Barney Frank.

Like the AHA, the *Center for Inquiry* (CFI) has been around for decades but has only recently become radicalized. Very much the creation of one man, the University of Buffalo professor of philosophy Paul Kurtz, the CFI has its roots in his 1970 Committee for Skeptical Inquiry, a group that included the scientist Carl Sagan, the writer Isaac Asimov, and the magician James Randi, who committed themselves to the scientific investigation of claims of the paranormal. In 1991 Kurtz founded CFI, bringing together the 1970s Skeptical Inquiry Committee and another of his groups, the Council for Secular Humanism, with its bimonthly publication *Free Inquiry*. Started by Kurtz in 1980, the journal, which had 27,000 subscribers, was aimed at nonbelievers. In its pages, Kurtz, the author of many philosophical studies of skepticism and founder of Prometheus Books, proudly embraced the label "secular humanist," rejecting its pejorative use by the Christian right to malign nonreligious intellectuals. The journal played a crucial role in publishing early arguments of the "New Atheist" intellectuals, discussed below, before their books were published and, after 2007, serving openly as their champion.

With its headquarters in Amherst, New York, near Kurtz's teaching job in Buffalo, CFI in the early 2000s had forty educational centers in the United States and around the world. In its recent, more assertive, turn it has remained true to Kurtz's lifelong quest to end the influence that religion and pseudoscience play in shaping public policy and to remove the stigma attached to being a nonbeliever. In 2006 *Free Inquiry* published four of the cartoons lampooning Muhammad that originally appeared in the Danish paper *Jyllands-Posten*, which ignited widespread protest in the Muslim world. Defending the publication, Kurtz wrote that "what is at stake is the precious right of freedom of expression." But in 2010 CFI's strident activism went too far for its founder. Kurtz, then age eighty-five and still on its board, felt that "angry atheism" had replaced his more positive secular humanist philosophy. He resigned that year when the new CFI president, Ronald Lindsay, announced the group's sponsorship of an annual International Blasphemy Day every September 30, when atheist individuals and groups are encouraged to express angrily and loudly their contempt for religion. Kurtz died in 2012; in 2016, the CFI merged with the Richard Dawkins Foundation for Reason and Science.

The *Freedom From Religion Foundation* (FFRF) is among the largest organizations of atheists and agnostics in America. It was founded in 1978 in Madison, Wisconsin, by Anne Nicol Gaylor, who, after graduating from the University of Wisconsin at Madison, owned and managed several small businesses, ran a suburban weekly newspaper, and was an abortion-rights activist. As head of the FFRF from 1978 to 2005, she grew its membership from the three people around her kitchen table to an activist group with 33,000 members in fifty states and Canada. Gaylor, who died in 2015 at the age of eighty-eight, has been succeeded by copresidents Annie Laurie Gaylor, her daughter, and her son-in-law, Dan Barker, an ex-evangelical Christian minister. The FFRF has published two popular books by Annie Laurie Gaylor, which echo Elizabeth Cady Stanton's atheist writing. *Woe to the Woman—The Bible Tells Me So* is about sexism in religion, and since publication in 1981 has been reprinted five times. The other, *Women Without Superstition—No Gods and No Masters* (1997), is a 600-page anthology of writings of nineteenth- and twentieth-century women freethinkers.

FFRF, as we note at length below, has become the preeminent gadfly of American civil religion in the last decade with its numerous lawsuits and in-your-face atheist billboard campaigns. Nothing better illustrates its role in the Atheist Awakening than its full-page ad in the *New York Times* on September 24, 2015, on the occasion of Pope Francis's address to a joint session of Congress. Under a huge picture of two tablets listing the ten "sins" of the Catholic Church, including "Banning Contraception," "Criminalizing Abortion," and "Denying Catholic Women's Right to Religious Equality," the ad text read:

Regardless of what Pope Francis' message is, Congress shouldn't be "blessing" him or handing him a government-endorsed pulpit. The framers of our godless Constitution wisely envisioned what John F. Kennedy described as "an America that is officially neither Catholic, Protestant nor Jewish—where no public official either requests or accepts instructions on public policy from the Pope . . . where no religious body seeks to impose its will directly or indirectly upon the general populace or the public acts of its officials.

The FFRF's 2015 ad, with its tear-out reply form to join the foundation at the bottom of the page, was a memorable highlight of a day rich in the symbolism and contradictions of the American secular government's embrace of God. Pope Francis spoke in the House of Representatives below the inscription "In God We Trust" and before, among others, nine Supreme Court justices, six of them Catholic and three Jewish. None was from America's Protestant majority. When the Pope later spoke to the throngs outside the Capitol from its balcony, he asked the crowd to pray for him and suggested that those who do not believe "send me your good wishes."

Not quite two years later, on May 25, 2017, the FFRF took out another full-page ad in the *New York Times* after President Trump delivered the commencement address at Jerry Falwell's Liberty University. The foundation replied to Trump's proud declaration there that "America is a nation of true believers." Above a huge caricatured head of the president that took up nearly half the page was the retort: "Mr. President—We are NOT a Nation of Believers." Below the president's picture, the text insisted "We are one nation under a Godless Constitution. We the people are free to believe or disbelieve," followed by the assertion that "a quarter of the U.S. population today is non-religious—true non-believers . . . Join the Freedom From Religion Foundation."

The latest newcomer to the alphabetical array of atheist groups is the *Openly Secular Coalition* (OSC), founded in 2014 by Todd Stiefel, dubbed by CNN "the money man behind atheism's activism." Born in Albany, New York, in 1974, Stiefel, raised a devout Catholic, went

to a Catholic high school. He lost his faith while an undergraduate at
Duke University and on graduation joined his family business, Stiefel
Laboratories, whose principal pursuit was developing products to fight
skin diseases. Stiefel worked for the company for twelve years, emerg-
ing as a driving force in its financial success that culminated in its sale
to GlaxoSmithKline for a hefty sum of money. With his new fortune,
Stiefel turned to philanthropic support of atheist activism, giving over
four million dollars to organizations like the American Humanist
Association and the Secular Coalition for America.

Financer of billboard campaigns and rallies, Stiefel's main involvement in the movement is through OSC, a coming together of more
than two dozen secular groups, which he chairs. Stiefel sees its purpose as raising public awareness of the numbers of nonreligious people in America and seeking "to eliminate discrimination and increase
acceptance by getting secular people—including atheists, free thinkers, agnostics, humanists, and non-religious people—to be open about
their beliefs." To that end the OSC funded several dozen YouTube
videos from people who describe themselves as happy nonbelievers.
Some of those feature average, hard-working and unknown Americans
talking about their nonbelief. And some spotlight well-known public
figures such as Barney Frank, Chris Kluwe, former punter for the Minnesota Vikings, who set eight team records in his eight seasons with
the Vikings, and Bill Maher, and the best-selling author and actress
Annabelle Gurwitch.

In addition to its as yet unsuccessful lobbying effort to get constitutional change in the eight states that deny public office to nonbelievers,
despite the unconstitutionality of those provisions, the OSC sponsors
on November 11, what it hopes will be an annual "openly secular day."
Intended to be a celebration by secular people of their secular worldview, and to reduce antiatheist prejudice, atheists are encouraged to
be open that day about their beliefs, to have meetings and parties, and
to pledge that they will tell at least one person of their nonbelief. This
"openness" is reinforced by the OSC's invocation of the omnipresent
mantra of the Atheist Awakening. "Being open has worked favorably for

the LGBT community; 68% of those who personally know gay or lesbian people favor marriage equality, as compared to 32% of those who
don't know anyone LGBT identified." By telling people about their atheism, nonaggressively, "in enlightening constructive conversation about
my identity," each openly secular person will help "dispel myths about
the secular" and contribute to changing how society views and treats
nonbelievers.

The *Secular Coalition for America* (SCA), one of the most important organizational expressions of the Atheist Awakening, was, as noted
above, founded in 2002 by Herb Silverman, the South Carolina math
professor who became the movement's heroic symbol after his fight
against his state's constitutional ban on nonbelievers holding public
office, the cause that inspired Stiefel's OSC. From his position on the
board of the AHA, Silverman proposed in 1998 a national coalition of
nontheist groups to counter the influence of the religious right. This
effort produced in 2000 the Coalition for the Community of Reason,
which in 2002 became the Secular Coalition for America. Its initial
members included the American Atheists, the American Humanist
Association, the Secular Student Alliance, and seven other groups.
Each of the groups had a member on the SCA's board of directors, and
Herb Silverman, who had brought the group together, was elected president for a term of ten years. He was succeeded at the helm of the SCA
in 2012 by David Niose, who had been president of the AHA.

The SCA has evolved into the movement's principal lobbying organization, now with seventeen members in the coalition, an office on K
Street in Washington, D.C., and a professional staff of six. Its mission
is that of its founder—to increase the visibility of and respect for non-
theistic viewpoints "and to show politicians, the press, and the public
that non-believers are organized to preserve the secular foundations
of American government." In its early years the SCA filed a complaint
to the Federal Communications Commission that DirecTV had given
five of its twelve set-aside "public interest" TV channels to religious
televangelists who used them to proselytize and raise money. The FCC
denied the SCA's complaint and without a hearing allowed DirecTV's

grant of "public interest" channels to the exclusively Christian religious programming.

Two years later, in 2006, the SCE held a contest to find and honor "the highest ranking elected official without a god belief" who would openly identify as an atheist or agnostic. The winner was Pete Stark, veteran Democratic congressman from the San Francisco area, who served from 1972 to 2012. Stark thus became the first member in the history of Congress to acknowledge his atheism. In 2008 he won the AHA's "Humanist of the Year" award and in 2011 he read a proclamation into the *Congressional Record* acknowledging May 5, set aside by congressional religious conservatives, as the "National Day of Prayer," as also "the National Day of Reason," defiantly noting that "reason and rational thinking have made our country great."

The SCA's lobbying efforts hit gold when its leadership met with Obama White House staff in February 2010 to discuss issues of concern to secular Americans. Topics covered were worries over faith-based initiatives, giving religion special treatment, and discrimination against atheists in the military. It was another first. The White House has always had meetings with religious leaders, but never before had an administration received a policy briefing from atheists and humanists. And the occasion was noticed. A group labeled "In God We Trust" blasted the White House "for plotting political strategy" with atheist activists who "represent some of the most hate-filled, anti-religious groups in the nation." Sean Hannity insisted on Fox News that the Obama administration gave "special treatment to atheists that religious groups have not received." As Herb Silverman then noted, "Hannity seems to have seen the two hour SCA meeting as more preferential than the two-day meeting a month earlier at the White House of some sixty religious leaders run by the White House Office of Faith-Based and Neighborhood Partnership." Not to be outdone in outrage, the Catholic League for Religious and Civil Rights issued a press release claiming "Obama Aides Host Catholic Bashers."

In addition to its lobbying efforts, the SCA sends out some 20,000 "alerts" to its own subscribers and many others to the members of its affiliated groups about news and political issues of concern to non-believers, while urging letters and emails to lawmakers and government officials. It publishes an annual scorecard rating on a scale of A to F how members of Congress voted on legislation of concern to the secular community. The SCA works closely on legislative matters with Democratic congressional members, for example Mike Honda, Democratic congressman from California, and Senator Elizabeth Warren from Massachusetts. Perhaps the SCA's most ambitious current initiative is its "Secular Decade Project," which aims to create a huge national grassroots network of affiliated secular groups in all fifty states with an army of local activists lobbying hometown, state, and federal political officials on issues of concern to the nonbelieving community.

An exciting and important part of the Atheist Awakening is the dramatic rise of nonbeliever student activism, presided over by the *Secular Student Alliance* (SSA), a national student organization founded in 2000 and headquartered in Columbus, Ohio. The SSA was, in many ways, a campus atheist reawakening. Three quarters of a century earlier the American Association for the Advancement of Atheism had organized a network of "junior atheist" clubs on twenty college campuses. So visible was their impact that the deeply religious filmmaker Cecil B. DeMille, who had already made a silent film of *The Ten Commandments* in 1923 and *The King of Kings*, also a silent film, in 1927, portrayed their sinister influence in his 1929 melodrama, *The Godless Girl*, a tale of a student atheist club where members take their oath with their hands reverently resting on a monkey's head. The AAAA and its junior atheist clubs had withered away by 1935, but their spirit reawakened with the SSA in 2000.

Less preoccupied than its predecessor with a defense of a besieged Darwinian theory of evolution, SSA's broader mission is to educate students "about the value of scientific reason and the intellectual basis of secularism in its atheistic and humanistic manifestations." More importantly, its affiliate chapters provide nonbelieving college students a safe space within which to proudly express their identity in welcoming communities where secular values prevail and encourage the defending and proselytizing of nonbelief. With a presence, to be sure, nowhere comparable to the Campus Crusades for Christ, the numbers of SSA college chapters have dramatically increased in its short life. The forty-two chapters that existed in 2003 increased by 2010 to 219, and by 2013 to 407 community college and university campus affiliates, many in the South and Midwest, as well as, more predictably, on the east and west coasts.

The dramatic recent increase of SSA college chapters can in large part be attributed to the significant financial gift made in 2011 by another atheist philanthropic angel, the Silicon Valley entrepreneur Jeff Hawkins, inventor of the Palm Pilot and distinguished brain scientist. A member of the Secular Coalition's board as well, Hawkins hoped his gift to SSA would be "an investment in our nation's future." Secular student groups, he stated, "give our youth the confidence to promote secular causes and to counter the demonization of atheists and secular advocates. The organization leading this generational change is the Secular Student Alliance." Hawkins' dual role in SSA and in the Secular Coalition for America is typical of the cross memberships in atheist activism. The SSA's advisory board includes Dan Barker of FFRF, Richard Dawkins, Fred Edwords, former executive director of the AHA, Herb Silverman, and Todd Stiefel.

The SSA has also had significant success in high schools. In 2001 it announced an initiative to support secular high school students in their efforts to organize and in two years there were thirty SSA affiliate chapters in American high schools and seventy others being created. Credit for the growth of high school atheist clubs must be given, paradoxically, to Jay Sekulow, the lawyer for the religious right who for a long time has run the American Center for Law and Justice, founded by Pat Robertson, which as we have noted defends the conservative religious agenda in the courts. Born a Jew in Brooklyn, Sekulow converted to Christianity, eventually becoming the general counsel for Jews for Jesus and subsequently an important lawyer in Trump's White House. Sekulow in 1990 successfully argued at the Supreme Court in *Westside Community Board of Education v. Mergens* on free-speech grounds that public schools cannot prohibit the formation of Christian clubs if other kinds of social clubs are allowed. This ruling, while it opened the door to high school Christian clubs everywhere, also proved to be a victory for atheist clubs. Thanks to Sekulow, clubs sponsored by the SSA, even when opposed by school boards who never say no to Baptist or Catholic clubs, are sprouting up all over the country.

As SSA-supported atheist identity and atheist organizations flourish in high schools and on college campuses, a parallel movement of nonbelieving humanist chaplains has emerged on nearly a dozen campuses to advise and nurture secular students. Encouraged by the popularity and impact of Harvard's Greg Epstein, author of *Good Without God* (and on the board of SSA), humanist chaplains can now be found at American University, Barnard College, Columbia, Rutgers, Stanford, Tufts, the University of Southern California (whose charismatic "atheist evangelist" chaplain, Bart Campolo, was profiled in the *Sunday Times Magazine* on New Year's Day, 2017), and Yale. Some colleges are even introducing atheism and secular studies into the curriculum. Pitzer College in Claremont, California, has a department of secular studies founded by the sociologist of religion Phil Zuckerman, and Trinity College in Hartford, Connecticut, has an Institute for the Study of Secularism in Society and Culture. In 2016 the University of Miami created the nation's first academic chair "for the study of atheism, humanism, and secular ethics," endowed by a $2.2 million donation from eighty-three-year-old Louis J. Appignani, the benefactor, as noted above, of the American Humanist Association and of the Secular Coalition for America.

Young children are just as much a part of the Atheist Awakening as are college and high school students. In 1996, attorney and former Eagle Scout Edwin Kagin, a member of a local Free Inquiry Group, in response to the Boy Scouts of America's enforcement of their requirement that members believe in God, decided to open a summer camp in Boone County, Kentucky, where children of atheist, agnostic, humanist, and free-thinking families could feel comfortable and accepted. Paul Kurtz, the national head of the Free Inquiry groups, supported the camp's creation; in its first summer, Camp Quest, as it was named, had twenty campers aged eight to twelve. Committed to "fun, friends, and free thought, featuring science, natural wonder and humanist values," Camp Quest, directed by Kagin and his wife Helen until their retirement in 2005, grew dramatically at multiple sites with the general surge in atheist activism after 2000. From the second camp in 2002 in Tennessee, and camps in Michigan in 2003 and Minnesota in 2004, the total grew to fifteen Camp Quests in 2017, with hundreds of campers all across America; small potatoes, to be sure, compared to the hundreds of Christian or Jewish summer camps. Still, no greater tribute to its success could be found than Stephen Colbert's satirical indictment of Camp Quest as a threat to America's security and moral identity in the "Threat Down" section of Comedy Central's *The Colbert Report* on July 24, 2006:

> I'm talking about Camp Quest, a network of summer camps dedicated to sunny day fun from a strict atheist and agnostic perspective. As their catch phrase says, "It's beyond belief!" Though Camp Quest provides regular camp activities like hiking and horseback riding, according to the *Cincinnati Enquirer*, children also "learn about the canons of rational thought, critical thinking and scientific inquiry." And in one activity, "[campers] must try to prove that invisible unicorns, as a metaphor for God, don't exist." The campers are also given other untenable philosophical challenges, like proving tetherball is fun. Well Camp Quest, here's another activity. How about canoeing on a lake of hellfire for all eternity!

While few reasonable late night fans would imagine the children of atheists adrift on a fiery lake in hell, Colbert's satire is funny only because we can imagine, alas, that some devout believers might predict this awful outcome for the Quest campers. Many might quietly believe that such a self-consciously proud dismissal of religious belief by parents, now bent upon proselytizing their young, had a whiff of smug pretention to it, or too cool an indifference to the tradition of valuing religious practice. Clearly the new activism among American atheists had its work to do, not merely in making its case for its reasonableness and its constitutional claims for equal treatment, but also for good public relations.

So it would be that the Atheist Awakening, energized by the atheist organizations described above, plus others—a subset of even more narrowly specific identity groups: African Americans for Humanism, Ex-Muslims of North America, Hispanic-Americans of Non-Belief, the Military Association of Atheist and Freethinkers, and the Secular Organization for Sobriety (a nonbelievers' alternative to Alcoholics Anonymous)—has used various strategies in its efforts to change attitudes to and treatment of nonbelievers. Since 2000 the movement has focused principally on four tactical approaches: intellectual, political, legal, and promotional, to enhance the public image of nonbelief in America and to counter its demonization.

In making the intellectual case for nonbelief, the Atheist Awakening has been the beneficiary of the New Atheist movement, the quartet of intellectuals—Richard Dawkins, Daniel Dennett, Sam Harris, and Christopher Hitchens—whose books mocking and attacking religion became best-sellers in the years between 2004 and 2007. Atheist activists Greg Epstein, David Niose, David Silverman, and Herb Silverman all have written books about their atheism, about atheists as moralists, and about the secular movement in general; but it was the strident assault on God from writers outside the movement per se that created the favorable context of ideas that helped inform the institutional activism of the Atheist Awakening. The very titles of the New Atheist books were music to the ears of nonbelievers: *The God Delusion* (Dawkins); *Breaking the Spell: Religions as a Natural Phenomenon* (Dennett); *The End of Faith: Religion, Terror, and the Future of Reason* (Harris); *god is not Great: How Religion Poisons Everything* (Hitchens).

The New Atheists argue that the existence of God is a scientific hypothesis that can be tested empirically and that the test reduces the possibility of God's existence to near zero. They go on to argue that religion is accorded too much respect in society since its impact is always pernicious and dangerous. Not only is belief in God mocked, but so is respect and tolerance for those who have faith, which is derived from what they consider a misguided assumption that faith is private and personal and thus cannot be criticized. Harris contends that "there is a multicultural, apologetic machinery that keeps telling us that we can't attack people's religious sensibility. That is so wrong and so suicidal." In bellicose, take-no-prisoners prose, the New Atheist Dawkins sums up Catholic education in these damning terms: "What teachers and priests are doing to children whom they encourage to believe in something like the punishment of unshriven mortal sins in an eternal hell is arguably more psychologically damaging than the publicized cases of sexual abuse by Catholic priests."

As appealing as the New Atheists root-and-branch dismissal of religion is to atheist activism, it also poses problems. Potential liberal and moderate allies of nonbelievers as well as some secularists themselves recoil from New Atheism, considering it as intolerant as the intolerance they are fighting. Then there are its contributions to the stereotype of the atheist as an elitist intellectual, seemingly insisting that theists believe in God because they are so dumb. Daniel Dennett, a philosophy professor, exemplifies to many observers an insufferable arrogance in his *Breaking the Spell* and *New York Times* op-ed "The Bright Stuff" (July 12, 2003). An important early advocate for atheists to come out of the closet, he suggested that self-identified atheists in America relabel themselves "brights," as Dawkins, the Oxford professor of evolutionary biology, was urging for British atheists. Brights, Dennett writes, see the world in naturalist, not supernaturalist, terms. "Brights don't believe in ghosts or elves or the Easter Bunny—or God." Despite Dennett's tortured effort to link the term to the skeptical Enlightenment ideals of light and reason versus religion and superstitious darkness, the unfortunate inference is that nonbrights are dim.

Further complicating the Atheist Awakening's total embrace of the New Atheism is the troublesome Islamophobia found in Dawkins and writers Harris and Hitchens. Their general abhorrence of religion seems to harbor a specific dislike of Islam, despite Harris's and Dawkins's claims to the contrary. Harris started writing *The End of*

Faith immediately after 9/11 and insists that "Islam is especially bel-
ligerent and inimical to the norms of civil discourse." Relative to other
world religions, he says, it has "a more dogmatic commitment to using
violence to defend one's faith." Hitchens's title *god is not Great* is an
intentionally insulting jab at Muslims who frequently recite in Arabic
"Allah Akbar," "God is great."

The atheist movement pursues secondly an assertive political strategy, now buoyed ironically by a 2015 Gallup poll (more recent than
the one cited earlier) which, while it showed that only 58 percent of
Americans would vote for an atheist presidential candidate—a figure
near their willingness to vote for a Muslim—was a big improvement
over the 18 percent who said they might vote for an atheist when the
question was first asked in 1958. Yet few politicians have embraced
the Atheist Awakening. As we have noted, in some polls 23 percent
of Americans describe themselves as religiously unaffiliated, which
the Pew Research Center defines as people who are atheist, agnostic,
or who describe their religion as "nothing in particular." Of the 515
members of the 115th Congress, convened in January 2017, which contains seven people who publicly identify as lesbians, gay men, bisexu-
als or transgender, only one member openly expressed her nonbelief.
Arizona Democratic representative Kyrsten Sinema, first elected in
2012 and sworn in with her hand on a copy of the United States Constitution, told the *New York Times* that while she advocated a secular
approach to government, she preferred the term "unaffiliated" to "nontheist," "atheist," or "nonbeliever."

The year Sinema arrived in Congress saw the departure of Pete
Stark, who in 2007 had come out as an open nonbeliever. Stark, eighty
years old, had served forty years in the House, and was defeated that
year by a thirty-one-year-old political novice and fellow Democrat,
Eric Swalwell. Stark's atheism does not seem to have been a factor in
the election; apparently it was never raised in the liberal San Francisco
Bay area district. What did Stark in was his age and a reputation for
crankiness that often turned into cursing and yelling. His congressional outbursts of temper and personal insults of colleagues, labeling a

female Republican House member a "whore for the insurance industry" or accusing Republicans of sending soldiers to Iraq "to get their
heads blown off for the President's amusement," played a much big-
ger role in the campaign than his atheism. Even so, it's doubtful that
his atheism helped free him from his reputation for being, as he was
described in October 2012 on the Bay area NPR station KQED, "among
the most despised members of Congress."

In 2013, a political action committee, the "Freethought Equality
Fund" (FEF), was formed by the Center for Humanist Activism, the
political and advocacy wing of the American Humanist Association.
The PAC, in its words, "seeks to change the face of American politics
and to achieve equality by increasing the number of open humanist and
atheists, and their allies in public office at all levels of government." FEF
also supports progressive candidates who are "strong advocates for the
separation of religion and government and the protection of American
civil liberties." In that latter category were five Democratic congressional candidates in 2014: Representatives Judy Chu (California); Rush
Holt (New Jersey), and Bobby Scott (Virginia) as well as Democratic
hopefuls from Massachusetts and California. In the 2016 election the
FEF PAC endorsed and supported a total of sixty-one openly secular
candidates, mostly in state elections; ten of them were elected to state
legislatures in Arizona, Colorado, Nebraska, New Hampshire, Oregon,
Vermont, Washington, and Wisconsin.

Meanwhile, the Secular Coalition for America, whose president
Herb Silverman, had told England's *Guardian* in 2011 boastfully that
there were twenty-nine nonbelievers in Congress (including Pete
Stark), but that he could not name twenty-eight of them because they
did not want to be outed, turned to local political work in addition to
its lobbying efforts in Washington. In the 2016 election cycle the SCA
emphasized forming secular caucuses in state political parties. It succeeded in Utah, where the Democratic Party approved the creation of
the party's first-ever secular caucus. Its most noticeable success saw
the Secular Coalition for Texas getting three resolutions onto the official 2016 Texas Democratic Party platform. One would repeal religious

exemptions to child protection laws, which exempt from prosecution people who abuse and neglect children based on religious belief. A second resolution would remove from the Texas constitution the requirement that public officials have to believe in God. The final resolution would remove all regulations and restrictions on women's reproductive health care, birth control, and abortion based on religious grounds.

Alongside their energetic political activism, atheist organizations have pursued thirdly an even more vigorous legal strategy rooted in an absolutist reading of church-state separation, and thus on many fronts that have received less publicity that the protracted legal assaults on "under God" in the Pledge of Allegiance. This atheist legal strategy has usually been independent of the American Civil Liberties Union's occasional although important defense of nonbelievers. The atheists have won some of their battles in court but lost many more. The AHA's Appignani Humanist Legal Center successfully sued the Federal Bureau of Prisons in 2015 on behalf of an Oregon inmate whose request to form a humanist study group, a right afforded prisoners of other faiths, had been denied. Under the settlement, nonbelieving prisoners in the federal system will have the same rights and recognition as inmates of other faiths, even to celebrating "holy days," including Darwin Day on the naturalist's birthday, February 12. However, in 2014 the AHA lost a case before the U.S. Fifth Circuit Court of Appeals in New Orleans, which upheld a lower court ruling in favor of a Texas school board that allowed students to offer public prayers at its board meetings. The Fifth Circuit panel held that student-led prayers at legislative bodies were different from prohibited prayers in public schools. In its decision the Circuit Court cited the "legislative prayer exception" pronounced by the U.S. Supreme Court in 2014 allowing prayers at town council meetings in Greece, New York. Finally, the AHA is the main plaintiff in the long Fourth Circuit legal battle over the constitutionality of the forty-foot-high "peace cross" that sits on state-owned land in Prince George's County in Maryland.

David Silverman's American Atheists is, not surprisingly, more litigious than the AHA. The AA in 2008 sued on behalf of ten Kentucky residents the state of Kentucky, which had placed over the State Office of Homeland Security the State Legislature's mandated inscription, "The safety and security of the Commonwealth cannot be achieved apart from reliance upon Almighty God." A Circuit Court judge ruled for the AA in 2009 that the legislature had violated the First Amendment's protection against the establishment of religion. The state's attorney general appealed the ruling to the Kentucky Court of Appeals. In 2011 it ruled 2 to 1 against the American Atheists. The AA, in turn, appealed for review by the Kentucky Supreme Court, which was denied in 2012, and then in 2013, to the U.S. Supreme Court, which also declined to hear the case.

In another case that received much more public notice, in 2011 the AA sued the World Trade Center Memorial Foundation, a recipient of a $10 billion grant from Congress, to prevent the installation in its Memorial Museum built on Ground Zero the two intersecting steel girders from the building wreckage that had been dubbed the "miracle cross." The seventeen-foot-high cross "formed by God" had stood in front of the nearby St. Peter's Catholic Church since 9/11, where it had been consecrated by a Franciscan priest. The United States District Court and the United States Court of Appeals for the Second District in 2013 and 2014 both accepted the World Trade Center Memorial Foundation's claim that the rescued steel beams was a "secular artifact."

What the AA had unsuccessfully demanded in its suit was the inclusion in the museum of an atheist memorial, for which it would pay, dedicated to nonreligious victims, because a small star of David, a Jewish prayer shawl, and some Hindu holy water had been included in the Memorial Museum; these clearly religious elements undermined the secular description of the huge "miracle cross." The request for equal treatment, rejected in New York, did succeed in Florida in 2013. Rather than engage in a lengthy lawsuit threatened by the AA over the placement of a large Ten Commandments display in the courtyard of the municipal building in Starke, Florida, the city administration agreed to the AA demand for equal time and equal prominence. In what is probably the first atheist monument built on public land in

America, the AA erected a stone "Atheist Bench" with quotes from AA founder Madalyn Murray O'Hair, the passage from the 1797 Treaty of Tripoli, signed by President John Adams, stating "that the government of the United States is not, in any sense, founded on the Christian religion," and quotes from the Bible describing punishments for breaking the Ten Commandments, most of which are death.

David Silverman, who proudly claims that RoadsideAmerica.com lists Starke's Atheist Bench as a "tourist attraction," acknowledges he would have preferred the city not to have erected the Decalogue monument and the AA not to have needed equality, just as he had hoped his World Trade Center suit had led to the removal of the "Miracle Cross." But sometimes even atheists have to see silver linings in the clouds. Several months after the 2014 Supreme Court rejected a challenge to the city council meetings of Greece, New York, beginning with prayers, the council gave equal time to an atheist who made the invocation at a board meeting there.

The AA's latest case, still unresolved, though one can hazard a guess about its outcome, is a suit against the state of Oklahoma for erecting a Ten Commandments monument on the State Capitol grounds. The AA argues conventionally that the monument is itself an unconstitutional establishment of religion but, more brashly and unusually, that the internal texts of several commandments ("Thou shalt not make unto thee any graven image," "Thou shalt not take the name of the Lord thy God in vain," and "Honour thy father and thy mother") violate the First Amendment's protection of free speech and expression as well.

Even more involved than the AA on the legal front has been the Freedom From Religion Foundation. It has won some important victories. Following a 1995 suit brought by it against its home state of Wisconsin for designating Good Friday a legal holiday, the federal District Court ruled in 1996 that the holiday was indeed a violation of the First Amendment because "the promotion of Christianity is the primary purpose of the law." In another case rich with historical symbolism, the FFRF brought suit against the Rhea County School District in Tennessee for allowing religious instruction in the county's public schools.

The Scopes trial put Rhea County on the world's map in 1925. The issue in 2001 was the county allowing students from Bryan College, named after the trial's religious hero, William Jennings Bryan, to teach the Bible to public elementary school students for thirty minutes a week during the school day in three county schools. Bryan College refers to itself as a Christian school and its motto is "Christ Above All"; its mission statement reads, "Educating students to become servants of Christ to make a difference in today's world." In June 2004 the Sixth Circuit Court of Appeals upheld a lower District Court judgment that the school board's practice of allowing the teaching of the Christian Bible as religious truth was a violation of the First Amendment's Establishment Clause. Not content with just its court victory, the FFRF has spent $150,000 to place a statue, erected in 2017, of Clarence Darrow, the famous agnostic lawyer who defended Scopes, in front of the Rhea County Courthouse to stand near the statue of Bryan put there in 2005 by Bryan College.

The FFRF wins 75 percent of its cases, but it sometimes loses on procedural grounds. The foundation in 2004 brought suit against President Bush's executive order establishing his faith-based initiative to fund religious charities, since faith-based organizations "are singled out as being particularly worthy of federal funding because of their religious orientation, and the belief in God is extolled as distinguishing the claimed effectiveness of faith-based social services." When *Hein v. FFRF* reached the Supreme Court in 2007, the court ruled 5–4 against FFRF, holding that taxpayers had no standing to challenge executive actions taken by the White House, only legislative governmental action.

In another case, *FFRF v. Obama,* in 2010, the foundation seemed to have triumphed when federal District Court Judge Barbara Brandriff Crabb ruled that the National Day of Prayer was an unconstitutional violation of the Establishment Clause. The court declared that "its sole purpose is to encourage all citizens to engage in prayer, an inherently religious exercise that serves no secular function. . . . The government has taken sides on a matter that must be left to individual conscience."

She likened it to a government resolution to encourage fasting during Ramadan, or attending a synagogue, or celebrating a national Day of Blasphemy. When the case was appealed to the U.S. Seventh Circuit Court of Appeals, however, that court ruled in 2011 that the FFRF did not have standing to challenge the National Day of Prayer and that only the president could be injured enough to challenge the statute creating it.

The FFRF has zealously attacked "In God We Trust," the nation's motto. In 2009 it filed a federal lawsuit to stop the engraving of the four words on a prominent area of Washington's new Capitol Visitor Center, which serves as the entrance and security screening area for tourists. "We are effectively being told that we (non-believers) are political outsiders . . . because we don't trust God," said Annie Laurie Gaylor. Jim DeMint, then the Republican senator from South Carolina, who had sponsored the resolution approving the inscription, claimed that "the Founders based the Constitution and our laws on religious faith and principles . . . our true motto, 'In God We Trust,' expresses this fact and we cannot allow a whitewash of America's religious heritage." Gaylor responded, "They want this up there because they think God is the foundation of our government. Boy are they misinformed." The lawsuit was dismissed. In 2013 the FFRF mounted a lawsuit against the U.S. Treasury Department and other government offices over the motto's presence on the nation's currency. The foundation was represented in court by Michael Newdow, who argued that its presence on money discriminated against nonbelievers who were "forced to proselytize— by an act of Congress—for a deity they don't believe in whenever they handle money." The case, *Newdow v. Peterson*, didn't go far. In 2015 the FFRF made an effort to have police in the South remove "In God We Trust" decals from their official vehicles because, as Gaylor told the *New York Times* on October 4, 2015, "the idea of aligning the police force with God is kind of scary. That's the first thing you'd expect to see in a theocracy." It was thoroughly quashed when the Texas attorney general upheld the practice in a three-page opinion, reported in the *New York Times*, "that courts have allowed it in other contexts because it reflects America's religious heritage. A law enforcement department's decision to display the national motto on its vehicles is consistent with that history."

Courts around the country are clogged with FFRF ongoing religion cases. In Kentucky, the foundation, joined by the ACLU, is defending a motorist whose requested vanity plate "I'm God" was rejected by the state DMV, first as "obscene or vulgar" and then as "not in good taste." In Pennsylvania, the FFRF is suing Leigh County to have a Latin cross removed from its official seal. In Washington, D.C., the district court is being asked to rule unconstitutional Congress's refusal to allow FFRF copresident Dan Barker to be a guest chaplain and give the House invocation, though invited to do so by U.S. Representative Mark Pocan. Congress said no because Barker had "announced his atheism publicly" and was thus "not a true minister of the gospel." In Pensacola, Florida, the FFRF, along with the AHA, is contesting a government-owned cross, while in Texas it is challenging the removal of a whimsical monument erected in the state capitol by the foundation commemorating the "birth" of the Bill of Rights, depicting the Founding Fathers and the Statue of Liberty crowded adoringly around a manger scene containing the constitutional document. In New Jersey it is challenging public grants of tax dollars to repair or maintain churches. In Indiana, again along with the ACLU, it is contesting an annual live Nativity performance at a public high school. And it has sued President Trump for rescinding the decades-old Johnson Amendment removing tax-exempt status from churches that engage in partisan politics.

The final strategy—promotional, public campaigns by which atheist activists seek to change American attitudes to atheism—had been the most visible and dramatic aspect of the Atheist Awakening. By promoting atheism in the public arena with "in your face" billboards and ads in newspapers and on television, the movement has tried to legitimate and normalize atheism as just another ordinary part of the American civic mosaic. This strategy, begun in 2005, has been pursued relentlessly and with no holds barred by David Niose, David Silverman, and Annie Gaylor on behalf of the AHA, the AA, and the FFRF.

The formerly staid AHA launched the public opinion initiative in 2005, after the arrival of Niose on its board, with full-page advertisements in liberal national publications like *The Nation, Mother Jones, The Progressive*, and *The American Prospect*. The ads, which sought to give a personal face to nonbelief without attacking religion, showed professional people above the caption, "My values? I'm a humanist" with further small-print descriptions of the importance of compassion, rights, and reason. This rather tame and nonconfrontational beginning was followed by a full-blown national campaign of antireligious billboards and posters on buses, coordinated by the United Coalition of Reason, a project of the AHA, but soon enthusiastically participated in by David Silverman and his AA, the "bad boy" of the movement, and the FFRF. Some examples:

- "Don't believe in God? You are not alone." (New Jersey Turnpike)
- "You know it's a myth: This season, celebrate reason!" (a Christmas billboard commenting on a Nativity scene, placed near the New Jersey entrance to the Lincoln Tunnel, which made the national news in nine countries and was covered by *The Colbert Report, The Daily Show*, and *Saturday Night Live*)
- "Tell your family you don't believe."
- "Imagine no religion."
- "Keep the merry, dump the myth." (Times Square)
- "Who needs Christ in Christmas? Nobody!" (a video billboard in Times Square showing a hand crossing out the word Christ")
- "Yes, Virginia, there is no God." (an FFRF billboard at Christmastime)
- "Why believe in a god? Just be good for goodness sake." (an AHA bus ad in Washington, D.C., showing a young African American man wearing a Santa Claus suit and a puzzled expression)
- "Are you good without God? Millions are!"
- "In the beginning man created God."
- "Dear Santa, all I want for Christmas is to skip church! I'm too old for fairy tales." (placed by the AA particularly in Bible Belt cities)

- "A 'Hail Mary' only works in football. Enjoy the game!" (a bill-board for Super Bowl Sunday, 2014, placed by the AA directly across from the game in Met Life Stadium in New Jersey)
- "I'm an atheist and I vote." (a two-week campaign in June 2016 on buses and ad kiosks in Washington, D.C., paid for by the FFRF)

Religious America has pushed back. Ministers in the Fort Worth, Texas, area called for a boycott of public transportation when ads proclaiming "Millions of Americans are good without God" appeared on the city's buses. Bloomington, Indiana, transit rejected as too controversial the same ad. Transit authorities in Des Moines, Iowa, ultimately pulled the "Don't believe in God? You are not alone" advertisement from its buses after numerous complaints. The same billboard was removed in Cincinnati after the owner of the land on which it stood received several death threats. Atheist billboards and bus advertisements have been vandalized in California, Colorado, Idaho, Massachusetts, Michigan, and North Carolina. In rural Chambersburg, Pennsylvania, a Christian group took a more constructive approach by responding to an "Imagine no religion" billboard with a huge nearby sign of its own, "Why do atheists hate America?"

Newspaper ads have been a particularly favored promotional tool for the FFRF, as demonstrated in its full-page ads in the *New York Times* on the occasion of Pope Francis's visit to Washington and President Trump's commencement address at Liberty University. Responding to a 2013 ad campaign by Hobby Lobby that praised God's purported role in the nation's founding, the FFRF took full-page ads in small city newspapers across the country on September 17, 2013, Constitution Day. The ads enjoined Americans to "Celebrate our Godless Constitution," on its 226th birthday, noting that there is no reference to a deity in the document. Large pictures of Thomas Paine, Benjamin Franklin, George Washington, John Adams, Thomas Jefferson, and James Madison dominate the ad, with quotations from them critical of revealed religion. Above the "sign up and send back" form on the bottom of the ad are the large words "In Reason We Trust."

The AHA, in an initiative funded by Todd Stiefel, ran ads in *USA Today*, the *Seattle Times*, the *Village Voice*, the *Atlanta Journal-Constitution*, the *San Francisco Chronicle*, and several magazines, juxtaposing passages from religious texts, the Old and New Testament, and the Quran, with notable humanist quotations. The intention was to show the moral superiority of humanism over religion. Paired, for example, is the Bible's "A woman should learn in quietness and full submission. I do not permit a woman to teach or to have authority over a man; she must be silent" (1 Timothy 2) with Robert Ingersoll in an 1878 letter, "The rights of men and women should be equal and sacred—marriage should be a perfect partnership." Another pairing describes particularly horrific actions by a vengeful God with a rationalist reading of the universe offered by Einstein. The ad then asks readers "to consider humanism." The AHA also ran these print advertisements on NBC and cable TV channels.

By far the most controversial atheist use of television occurred in 2014, when the FFRF produced a thirty-second commercial with President Reagan's son, Ron Reagan, proudly proclaiming his atheist convictions. It was refused by CBS, NBC, ABC, Fox, and Discovery, and shown only on CNN and Comedy Central. Three years later, in 2017, NBC finally agreed to run it along with CNN again. In it the president's son says to the TV audience: "Hi, I'm Ron Reagan, an unabashed atheist, and I'm alarmed by the intrusion of religion into our secular government. That's why I am asking you to support the Freedom From Religion Foundation, the nation's largest and most effective association of atheists and agnostics, working to keep state and church separate, just like our Founding Fathers intended. Please support the Freedom From Religion Foundation. Ron Reagan, lifelong atheist, not afraid of burning in hell." Michael Reagan, the adopted son of the late president and a conservative commentator, is now boycotting NBC and CNN for airing this commercial and took to Twitter to note that "our father is crying in heaven."

These tears notwithstanding, the movement's promotional activism helped bring thousands of nonbelievers to Washington's National Mall at the steps of the Lincoln Memorial in 2012 and 2016 for exuberant all-day Reason Rallies, a sign of both how strong the Atheist Awakening is and of nagging concerns that beset it. Dubbed "Woodstock for Atheists" by the press and "coming out parties" by their sponsors, the Reason Rallies, both funded by Todd Stiefel, received extensive media coverage. Their predecessor in 2002, the "Godless Americans March on Washington," sponsored mainly by the American Atheists, had a turnout of perhaps 2,000 people, and fell below the radar of national attention. Not so the Reason Rally of March 24, 2012, which despite day-long rain and disagreement over its size—sponsors claiming 30,000 attendees, the press judging 20,000—was, as the international media described it, agreeing with the event's website, probably "the largest gathering of secular advocates in American history."

What had changed was not only Stiefel's money, but also Dave Silverman of American Atheists, still the event's point person, reaching out to the panoply of atheist organizations that had emerged in the past decade, to cosponsor the event. Silverman promised "a party or a celebration. The largest atheist party ever." The official goals were to encourage attendees to come out of the closet, to dispel stereotypes about nonbelievers, and to put secular values on the legislative agenda of American voters. Privately, the sponsors hoped that the atheist gathering would be a more diverse group than the mainly over-forty-year-old white male attendees of the Godless rally in 2002. This goal was realized. The attendees at Reason Rally 2012 were mainly under thirty, at least half were female, and there were many people of color.

Music was provided by the popular punk rock band "Bad Religion," whose front man and songwriter for thirty-three years, Greg Graffin, a Cornell PhD in zoology, opened the rally by singing "The Star Spangled Banner." The crowd then recited the Pledge of Allegiance, omitting, of course, the phrase "under God." The emcee was Paul Provenza, the English stand-up comic, actor, and Labor Party activist, who presided over a lineup of pop culture comic personalities, including Tim Minchin, Adam Savage, and Eddie Izzard. Bill Maher and Pete Stark spoke to the group by video link. The press tended to emphasize in its reporting of the event, in addition to the size and good spirits of

the rain-soaked crowd, the injunction from keynote speaker Richard Dawkins that the attendees hold nothing back in confronting the
"most absurd beliefs, for example, transubstantiation. . . . Mock them,
ridicule them in public. Don't fall for the convention that we're all too
polite to talk about religion. Religion makes specific claims about the
universe which need to be substantiated and challenged."

Four years later, on June 4, 2016, a second Reason Rally was held
using the same celebrity format of comics and scientists, the best known
being Bill Nye, but this time emphasizing nonbelievers as an important voting bloc in that fall's election. To that end two members of the
House of Representatives—with religious ties, to be sure, but friends of
secularism—Tulsi Gabbard, a Democrat from Hawaii and a Hindu, and
the churchgoing Bobby Scott, a Democrat from Virginia, spoke to the
crowd on the importance of reason in policy making. Speaking, as well,
was the putative heir to Pete Stark as the only openly nonbeliever in
Congress, Jamie Raskin, who would, in fact, be sent to Congress from
Maryland that fall. Raskin, a law professor and member of the American Humanist Association, and an outspoken advocate of dropping
the Maryland constitution's ban on nonbelieving state officials, has
denied that he is an atheist, telling the *Washington Post*, "I'm Jewish
and a humanist with a small 'h'—I've never called myself an atheist . . .
I've never pronounced on the existence of a divinity." Raskin told the
crowd, "It is time for all Americans to stand up for our most essential
public values against science deniers and theocrats all over the world."

Despite Stiefel's renewed financial generosity, despite the absence
of rain, despite the cosponsorship by all the alphabetic secular organizations, attendance at Reason Rally II in 2016 was substantially lower
than at its predecessor in 2012, with the consensus estimate made by
observers of between 7,500 and 10,000. Explanations offered for the
surprisingly lower turnout vary: potential attendees decided not to
come when they heard some of the scheduled big-name celebrities,
including actor Johnny Depp, comedian Margaret Cho, and scientist
Richard Dawkins, could not participate; the rally occurred in June,
whereas the 2012 rally held in March attracted college students still

on nearby campuses; the presidential campaign of 2016, for whatever other fears it generated, featured Trump, Clinton, and Sanders, who didn't talk endlessly about their faith, as opposed to 2012 when the Mormon Mitt Romney and the Bible-friendly Obama did. What would the attendance have been if Cruz were still a contender?

The decline in attendance may, however, speak to larger issues and concerns about identity and community that bedevil the nonbeliever movement. Reason Rallies serve the same identity- and solidarity-building roles for atheist activism that parades do for gay pride, that "black is beautiful" rhetoric did for black pride, and that consciousness-raising coffee sessions did for feminist identity. Not unlike the huge rallies for Trump supporters, the face-to-face solidarity of Reason Rallies provides a safe place for atheists whose identity places them so outside the American mainstream. But as with the Trump faithful, despite the large attendance at some post-election rallies, atheist identity and solidarity often tend to assert themselves more in virtual reality, on the internet, than in face-to-face community,

Whatever the reasons, atheists are more likely to find one another on social media than in the flesh. There are some 150 secular websites, and with two million subscribers, its forum "/r/atheism" is one of the largest communities on the social and entertainment website Reddit. Popular atheist blogs, such as PZ Myers, the biology professor from Minnesota's "Pharyngula," and YouTube video sites like "The Amazing Atheist" are central to building atheist identity and activism, while "Atheist Republic," an internet site, prides itself in providing "a community for atheists worldwide" by offering online discussion forums, blogs, and "image macros of thought-provoking, funny or inspirational quotes." The internet lets nonbelievers know that they are not alone, that they share an identity with millions of others.

But there are worrisome issues around atheist identity, and not the least of them is the image of the solitary atheist finding virtual community on the computer screen and thereby perhaps less likely to show up for an outdoor rally. Solidarity and collective identity may not come easily to nonbelievers, who are by nature, we suspect, individualistic and self-directed in their beliefs and actions. Nonbelief is usually the product of deep introspective individual choice, often against familial and communal conviction, which might make the nonbeliever less likely to be a joiner. And this individualistic orientation speaks to the obvious problem with atheist activism's constant use of the LGBT activist model and its coming-out strategy. Nonbelief is a voluntary choice. Atheists are discriminated against, stigmatized, and bullied, but unlike sexual orientation and racial identity, atheist identity, as judges in the state pledge cases point out, is a matter of individual choice, not an intrinsic identity with which one is born.

Finding cultural identity and community online, so much a part of the Atheist Awakening, may undermine opportunities for face-to-face supportive gatherings, meetings, and actions as the basis for building solidarity. It allows private affirmation on the internet to replace the collective and social dimension of a movement and could threaten the continued success of atheist activism. Similarly worrisome is that the deeply individualistic foundation of atheist commitment is usually accompanied by a rationalist and empirical worldview, which leads to what Richard Cimino and Christopher Smith call atheism's "affective deficit." Privileging an intellectual and scientific view of life while rejecting rituals and spirituality, atheists have tended to overlook the importance of the emotional and the aesthetic. Instead of simply mocking religion, atheists, according to Cimino and Smith, need to produce an alternative positive "secular spirituality" as the basis of nonbeliever identity.

So it is that some movement activists are trying to focus atheist identity on affective rituals, around which they assume a sense of community thrives. The FFRF, for example, has pushed for the observance of Winter Solstice Day by atheists during the Christmas and Hanukkah season, and recommends legal initiatives such as its successful one in Wisconsin at the State Capitol to have placed, alongside displays of crèches and menorahs, atheist signs that read:

At this season of the Winter Solstice may reason prevail.
There are no gods, no devils, no angels, no heaven or hell.

There is only our natural world.
Religion is but myth and superstition that hardens hearts and
    enslaves minds.

Another approach to enhancing the affective dimension of atheist identity focuses on the celebration of Darwin Day on February 12, an approach invariably more meaningful to student and academic atheists, especially scientists. A strategy to create an atheist identity ritual quite popular among internet atheists is the "Scarlet A" initiative. Proposed originally by the Richard Dawkins Foundation for Reason and Science, this play on the title of Hawthorne's novel proudly emblazons atheist identity on pins, apparel, and especially social media profiles, with a scarlet letter A. There is also the dream of David Niose of the AHA and the SCA, who, in the spirit of Felix Adler, would love to see "Humanist Centers" in every American community for nonbelievers to gather together, as believers do in their congregations "with all the benefits but none of the dogma and creed." Harvard's fabled humanist chaplain Greg Epstein, in the name of a more affective "secular spirituality," calls on nonbelievers to come up with alternative secular versions of weddings, baby namings, and funerals.

But a more emotionally satisfying and positive freethinking affective experience must not jettison what got atheist activism to where it is now, the fortress of reason, facts, and science in a world too much ruled by unreason and superstition.

Atheists and a Virtuous Republic

So HOW DOES it stand today with nonbelievers in the United States? Legally and culturally atheists and all others who have put God aside as a useful concept have gained ground since the adoption of the Constitution. Measured by numbers, the Atheist Awakening has been astonishing. Nontheists are no longer a tiny minority of the American population but constitute a substantial plurality. At the same time their negative rating remains high in this self-proclaimed godly republic. Close to a majority of Americans believe that atheists cannot be good citizens or trusted with high public office. The courts, the legislatures, the executive branches at both the federal and state level are slow to honor the complaints of "godless citizens." Those who govern cling to a formula that turns many obvious state endorsements of religion into "merely" ceremonial utterances that don't violate the First Amendment or the principle that government cannot favor religion over nonreligion. Nontheists are free to believe what they like. However they have not successfully challenged the public pronouncement, and not just in the Pledge of Allegiance, that America is "one nation under God."

Although formidable lobbying groups in the last twenty years have pursued the quest for a "secular" America through court battles, court decisions, even if they were all to come down on the side of nonbelievers, do not by themselves win the hearts and minds of democratic majorities. Religious Americans have one strong point to back up a claim that they deserve preferred treatment. They argue that they are uniquely equipped to bring moral principles to America's public square. It's a claim with a lineage stretching back to the country's founders. Our forebears believed that the novel experiment of a democratic republic could not function without a consensus around moral principles rooted in theistic religion. Whatever their disagreements about the content of religion, they were united in the conviction that a heavenly Creator had laid down a plan for virtuous living which democratic citizens could discover by reason, or faith, or a combination of the two. Given this historically grounded belief—and it amounts to far more than a ceremonial deism, a phrase that would have meant nothing to our founders—it's worth dwelling on the question of what exactly people who dismiss the idea of a heavenly Creator can offer a democratic society.

Saying that God does not exist, and saying it rudely, may make nonbelievers feel better. The ritual of coming out can be a heady experience that pushes aside politeness. You shouldn't need to apologize meekly for holding unpopular beliefs. Even so, negative pronouncements about why theists have it all wrong and are wedded to outdated superstitions aren't enough to gain respect. Even if all of the complaints about religion made by Richard Dawkins and other New Atheists were true—and they aren't—and even if those complaints never applied to secular philosophies—though they frequently do—statements suggesting that people who believe in God are idiots constitute a condescending intolerance that reinforces a perception that nonbelievers are unfeeling elitists. Atheists who have never found occasion to respect people who believe in and pray to an Almighty God need to seriously reevaluate the breadth of their experience.

Nontheists might argue that they are merely giving back the sort of disrespect that has long been directed at them. Yet however good payback might feel, it can't substitute for a positive program. Whatever else is true, theists are not going to disappear or become marginal to American society and culture. Nonbelievers must address theists by demonstrating that they too are concerned with a virtuous nation. Sure, plenty of evidence tells us that the formula "one nation under God" hasn't guaranteed a high level of public morality. A widespread belief in God hasn't saved the country from greed and the corruption of its public and private spheres by money, lots of money. But that does not answer the observation once posed by Benjamin Franklin that if we are this bad with a professed allegiance to religion, wouldn't we be much worse without it. Nonbelievers have work to do in convincing the general public that Franklin was wrong.

Let's begin with the strongest positive claim of nontheists. It's no accident or coincidence that they are strongly overrepresented among scientists and people who work in almost any creative field or area of research. The search for new knowledge requires minds that are skeptical of received truths, including the dogmatic ones encoded in many organized religions. People who believe that change occurs by divine miracles, that evolution is a godless hypothesis, or that human beings have done nothing to bring about disastrous climate change are not helping the cause of democracy. It is not elitism, only common sense, to insist that the first principle of any public morality, whether theistic or nontheistic, is that human beings bear responsibility for what they do. Prayer, when it comes to public policy, is no substitute for long years of education. A respect for education and learning shouldn't divide Americans, but it does.

Politics has long made clear that the claims of knowledgeable experts don't fit easily into democratic procedures. Even if they did, experts can be wrong. But human fallibility suggests an important attitude that theists and nontheists might discover they share. Whatever human beings think they know, whatever they imagine they might accomplish, they threaten to do more harm than good if they forget about the danger of hubris, or excessive pride. Theologians of many religious traditions regard hubris as a sin, for it defies God's power over us, but the Greeks spoke about it in their mythology even earlier than Jews, Christians, Muslims, or secular humanists. The story of Icarus suggests that if human beings learned to fly, they would need to restrain their sense of arrogance about the achievement. Otherwise, our flight takes us too near the sun and we will perish. Theists might see that result as a fall into hellfire. Nontheists think instead of atomic explosions visited upon innocent civilian populations or rising tides from a warming planet. God or no God—it doesn't matter. Unchecked arrogance makes disaster a certainty, if not for us then for our grandchildren and their children and grandchildren and so on for as many years as human life can sustain itself.

Felix Adler thought that for nonbelievers to gain recognition for their commitment to public morality, they needed to organize. He founded the Society for Ethical Culture because nonbelief in God, no more than theism, necessarily breeds virtue. Atheists in America can be racists or intolerant. They can be hedonistic or soullessly greedy no matter what the cost to others. They may fall into a despairing cynicism. Adler recognized that a commitment to morality turned to public service and charity requires all the help it can get. Organization is a tested and effective way for human beings to brace themselves to work on common endeavors. Americans used to be joiners. They aren't so much any more. Members of what were once the largest religious bodies in America know that as well as anyone.

It's a good thing that nonbelievers have created lobbying organizations. It's also a good thing that in recent years courts have tended to accord the conscience of nonbelievers the same gravity as the conscience of believers. The strong pacifist beliefs of Daniel Seeger and Elliott Welsh during the Vietnam War convinced the Supreme Court that moral beliefs based on secular philosophies were equivalent to the strong beliefs of people raised in traditional religious denominations. What the godless citizen now needs to do is to seize the opportunity to demonstrate that secularism doesn't mean that morals are irrelevant to issues of public policy. It only means that disputes among moral positions have to be resolved by democratic processes that don't rank the morals of a humanist less worthy of consideration than the morals of a Presbyterian or a Catholic or a Jew or a Muslim.

Yet, as noted in the previous chapter, it hasn't been easy for non-believers to find a positive agenda that has emotional drawing power. Celebrating a national day of reason might bring out the troops once or twice, but then the initiative fizzles. Nontheists have clogged court dockets and have won important victories. Those legal battles are necessary, but how many nonbelievers spend their days worrying about the erection of a stone tablet listing the Ten Commandments on the grounds of the capitol building in Austin? They might sign a petition that the monument violates the principle of secularity and that taken together with dozens of other government-sponsored religious endorsements it blunts any aspirations they might have to seek a political career. Nonetheless, although the hard lessons learned by Robert Ingersoll are still relevant, by and large nonbelievers allow their legal battles to be fought by others.

In what might seem the highest touch of irony, the campaign to take atheism seriously may rest on convincing the courts and the American people to take religion seriously. Judges who decree that the phrases "in God we trust" and "one nation under God" are ceremonial and have no religious significance are in effect saying that religion is a secular construct of political figures rather than the work of religious leaders. Worse, they are saying that religion is trivial, which, when you think about it, may be the most dangerous form of blasphemy. Most religious Americans understand the difference between their religious faith and nationalism. The Supreme Court needs to learn that lesson. When people pray or read from a text that they consider sacred, they are doing something with religious meaning and therefore something that nonreligious people cannot and should not share. Empty formulas, which are what the tenets of "ceremonial deism" amount to, are of no use to believers or nonbelievers. When repeated again and again, they seriously damage the clarity of our language and thought.

Some Supreme Court jurists cite "original intent" as their guide to constitutional interpretations. In dealing with religious cases, they find it relevant that Thomas Jefferson referred to an Almighty Creator in his public addresses. Jefferson did, but he also belonged to a generation of revolutionaries. How easily Americans seem to forget that. First among Jefferson's intentions, and of the men who wrote the Constitution, was not to bind those who came after them into a straitjacket. Crucial to the faith of the founders was a belief that human reason could bring people together. Reason did not eliminate differences or selfish motives, but it made compromise possible. Reason could create a political space where citizens might convene to consider the general welfare, putting self-interest aside as much as possible.

Clearly, limits imposed by the world they lived in bounded the ideals of our founders. To their shame, their reason failed to recognize the intolerable wrong represented by the buying and selling of black Africans as property. Even so, their confidence in reason was not misplaced. Science advances by the discovery and correction of error, and by discarding formulas that no longer work. A changed historical context necessitates a reevaluation of assumptions. Religious freedom meant one thing to a generation when few nonbelievers existed. It means another when nonbelief is no longer unusual.

Let's be absolutely clear that religious liberty, everybody's religious liberty, requires vigilant protection. Members of small or unpopular religious groups can face the same sorts of arbitrary discrimination that Herb Silverman faced when he applied for a notary's license in South Carolina. A Sikh student at Hofstra University was told he couldn't join the ROTC unless he shaved his beard and discarded his turban, despite the necessity of them to his religion. In Texas a kindergarten student of Native American heritage was barred from school for wearing long braids consistent with his religious identity. The cases are equivalent to the practice of the city government in Warren, Michigan, which allowed a "prayer station" in its city hall but refused the request of an individual who wanted to erect a "Reason station," or that of a police officer in Puerto Rico who was punished because of his refusal to line up with other officers and pray.

Courts found all these official actions unconstitutional and treated them as simple matters. However, arbitrary actions and regulations, even when clearly wrong and doomed to be struck down by the courts, are more than nuisances. Someone has to take a complaint to court, a time-consuming practice requiring expensive legal services and a lot of patience waiting for a decision. For every case where the ACLU and/or an atheist organization helps a plaintiff to sue, dozens of other complaints simply get buried and citizens have to accept the injustice. Local customs and attitudes dictate discrimination, and judges cannot fix even all the easy cases. And of course in many harder cases, as we have seen, courts are often content to sanction the discrimination rather than challenge the force of custom and deal with ensuing storms of protest. Yet the United States has weathered seasons of protest and emerged on the other side of them a more just nation. The force of public opinion directed at nonbelievers as well as at the practices of unpopular religious groups works to keep the ideal of full religious liberty and equal protection of the law an elusive goal.

Nonbelievers have been waiting a long time for American public opinion to change. What else can they do to discourage politicians from attacking atheism as a menace to American ideals? Here is one modest suggestion. Why not, in addition to Darwin Day rallies and establishing more lobbying organizations to bring to court the complaints of nonbelievers, a campaign to solicit a generous endowment for what we might call "The Secular Project." The purpose of this foundation would not be to promote atheism or nonbelief per se, but to seek applications from nonbelievers who need funding for projects that in some way, either through research or practice or a combination of the two, aim to safeguard our planet, to eliminate human suffering anywhere in the world, and to promote peace. What better way for nonbelievers to accentuate the positive than by supporting plans that demonstrate the creative ways in which nonbelief can be a secular equivalent not to religious worship but to religious charitable work. The Secular Project would demonstrate, by the proposals it funded, that atheism, agnosticism, and other labels used to designate nontheistic beliefs are not just fallback positions for people who can't square the world they live in with beliefs in religious prophets, or the "power of prayer," or heaven and hell. It would do something to correct the atomized identity of the "nones."

It may be that trying to recommend a strategy to the millions of nonbelievers in the United States is akin to the project of herding cats. The men and women who lead the organizations spawned by the Atheist Awakening have made skillful use of social media to try to give nonbelievers a collective identity they have never quite found in the past. Yet compared to the Civil Rights movement or the Feminist movement or the Gay Pride movement, it remains a movement without charismatic national leaders. That is in part because the forms of legal discrimination nonbelievers face today, while important, are not on the order of denying African Americans the vote, or allowing unequal pay for women doing equal work, or preventing gays and lesbians from marrying or obtaining spousal benefits for their partners. In their struggles for equal rights these groups often had to deal with violent reprisals. Yet one important consideration joins the Atheist Awakening to these other protest movements. Their fight is not just about ending discrimination for themselves. All of them, as they are managing to break through false stereotypes and biases that curtail the contributions they have to offer, bring enormous creative resources to American public life. Unwarranted discrimination hurts everyone.

Our book then is not just a plea to end discriminations against atheists, agnostics, and nontheists because of the burdens placed upon them. It is an argument about the cost we pay as a nation because of that discrimination. Every political speech and every ceremonial occasion excluding nonbelievers or suggesting that they are second-class citizens demeans our democracy. Every textbook that discusses the contributions of Elizabeth Cady Stanton, Thomas Edison, and Luther Burbank while deliberately excising any mention of their religious doubts does harm. No nation can claim a high standard of education without recognizing that people who don't subscribe to a theistic religion often possess knowledge that is crucial to solving the myriad problems that beset our world. Our survival demands the application of scientific and humanistic research. We need the creativity of nonbelievers, and harnessing that energy requires an end to the use of atheism as an epithet, a usage that began with the obloquy unfairly heaped upon Thomas Paine. In fact no one better represented the boldness, the rudeness if you like, of the American experiment than Paine. A national monument to his memory is way overdue, one perhaps inscribed with words he penned in 1775 that were not controversial to our revolutionary forebears and should not be controversial now: "When we yield up the exclusive privilege of thinking, the last shadow of liberty quits the horizon."

NOTES, CITATIONS, AND USEFUL READING

Chapter One: The Invention of Religious Liberty

The documents written by our founders that are cited in this chapter are published in many places and are easily accessible online. Roger Williams is a little different. The quotations in this chapter are taken from *The Complete Writings of Roger Williams* (New York, 1963), vol. 1, p. 108, and vol. 3, p. 399. Quotations documenting the trials of colonial dissenters and the opposition of colonial leaders to church-state separation appear in William McLoughlin's magisterial two-volume work, *New England Dissent, 1630–1883. The Baptists and the Separation of Church and State* (Cambridge, MA, 1971), pp. 105, 376, 621, 1004. Another book that provides indispensable background to the material about colonial America is Leonard W. Levy, *Blasphemy. Verbal Offense Against the Sacred from Moses to Salmon Rushdie* (New York, 1993). On the relative invisibility of nonbelief prior to the nineteenth century, see James Turner, *Without God, Without Creed: The Origins of Unbelief in America* (Baltimore, 1985).

Chapter Two: Atheism Becomes Un-American

Most of the cited material in this chapter is taken from the database collections of the *New York Times*, the *Boston Globe,* the *Chicago Tribune,* and the *Washington Post.* The most useful source on Kneeland, from which the quotations are taken, is Mary Whitcomb, "Abner Kneeland: His Relation to Early

Iowa History," *The Annals of Iowa* (1904), pp. 340–63. But a number of historians have paid attention to Kneeland. See, for example, Susan Jacoby, *American Freethinkers: A History of American Secularism* (New York, 2004); David Sehat, *The Myth of American Religious Freedom* (New York, 2011); Eric R. Schlereth, *An Age of Infidels: The Politics of Religious Controversy in the Early United States* (Philadelphia, 2013); and Leigh Eric Schmidt, *Village Atheists: How America's Unbelievers Made Their Way in a Godly Nation* (Princeton, 2016). For Ingersoll's advice to Black, see Susan Jacoby's *The Great Agnostic: Robert Ingersoll and American Freethought* (New Haven, 2014), p. 162. The best modern biography of Paine is Eric Foner's *Tom Paine and Revolutionary America* (New York, 1976). On the Haymarket episode, see Paul Avrich, *The Haymarket Tragedy* (Princeton, 1984). The press covered all of the trials discussed in this chapter; in addition to the citations in the text, see the *Chicago Tribune*, August 24, 1886; the *Boston Globe*, May 10, 1886; and the *New York Times*, May 20 and 21, 1887, August 18, 1928, and October 16 and 22, 1929. See also Jill Lepore, "The Sharpened Quill," *The New Yorker*, October 16, 2006.

Chapter Three: The Political Cost of Nonbelief in Nineteenth-Century America

American newspapers, as should be clear from citations in the text, gave extensive coverage to Ingersoll's career. For quotations from Ingersoll not taken from newspapers, see (in the order they appear) *The Works of Robert Ingersoll*, 12 volumes (New York, 1902), vol. 1, p. 164; vol. 1, pp. 15–16; vol. 8, p. 293; vol. 1, pp. 377–78. For the quotation from Thomas Talmadge, see Susan Jacoby, *The Great Agnostic: Robert Ingersoll and American Freethought* (New Haven, 2014), p. 54. All autobiographies are self-serving, and Elizabeth Cady Stanton's *Eighty Years and More* (1898; repr. New York, 1980) is no exception. It is indispensable reading for anyone who wants to understand her life, and it is the source of many quotations in the text (pp. 13, 25–26, 41–44, 72, 88, 285, 318, 389). The best biography of Stanton is Elisabeth Griffith, *In Her Own Right: The Life of Elizabeth Cady Staton* (New York, 1985). Equally important is Kathi Kern, *Mrs. Stanton's Bible* (Ithaca, 2001). Ellen Carol DuBois has put together a very useful collection, *Elizabeth Cady Stanton, Susan B. Anthony: Correspondence, Writings, Speeches* (New York, 1981), which records Stanton's complaint about the lavish attention heaped upon Anthony, p. 191. The 1896 *Proceedings of the NAWSA* is the source for material about the organization's decision to distance itself from *The Woman's Bible*. See also quotations in the two volumes of Stanton's papers edited by two of her children, Theodore Stanton and Harriot Stanton Blatch, *Elizabeth Cady Stanton: As Revealed in Her Letters, Diary and Reminiscences* (New York, 1922), vol. 2, p. 224 (Anthony's remark to Reverend Patton); p. 340 (Stanton's assessment of Ingersoll); p. 195 (Stanton's musing on Catholic community).

Chapter Four: A Secular Equivalent of Religious Worship

For the quotations about Mark Twain's religious views, see Thomas D. Schwartz, "Mark Twain and Robert Ingersoll: The Freethought Connection," *American Literature* (May 1976), p. 191. Columbia University holds the largest collection of the papers and letters of Felix Adler. The lectures cited in this article are "What is Atheism," April 6, 1879; "The Essential Difference Between the Ethical Society and Churches," March 4, 1900; "Sketches of a Religion Based on Ethics, Introductory Discourse," August 30, 1884; "How Far Does the Ethical Society Take the Place of a Church," (March 1897). "Some Characteristics of the American Ethical Movement" is contained in *Fiftieth Anniversary of the Ethical Movement, 1876–1926* (New York, 1926). The best study of Felix Adler is Benny Kraut, *From Reform Judaism to Ethical Culture: The Religious Evolution of Felix Adler* (Cincinnati, 1979), which includes an account of Adler's appointment at Cornell. For Jane Addams, see *Forty Years at Hull House* (1935). Victoria Brown, *The Education of Jane Addams* (Philadelphia, 2004) contains Stead's appraisal of Hull House, p. 275.

Chapter Five: One Nation Under God

The history of the Pledge of Allegiance and its transformation in 1954 is ably described in Richard J. Ellis, *To The Flag: The Unlikely History of the Pledge of Allegiance* (Lawrence, KS, 2005). Congressional and political comments about the Pledge are found there, in the *Congressional Record*, the contemporary newspapers cited in the text, or embedded within the court cases that are named. The two Circuit Court cases and the Supreme Court case, which form the heart of the chapter, contain the quotations in the text. The Neuhaus comments are from his journal *First Things* (March, June/July 2004). Thomas Berg's article "The Pledge of Allegiance and the Limited States" is in the *Texas*

Review of Law and Politics, vol. 8 (2003). The Samuel Huntington quote is from his *Who are We? Challenges to American National Identity* (New York, 2004) and that of Herberg from his classic *Protestant, Catholic, Jew* (New York, 1955). The best study of atheists as "others" in a spiritual America is Penny Edgell, Joseph Gertels, and Douglas Hartman, "Atheists as 'Other': Moral Boundaries and Cultural Membership," *American Sociological Review,* vol. 7, no. 2 (April 2006). The study of children and the Pledge is from Eugene Freund and Donna Givner, "Schooling, The Pledge Phenomenon and Social Control," *American Educational Research Association Working Paper* (1975). The Robin Williams comic rewrite is from "Live on Broadway" (2002).

Chapter Six: Fifty States Under God

The direct quotations are mainly from the three court cases discussed or the law-review articles cited. The "expressivist" theory is elaborated in Richard H. Pildes and Elizabeth S. Anderson, "Expressive Theories of Law: A General Restatement" (*University of Pennsylvania Law Review* 148 (2000). For the efforts that sought to add Christian language to the Constitution during the ratification process and during the Civil War, see our *The Godless Constitution* (1996, repr. New York, 2006). The Ellsworth quote is also from that text. The quotations associated with Herb Silverman are from his book *Candidate Without a Prayer* (Durham, NC, 2012).

Chapter Seven: Unequal Citizens Under God

Most of the material in this chapter rests on the cited court cases. Reading them in their entirety—the majority opinion, the concurring opinions, the dissents—is the only way for readers to make up their own mind about the issues. On the subject of conscientious objection, Lillian Schlissel has edited an invaluable collection of documents in *Conscience in America: A Documentary History* that cover conscientious objection from 1757 to 1967 (New York, 1968). Quotations we have used, especially on Fraina, are on p. 47 and p. 184 of her book. We have also relied on Mulford Sibley and Philip Jacob, *Conscription of Conscience; The American State and the Conscientious Objector: 1940–1947* (Ithaca, 1952), which sums up the view of General Hershey, p. 68. We do not always agree with Douglas Laycock, but no one has written more thoughtfully about the issues that underlie RFRA. His numerous articles are collected in two volumes, *Religious Liberty* (Grand Rapids, 2010, 2011). The statement cited in this chapter is from his, "Free Exercise and the Religious Freedom Restoration Act," *Fordham Law Review* (1994).

Chapter Eight: The Atheist Awakening

Much of the data and details informing this chapter can be found in the books written by contemporary atheist activists: David Niose, *Non-Believer Nation* (New York, 2012); David Silverman, *Fighting God* (New York, 2015); Herb Silverman, *Candidate Without a Prayer* (Durham, NC, 2012). But an equally valuable source was Richard Cimino and Christopher Smith's important scholarly study, *Atheist Awakening* (New York, 2014), the title of which we appreciatively borrowed in naming this chapter. Also useful was Caroline Corbin, "Nonbelievers and Government Speech," *Iowa Law Review* (2012), and Nelson Tebbe, "Nonbelievers," *Virginia Law Review*, vol. 97 (2011). The Barney Frank remarks are from a 2017 telephone interview with the authors. Quotations from court cases can be found in the records of the particular court. The Martha Nussbaum quote is from "Under God: The Pledge, Present and Future," *University of Chicago Law School Alumni Magazine, The Record* (Fall 2008). The Zuckerman summary of cross-national studies is from his "Atheism, Secularity, and Well Being: How the Findings of Social Science Counter Negative Stereotypes and Assumptions," *Sociological Compass* (2009). For Charles Tilly, see his "Social Movements and National Politics," Charles Bright and Susan Harding, eds., *Statemaking and Social Movements* (Ann Arbor, 1984).

ACKNOWLEDGMENTS

We would like to thank the following people for the helpful interviews we conducted with them during the course of writing our book: Maggie Ardiente, Director of Development and Communications, and Ray Speckhardt, Executive Director of the American Humanist Association; Diana Castillo, Legislative Manager of the Secular Coalition for America; Barney Frank, former congressman; Daniel Mach, Director of the ACLU Program on Freedom of Religion and Belief in Washington; David Silverman, president of American Atheists: Arthur Spitzer, director of the Washington office of the ACLU. Barbara Donnell of the Cornell History Department helped us keep track of the drafts of various chapters of the book and managed to get our writing, done on various computers, into a single format. Every author knows how big a difference a good editor can make. Amy Cherry, our excellent editor at Norton, helped us in numerous ways to sharpen our analysis and clarify our arguments.

INDEX